D1612263

Inside Right

It is seldom that liberty of any kind is lost all at once.
David Hume: 'Of the Liberty of the Press'

In a word, a wild and growing notion prevails that governments, and all things pertaining to them, are of less use than had been always supposed.
John Galt: *The Member,* 1831

BY THE SAME AUTHOR

The Body Politic

Inside Right

A Study of Conservatism

Ian Gilmour

Hutchinson of London

Hutchinson & Co (Publishers) Ltd
3 Fitzroy Square, London W1P 6JD

London Melbourne Sydney Auckland
Wellington Johannesburg and agencies
throughout the world

First published 1977
© Ian Gilmour 1977

Set in Monotype Times/Univers

Printed in Great Britain by
The Anchor Press Ltd
and bound by
Wm Brendon & Son Ltd
both of
Tiptree, Essex

ISBN 0 09 131760 6

Contents

Preface

In the following pages there is no attempt to set out a Conservative programme. This book is in no sense a manifesto. It contains no detailed policy prescriptions.

Nevertheless I hope a book on Conservatism may be pardonable. Britain is in great economic and constitutional difficulties; Socialism is in intellectual disarray; a number of myths have grown up around the history of the Tory Party since 1945, many of them clustered around the Conservative Government of 1970–4. There might therefore, it seemed to me, be some value in considering what Conservatism had been about in the past and what Conservative writers had said. In the light of that knowledge, I have tried to describe the nature of Conservatism. The book then shows how Conservatism differs from beleaguered social democracy, and goes on to discuss what Disraeli laid down as the abiding concerns of Toryism: 'the institutions of the country' and 'the condition of the people'.

The word Conservative came into general use only in the 1830s, whereas the word Tory dates from the seventeenth century. Some people have attached slightly different meanings to them. But, except occasionally when referring to the history of the party, I have treated the words Tory and Conservative as interchangeable.

Many people have helped me. I am chiefly indebted to Mr Christopher Patten, Lord Blake, Dr John Patten and Mr Iain Hamilton. Mr Christopher Patten prompted me to write the book, scrutinized the manuscript at every stage and made a host of valuable suggestions. Lord Blake was once again kind enough to read my manuscript and to give me the benefit of his unrivalled knowledge of the subject; his detailed criticisms greatly improved what I had written. Dr John Patten and Mr Iain Hamilton read the whole manuscript and gave much useful help and advice. I am also deeply grateful to Mr James Douglas, Mr David Nicholson, Mr Adam Ridley and Mr Stephen Sherbourne, who read parts of the manuscript and made many helpful suggestions and criticisms. Naturally, however, the errors and the opinions are mine and mine alone.

I should like to thank Professor Oakeshott and Lord Hailsham for permission to quote from their writings, and Lord Salisbury for permission to quote from Lord Hugh Cecil's *Conservatism*.

Two passages in this book first appeared in slightly altered form in articles I contributed to *The Times*, and I am grateful to Mr William Rees Mogg for permission to reproduce them here. I have also reproduced with only minor alterations one passage on the history of the Tory Party from my book *The Body Politic*.

The Library of the House of Commons continues to be one of the efficient (and courteous) parts of the constitution.

I owe Pamela Milne my warm thanks for undertaking the arduous task of typing and retyping the bulk of the manuscript with fortitude and skill, and I should like to thank Mr Harold Harris and Mr Julian Watson of Hutchinson for their many kindnesses and for speeding up the process of publication.

My wife and all my children helped in very different ways, and to them I offer this book.

Part One

By Conservative principles we mean the maintenance of our settled institutions in Church and State and also the preservation and defence of that combination of laws, of institutions, of usages, of habits and of manners which has contributed to mould and form the character of Englishmen.

Sir Robert Peel[1]*

*Superior numbers indicate the references listed on pp. 273–84.

1. Post-War Conservatism

Any policy which is approved by the mass of the nation is certain to be promptly accepted by its rulers.
Salisbury in 1864[1]

> Nations melt
> From power's high pinnacle, when they have felt
> The sunshine for a while, and downward go . . .

Byron[2]

In legislation it is not merely reason and propriety which are to be considered, but the temper of the times.
Disraeli[3]

'I confess much doubt', Hicks Beach, the Chief Secretary for Ireland, wrote in 1886 to Salisbury, the Prime Minister, 'whether the country *can* be governed nowadays by persons holding opinions, which you and I should call even moderately conservative.'[4] Since 1945, many people have come to share Hicks Beach's doubts. But mostly their concern has not been with the philosophical question whether the country can now be governed by people holding such views. Their doubts have been directed to the more practical question whether in recent times the country has in fact been governed by people who held 'even moderately conservative opinions'.

In other words they believe that since 1945 the Conservative Party, and with it of course the country, has been following a false and non-Conservative trail. In their view the Conservative Party has forsaken its true principles, ideas and traditions, and instead of preserving a free and competitive society has been merely paving the way for tyranny and Socialism.* According to them, therefore, the

---

*For the view that the Conservatives have been on the wrong track, see, for example, Lord Coleraine's 'For Conservatives and Others', some of the essays in *1985: An Escape from Orwell's 1984*, edited by Rhodes Boyson, MP, and the *Daily Telegraph, passim.*

Tory Party has partly fulfilled Bernard Shaw's prophecy that 'at least half' of the steps towards Socialism in England would be taken 'when the anti-Socialist party [was] in power'.[5]

Nobody but the most bovine party hack believes that all the policies and actions of his party have always been right, or that all the actions and policies of other parties have always been wrong. Yet an admission of occasional error is a very different thing from the suggestion that almost the whole Tory Party has been marching in the wrong direction for thirty years. And certainly the allegation that Toryism has been betrayed does raise some apparently awkward problems.

For one thing it implies that Churchill, Eden, Macmillan, Butler, Douglas-Home, Heath and Macleod were all either grossly misguided or were not true Tories. This seems improbable. For another, there is some incongruity in a party which gives intellectual speculation a lower place in politics than do its opponents and which believes that policies grow out of the needs, fears, hopes and wishes of the people and out of the demands of the time, coming to the conclusion that it has been intellectually in error since 1945. For a third, there are obvious dangers in a party proclaiming that it has been badly mistaken over a long period of time. If it has been so wrong in the past, why should people flock to support it in the future? Besides, any such confession is particularly hazardous for a Conservative Party. If Conservatives, who almost by definition have some reverence for the past, discountenance both the country's and also their own party's past, there is not much left for them to conserve. A decisive break with what has gone before is obviously congenial to a revolutionary or an extreme left-wing party; it should have few attractions to a party which favours continuity and gradual change.

Nevertheless these difficulties do not dispose of the right-wing case.* Britain's dismal economic performance, the declining standards of public behaviour, the rise in crime, the increasing bitterness of sectional conflict, the apparent inadequacy of the country's political system, all demonstrate that much is badly wrong. Confronted with the Britain of the 1970s even Dr Pangloss would have hesitated to say that everything was for the best in the best of all

---

*It is almost impossible to define 'right wing', 'left wing' and 'centre' in the Conservative Party. But though 'right wingery' cannot be exactly defined, it is, like the elephant, easily recognized when it is seen.

possible worlds, and would instead have had to join the army of the unemployed.

Some national decline was of course inevitable. Even before the war, Britain held a position in the world which her power did not warrant. Her Empire looked wonderfully impressive on the map, but she was in reality greatly overstretched. Her world-wide commitments, combined with her weakness, made it impossible for her to intervene effectively in the Far East or in Europe. The price she paid for being a world power was impotence. Hence, the policy of appeasement, as Mr Michael Howard has pointed out, was at least as much due to the requirements of imperial defence as to the shortcomings of British statesmen.[6] The British Empire could not have survived after the war, even if the Japanese victories had not taken place. Considering that in 1907 the Permanent Under-Secretary at the Foreign Office thought the British Empire had 'gouty fingers stretched in every direction', and Jan Christian Smuts had earlier described it as a 'ramshackle structure . . . without any adequate military organisation . . .',[7] the Empire did well to last as long as it did. The rise of the two super-powers, America and Russia, merely accentuated Britain's loss of status and power.

Britain's economic decline also began in the nineteenth century, but it was accelerated after the war by certain national habits and attitudes. In the words of the late Lord Nuffield in 1959, Britain has seemed 'a nation in semi-retirement'.[8] This mood probably ran too deep to be easily changed by the exhortations of politicians. Yet politicians in general and the Tory Party in particular cannot escape their share of the blame. Over Europe, for example, many chances were lost from 1945 onwards. Had they been taken, British influence in the world would today be far greater and her economy much less weak.

Arguably up to 1964 the nation's decline was little more than was in the nature of things inevitable. Unquestionably, it has been much more pronounced since 1964; and it is inseparably interwoven with the personality and performance of Sir Harold Wilson. Yet Sir Harold only scraped into office through the mistakes of the Conservatives. Suez, Lord Blake has pointed out, by offending the intellectuals, had the same adverse but delayed effect on Conservative electoral fortunes in 1964 and 1966 as did the Jameson Raid on the South Africa war in 1906.[9] All the same, the Tories should still have been able to beat a Labour Party which, after the rows over Clause 4 and nuclear disarmament, looked divided and in decline.

But in the early sixties Toryism lost momentum. There was much criticism of the way the economy was being run. A tight financial policy and a pay pause were unpopular though necessary. Indicative planning, the National Economic Development Council and an incomes policy raised some right-wing ideological hackles. The 'winds of change' policy in Africa of Macmillan and Macleod produced similar discomfort and opposition on the Right. Perhaps through overconfidence bred by the striking electoral victory in 1959, some Conservatives became impatient of the 'Butskellite' consensus. The Monday Club was founded by right-wingers to stop what they saw as the party's drift to the Left since 1945, though where the drift was from was never precisely clear. Mr Macmillan purged one-third of his cabinet in 1962 which eroded rather than restored confidence. General de Gaulle vetoed British entry into the EEC in January 1963, and shortly afterwards there was a strong move in the parliamentary party to get rid of Macmillan. No capital tax was placed on deals in land development. The Vassall and Profumo cases were badly handled, and some of the Labour Party made profitable if disreputable use of them. And following Mr Macmillan's resignation during the Tory Conference in 1963, there was a bruising struggle for the leadership.

As a supporter of Lord Hailsham, I thought that quite apart from the other reasons for backing him he would win the approaching election for the Conservative Party. The supporters of R. A. Butler thought that he, too, would win. Nobody now can know whether either or both of them would have won. But, as the supporters of the other candidates had feared, under Sir Alec Douglas-Home the party was defeated. All the same, Sir Alec only just lost; and it may well be that he would have won had Iain Macleod and Enoch Powell joined his Government. Alternatively he might have won, even without them, had not Edward Heath in the last session of that Parliament insisted on abolishing resale price maintenance.[10] There is therefore a fairly wide range of possible culprits. But the choice of Sir Alec, who deservedly enjoyed high popularity throughout the Conservative Party, indicated that the party was more intent on pleasing itself than on furthering its electoral prospects.

In any case the result of the 1964 election was ruinous. If Labour had been defeated yet again, it would almost certainly have been forced to drop nationalization, to modernize itself, and to become like the other European Socialist parties. Victory enabled it to stay as it was, and under Sir Harold Wilson to inflict six years of government barren of achievement upon the British people. In those years Britain slipped much further behind its neighbours, and by 1970 was weaker in every way than she had been in 1964. Readers of the Crossman diaries may be surprised that the results were not even worse. But that is small consolation. By letting Wilson into office, the Tories were accessories before the fact and therefore in some measure to blame.

Right-wing hostility to the Tory leadership is not confined to the post-war years. Almost all Tory leaders have faced criticism and attack from the right wing or from what the early nineteenth century called 'ultras'.* Wellington showed later that he was not an ultra, but he was so opposed to Canning's policy towards South America that he suggested in 1825 that the King might prefer a government formed by the Whigs to one formed by a Tory Party that had been 'tricked' by Canning.[11] When Canning became Prime Minister, 'the real opposition', wrote Palmerston, sat 'behind the Treasury bench'.[12] Wellington and Peel in their turn had similar trouble with the ultras over Catholic emancipation. Wellington had to fight a duel with one, while Peel lost his seat at Oxford University.[13]

Later, when he was Prime Minister, Peel wrote that 'the true friend to the . . . complaining ultra is the man who would avert the consequences which would inevitably follow if some of them could have their way'. In the same year, 1842, the Tory MP, Henry Drummond, declared that Conservatism had become 'simply a profession of toryism and a practising of radicalism'.[14] Much more than Wellington, Disraeli was later to show that in power he was anything but an ultra, yet his attacks on Peel are the best as well as the most famous of the polemics against Conservative leaders who have allegedly betrayed Conservatism. Disraeli made the perennial accusation that under Peel the Tories had become 'a party without principles', and he posed the perennial question what in practice 'will you conserve'? The Conservative cause, he wrote, 'is the great constitutional cause that refuses everything to opposition; yields everything to agitation; conservative in Parliament, destructive out of doors;

*Canning coined the word 'ultrageous'.[15]

that has no objection to any change provided only it be effected by unauthorised means'.[16]

Appropriately enough, when he became a leader of the party, he had to put up with similar criticism. Derby and Disraeli, wrote Peel's critic, Henry Drummond, in 1859, 'have led the Conservative Party to adopt every measure which they opposed as Radical ten years ago . . . I do not think it creditable to the intelligence of the country gentlemen of England to vote black to be white or white to be black at their bidding.'[17] Salisbury was more wounding still. When, he wrote, the party lost the Peelites, 'it went into the market and bought such articles of the kind as were for sale – mostly damaged goods of unprepossessing appearance, which other buyers had rejected and whose subsequent wear has hardly made good their original cost'.[18] And in 1867 he thought there was nothing 'of which the Conservatives are in any special way the protectors'.[19] Some of the Conservative leaders had 'shown a freedom from scruple surpassing all former example' and he added that they could 'seldom be persuaded that any political principle is worth the sacrifice of their own careers'.[20] Even Salisbury himself, when party leader in 1884, was accused of turning Socialist.[21] Of his Government's Workmen's Compensation Act in 1897, Alfred Cripps, then a Conservative MP, told Beatrice Webb that Salisbury was 'cynically indifferent to home affairs' and Balfour had 'no principle'.[22] As leader of the opposition after the Tory defeat in 1906, Balfour was highly partisan, but he could not satisfy his more extreme right-wing critics and was ditched as leader in 1911.

Though he had trouble over the free-trade protection issue, his successor, Bonar Law, did not favour social reform and was not open to right-wing assault.[23] He even said in relation to Ulster that 'there are things stronger than Parliamentary majorities'.[24] But under attack from Carson when his leadership of the party as well as the existence of the coalition were at stake shortly before Asquith's fall in 1916, he was only supported by seventy-three Conservatives.[25]

Bonar Law had resigned because of illness before Lloyd George's coalition government signed the Irish Treaty in 1921. The behaviour of his successor, Austen Chamberlain, over the treaty was described by Carson, the Ulster leader, as 'very like, after having shot a man in the back, going over to him and patting him on the shoulder and saying: "Old man, die as quickly as you can, and do not make any noise." ' In Carson's view, Ulster had been only a puppet in the political game 'to get the Conservative Party into power'.[26] Chamberlain lost the leadership a year later when a majority of Conservative MPs rejected his advice to continue the coalition with Lloyd George.

'My party,' said Baldwin, 'what is my party? Diamond Jubilee Diehards and Tory democrats pulling me two ways at once.'[27] But it was the Diehards or 'the forty thieves' who caused Baldwin trouble. After he had lost the 1929 election, the *Daily Mail* said, that 'it was the semi-Socialist policy that went down in the great defeat',[28] and Baldwin was nearly driven out of the leadership. In the early thirties, Neville Chamberlain had hoped to move towards a 'fused party under a National name', and to 'get rid of that odious title of Conservative'.[29] Nevertheless, he did not as Prime Minister face pressure from the Right. This time the resentment came from the Left. Duff Cooper complained to Baldwin that Chamberlain had 'come to make that fatal error of relying on his Right Wing and believing that they represent the party'.[30] And had Chamberlain called an election in 1938 after Munich, Anthony Eden would not have supported him but would have stood as an Independent Conservative.[31]

Even Churchill was told in 1947, by his Chief Whip, James Stuart, that a number of his senior colleagues wanted him to retire. Churchill 'reacted violently, banging the floor with his stick'.[32]

There is therefore nothing new in right-wing accusations that Conservative leaders have forsaken Conservative principles. The leadership of the Conservative Party has nearly always been criticized by party zealots for conceding too much. Indeed contemporary Conservatism as practised by the leadership is, like contemporary art, seldom much admired at the time; it only achieves acceptance and admiration in retrospect. But for the moment we are concerned with the Conservatism of the post-war party; and the right-wing criticism of the Tory leadership since the war seems to carry the following implications: the last thirty years have been disastrous for the British people, and most previous periods were much better; the disaster has been brought about by socialist policies; the Conservative Party has favoured socialist policies in contrast to the policies it favoured during the rest of its history; it has done little to slow the long march to socialism, let alone reverse it; the Tories could have ignored what Johnson called 'the clamour of the times',[33] and evolved radically different policies; and a Tory Party espousing such policies could have won elections and successfully governed the country.

For the contemporary right-wing belief that the Tory Party has been profoundly misdirected to be a true indictment, all those propositions would have to be true. Yet at least some of the right-wing resentment seems ill-founded. Sir Winston Churchill, as Prime Minister, was not greatly interested in carrying out the denationalization part of the Conservative programme.[34] Nevertheless, the electoral pledges of 1951 were honoured, and steel and road haulage were duly brought back into the private sector. And plainly there was none of the so-called 'ratchet' effect of Socialism during the thirteen Tory years. The first Wilson Government did not greatly extend state ownership except for steel, and the Conservative Government of 1970 could not have subjected that industry to yet another upheaval only three years after the previous one. Admittedly, the Heath Government hardly denationalized anything at all, but a full-scale scheme of denationalization could scarcely have been superimposed upon all its other tasks. In other words the ratchet effect of Socialism is largely a phenomenon of the last three years.

Again, the breakdown of Keynesianism today does not imply either that Keynesian policies after the war should not have been followed or that it was possible to avoid following them. Probably, the chief reason for the party's heavy defeat in the 1945 election was the high unemployment between the wars. The Tories were blamed, and the voters were determined to avoid a repetition of the thirties. The fact that very different policies have led to high unemployment in the seventies has no bearing on the political situation thirty years ago. As R. A. Butler has pointed out, the Tories had to convince the electorate that they had a policy 'which was viable, efficient and humane, which would release and reward enterprise and initiative but without abandoning social justice or reverting to mass unemployment'.[35] Even with such a policy, the party only just scraped into office in 1951 at the second attempt. A different policy would have kept the Tories in the wilderness indefinitely. For both political and economic reasons Keynesianism was imperative.

There is, however, a much wider historical misunderstanding at the root of right-wing criticisms. Right-wingers are inclined to forget that the pattern of British post-war politics was set by Churchill's great wartime Coalition, not by Attlee's post-war Government. 'In the course of time', Dr Addison has written, 'the Coalition proved to be the greatest reforming administration since the Liberal Government of 1905–14 . . . Social security for all, family allowances, major

reform in education, a National Health Service, Keynesian budgetary techniques, full employment policies, town and country planning closer relations between the state and industry – all these had been set on foot by the spring of 1943.'[36] The 'Butler' Education Act was passed in 1944. And Churchill himself told the House of Commons at the end of that year, 'We shall press forward perseveringly with the great programme of legislation which this remarkable coalition has framed . . .' 'All the leading men,' he added, 'in both the principal parties – and in the Liberal Party as well – are pledged and committed to this great mass of social legislation, and I cannot conceive that whatever may be the complexion of the new House, they will personally fail to make good their promises and commitments to the people.'[37] In Dr Addison's words, 'A massive new middle ground had arisen in politics.'[38]

Nationalization was of course not part of the Coalition consensus. Indeed even the Labour element in the Coalition were ready to drop it. The National Executive's main economic resolution at the Labour Party Conference in December 1944 did not even mention state ownership, and moving it Mr Shinwell said that the executive did not think nationalization essential for post-war reconstruction.[39] Only a revolt from the floor, which was led by Ian Mikardo and supported by the young James Callaghan,[40] foisted state ownership with all its baleful results upon the Labour leadership and the country.

Nationalization apart, the main lines of post-war policies were laid down by Churchill's wartime Coalition. The Conservative political stance since 1945 may be summarized as: general welcome of the welfare state, though such acceptance does not preclude alteration, improvement or pruning; full employment, however defined, as a prime aim of economic policy; the encouragement of ownership of property; the acceptance of trade unions as an important estate of the realm coupled with the recognition that many of the activities of trade unionism are economically damaging, and, lately, constitutionally unjustifiable; the conviction that Britain must play her proper part both militarily and diplomatically in the defence of the West; the belief that the mixed economy is a condition both of political freedom and of social stability; the judgement that private enterprise is not only essential to the preservation of political freedom but also when applicable the most efficient form of economic organization, coupled with the recognition that here as in other countries the state is bound to play an important part in the economy. All this

was explicit or implicit in Tory policy and attitudes during the war.
There was, therefore, no break in continuity between the post-war
Tory Party and the Tory Party of 1940–5. Indeed it would have been
surprising if there had been: after all, up to 1957 the leaders of the
party were the same men who had led it during the war.

Churchill was the greatest Conservative of this century. Earlier, he
was for twenty years a Liberal. He was never a Socialist. Yet 'Party
differences', he wrote in 1953, 'are now in practice mainly those of
emphasis . . .'[41] He would not have been so complacent, had he
believed he was presiding over the end of Conservatism and merely
providing a transition to Socialism. And he had good reason to
write and act as he did. After all, neither Keynes nor Beveridge, the
two chief architects of the consensus, was a Socialist; and the consensus was founded upon making capitalism work, not upon destroying it. Seemingly, therefore, it was rather more of a Tory than a
Socialist consensus. Indeed, according to the authors of the Nuffield
Study of the 1970 election, 'The Labour Party had adopted so many
Conservative policies that it left Mr Heath little room for man-
oeuvre if he did not wish to break the consensus by moving to the
right.'[42]

Conservatives who are worried by what they think their party has
sacrificed are often blind to the great changes in the policies of their
opponents. Before the war Cripps said he 'did not believe it would be
a bad thing for the British working-class if Germany defeated us'.[43]
Even Attlee could say in 1934 that his party 'had absolutely abandoned any ideas of nationalist loyalty',[44] and many other statements
of similar absurdity were made by Labour leaders. Attlee criticized
every proposal for rearmament down to the outbreak of war,[45] and
the Labour Party even opposed the introduction of conscription in
1939. Since the war, Labour's conduct of foreign policy except
during the days of Bevin and Attlee has been undistinguished, and
there have been some great follies due to left-wing influence, particularly in the sphere of defence. But in general there has been no
nonsense about following a 'Socialist' foreign policy. Labour have
maintained the Western Alliance with 'capitalist' America against
'Socialist' Russia. They have thus adopted Tory foreign policy in the
sense of seeking to promote the British national interest.

A consensus implies that both parties have diluted their policies.
Almost certainly a two-party system cannot work in the absence of
such a consensus and dilution; and obviously either party is likely to

want the proportion of the mixture altered so as to contain more of its own ingredients. The Conservatives moved slightly to the Right from 1964 to 1970, but they did not depart from the consensus; nor did Labour. A shattering, however, of the consensus by one of the parties can only indicate its belief that the consensus was not further-ing its aims. If the consensus was producing Socialism, why should Labour have broken it? In other words, Labour's metamorphosis in the last few years shows that the consensus was not a Socialist one. Even so, Labour's breaking of the consensus would not perhaps be quite enough to absolve the Tory Party of Socialist deviationism, if Labour's swing to the Left since 1971 could be shown to have been inevitable. If it was foreseeable, then moderate Tory policies could be accused of having prepared the way for the imposition of Socialism, and Tory politicians could be accused of lack of foresight. But there is nothing in post-war history to suggest the inevitability of that swing. After all, most of Labour's counterparts on the Continent had for some years been becoming less Marxist and dogmatic – not more. Labour's behaviour was not predictable; it was an aberration. Hence, the Leftward lurch of the Labour Party is more of a vindication of Tory policies since 1945 than a condemnation of them. Or rather it seems to clear them from the charge of being Socialist – it does not prove that they were right.

2. Origins

New parties arose, under the appellation of Whig and Tory, which have continued ever since to confound and distract our government. To determine the nature of these parties is perhaps one of the more difficult problems that can be met with and is a proof that history may contain questions as uncertain as any to be found in the more abstract sciences.

David Hume[1]

A wise Tory and a wise Whig, I believe, will agree. Their principles are the same, though their modes of thinking are different.

Samuel Johnson[2]

The Duke was what, in the confused phraseology of the revolutionary war, was called a Tory.

Disraeli: *Tancred*.[3]

Before coming to a conclusion on the Conservatism of the post-war Tory Governments, and before deciding whether Hicks Beach's pessimism was justified, it may be wise to look back beyond recent policies and events. We need rather more guidance as to what is and what is not Conservatism than the continuity of the last thirty years. Guidance can be sought in the origins of the Tory Party, in its history, and in the views of Conservative writers.

We may begin by going back to the origins of the party which is of course strictly a radical rather than a conservative activity.[4] The difficulty is that there is no agreement as to when the Tory Party began. Dr Johnson thought the first Whig was the Devil.[5] Lord Acton thought it was 'not the Devil but St Thomas Aquinas'.[6] Tories cannot claim such distinguished ancestors. Their parentage is uncertain, and the date of their birth is obscure. Perhaps the Tories, like the poor, have always been with us. Some intrepid explorers have found the beginnings of Toryism in Tudor times. But Henry VIII, for all his political skills, is not an appealing founder – at least for those who believe that the family is an integral part of Toryism. The prevalent gangsterdom under Edward VI and the *autos-da-fé* of Mary are even less tempting. Elizabeth is more promising, and some Elizabethan social legislation to relieve the poor can be viewed as effective Tory paternalism. Yet plainly no such thing as a Tory Party then existed.

A more popular choice for the beginnings of Toryism is 1642 and the Cavaliers. 'Church and King' was for long the foundation of Toryism. And certainly Falkland and Hyde were attractive and moderate men. They declared ship money illegal and like the rest of the moderate Royalists they were opposed to the arbitrary rule by the King and to the excesses of Laud and the bishops. They even voted for the attainder of Strafford.[7] It was only the extremism of 'King' Pym and his followers that drove them over to the side of Charles, and they voted against the Grand Remonstrance. Having dismantled the so-called royal tyranny, they declined to set up a new one. 'When it is not necessary to change,' said Falkland, 'it is necessary not to change.'[8] Macaulay, an unfriendly critic, summed up their attitude in his 'Battle of Naseby':

> 'For God, for the Cause, for the Church, for the laws,
> For Charles King of England and Rupert of the Rhine.'

Yet neither the Church nor the King was worthy of such men. Charles I was genuinely religious, had a fine collection of pictures and unlike Henry VIII was a good husband and father.* But he was incompetent in his duplicity, his attempt to govern without Parliament was a failure, and under him the Church of England was a persecuting Church. And even if he is given the benefit of every doubt about the start of the first civil war, he was certainly to blame for the second. After the Bill of Attainder had passed the Commons, Charles gave Strafford the word of a King that he would 'not suffer in life, honour or fortune'.[9] If Toryism is, as Cardinal Newman thought, loyalty to persons,[10] Charles's betrayal of Strafford excludes him.†

---

*'He had so many virtues,' scoffed Macaulay, 'and what, after all, are the virtues ascribed to Charles? A few of the ordinary household decencies which half the tombstones of England claim for those who lie beneath them.'

†It was said of Balfour that 'he smiles upon his friends and leaves them to the wolves'.[11] But it was only their political lives that were then at stake.

In some ways, indeed, Oliver Cromwell has better claims to being a conservative than Charles I. Admittedly to cut off the head of one's sovereign is not in general a conservative mode of behaviour. Yet Cromwell might have said with the Spanish conservative Cambó: 'Considering the circumstances in which the country finds itself, the most conservative thing is to be a revolutionary.'[12] And like that other erstwhile revolutionary, George Washington, Cromwell was often highly conservative. He always wanted 'a settlement of somewhat with monarchical power in it',[13] but he was admirably undogmatic about forms of government. 'If you make the best of it,' he said in the Putney debates, 'if you should change the government to the best of it, it is but a moral thing. It is but, as Paul says, "dross and dung in comparison of Christ".'[14] He was profoundly aware of the limitations of politics. He did not think 'when I undertook the Place [the Protectorate], that I could do much good; but I did think I might prevent imminent evil'.[15] He had no preconceived plan or system of abstract ideas. 'No one rises so high,' he said, 'as he who knows not whither he is going.'[16] He was always empirical and cautious. He was also, as the German theologian Döllinger pointed out, 'the first among the mighty men of the world to set up one special religious principle, and to enforce it so far as in him lay: . . . the principle of liberty of conscience and the repudiation of religious coercion'.[17]

Cromwell was not a philistine. He did not desecrate cathedrals. The theatre was not banned during the Protectorate. Indeed it was during his rule that actresses first appeared on the London stage. His Court was an important patron of music. Milton and Marvell were his secretaries, and the miniaturist Samuel Cooper held office under him.[18] Nevertheless he was a dictator and a Puritan, and the most that can therefore be said of him is that he was a Tory *manqué*.

The term 'Tory' dates from the Exclusion controversy of 1679–81 and has been in common use ever since. (A Tory was originally an Irish robber and outlaw; a Whig was a Scottish outlaw.) Some of those who supported Charles II in that crisis, notably Halifax, were men of fine conservative judgement. Charles himself, whose concern for the family ranked about midway between that of Henry VIII and Charles I, was good company, he liked dogs and horses, and he was politically skilful. Yet, during his reign any chance of the Church becoming genuinely comprehensive was finally thrown away; as Halifax said, the Church sacrificed 'their interest . . . to their revenge'.[19]

And Charles II's position of pensioner of Louis XIV and his efforts
to earn that pension are not consonant with one of the fundamental
Tory virtues, patriotism. But whatever may be thought of Charles
and his brother, there was from about 1680 a Tory Party in existence.

Between 1690 and 1710, according to Professor Plumb, 'the Tory
party acquired a recognisable *persona*'. Tories 'stood for free and
frequent elections, sharp punishment for bribery and electoral corruption, low taxation, financial rectitude, accountability to Parliament, the exclusion of all place-holders, and a sound land qualification for members. They also had a reluctance to large-scale
continental war and an aversion to dissent.'[20] But the old Tory Party
was virtually broken by Bolingbroke's cowardice in fleeing the
country to serve the Pretender and by the attachment of many
Tories to Jacobitism. As a result of Tory folly, Walpole was able to
end the two-party system;[21] and therefore, though something of the
tradition lingered on, there is no continuity between that Tory Party
and the Tory Party of the present day.

Up to 1760 the Government was called Whig, and after 1760 the
Government party was called Tory by its opponents.[22] But the labels
tell us nothing about the principles and outlook of those to whom
they were affixed. In the middle of the eighteenth century the continuity was of power and opposition not of names and parties.* The
Younger Pitt never called himself a Tory and only once 'an independent Whig'.[23] After Pitt's death, Canning was the first Cabinet
Minister for nearly a century to describe himself as a Tory.[24]†

*A song put into the mouth of North by the *Morning Chronicle* gives a good
illustration:
> 'Then Whigs we'll be and coalesce
> And change our former faces;
> For Whiggish principles are best
> Till we're in Tories' places;
> But should kind heaven my power restore
> I'll change the present story;
> Make me but absolute once more,
> And then I'll turn a Tory.'[25]

†This confusion about party names is not confined to England. The oldest
party in America, the Democratic Party, was at the end of the eighteenth century
called the Republican Party. Later it became known as the Democratic–Republican Party. Then in the time of Jackson the word 'Republican' was dropped.[26]
The present Republican Party calls itself the GOP (the grand old party), presumably because it is in fact younger than its rival.

Yet Lord Blake has good grounds for thinking that traces of a new Tory Party can be discerned though it lacked the name,[27] and he dates the continuous existence of the Conservative Party from the crisis of 1782–4. But ten years later one of the greatest conservative thinkers, Burke, was led by his hatred of the French Revolution and his differences with Fox to cross the floor of the House in company with the Portland Whigs; that seems to me to make 1794 as good a date for the birth certificate of the modern Tory Party as any other.*

The darkness surrounding the party's origins clearly makes the search for its first or original principles fruitless. The ideas of all those who lived before the age of Pitt and Burke should not be ignored – some of them will be considered in the next part – but any attempt to draw lessons from the early or pre-history of the party is mere ancestor-worship, without even the certainty that the right ancestors are being worshipped.

---

*There are of course other possibilities such as 1809, which saw the formation of what can probably be called the first almost purely Tory administration, though its leader Spencer Percival never called himself a Tory; 1832, which saw the Tory Party's greatest *débâcle* and from which Conservatism, as opposed to Toryism, is sometimes dated; and 1846, when the split over the Corn Laws caused a gap in the organizational continuity of the party.[28]

3. A Glance Backwards

I have constantly observed that the generality of people are fifty years, at least, behind hand in their politics . . . In books everything is settled for them without the exertion of any considerable diligence or capacity. For which reason, men are wise with but little reflection, and good with little self-denial in the business of all times except their own.

Edmund Burke[1]

History is philosophy teaching by examples . . .

Bolingbroke[2]

Foot after foot ye go back and travail to make yourselves mad;
Blind feet that feel for the track where highway is none to be had.

Swinburne: *Hymn of Man.*[3]

To place the origins of the Tory Party in 1794 or 1784 is not of course to suggest that there was then or for many years afterwards anything resembling the present party system. Until 1832 the King, not the Prime Minister, was the head of the Government; and politics were still a matter of groups, proprietary factions and changing and conflicting loyalties.* All Governments were to a greater or lesser extent coalitions. Yet without undue arbitrariness, the party's history can be divided into three periods: 1794–1827, 1827–74, and 1874–1945. Save for one short interval it governed for the whole of the first period. It thus presided over the British wars against the French Revolution and against Napoleon. The Tories could look back, Canning said, to 'nations rescued and thrones re-established, battles won with matchless courage, and triumphs un-paralleled in their splendour and consequences'. In contrast, he said,

*'Our danger is not from opposition,' the Prime Minister, Liverpool, wrote to Peel in 1812, 'but evidently from the third parties headed by Lord Wellesley and Canning.'[4]

the Whig record was a 'series of persevering objections to every measure by which these glories and benefits have been obtained, [and] a succession of theories refuted by facts and of prophecies falsified by experience'.[5]

From 1812 to 1827, Liverpool was Prime Minister. The Frenchman who remarked of him that if he had been present at the creation of the world he would have said, *'Mon Dieu, conservons le chaos'*,[6] was unjust. Admittedly, after fairly mild disturbances in 1816 and 1819, the Liverpool Government passed some repressive legislation, including Sidmouth's notorious 'Six Acts'. But with Canning and Peel joining the Cabinet in 1822 as Foreign and Home Secretaries, and Huskisson joining it a year later as President of the Board of Trade, the Government became much more liberal as well as more divided.

Canning pursued a popular foreign policy designed to raise British prestige. 'Every nation for itself, and God for us all',[7] was his cry. Peel reformed the barbarous criminal law, abolishing the capital sentence on over a hundred offences, and began reform of the prisons and the legal system. 'What I propose,' he said, 'is to break this sleep of a century.'[8] And Huskisson greatly reduced tariffs, relaxed the navigation laws and allowed the colonies to trade direct with foreign countries. At the same time the Combination Acts were repealed so that trade unions could legally combine and strike for higher wages or improved conditions. This was, however, the work of Francis Place, not the Government. Indeed Liverpool was apparently ignorant of what had happened.[9] Nevertheless the Radical Place considered Liverpool's Government 'less exceptionable than any former Administration' and did not think 'a change in favour of the Whigs desirable'.[10] But the reforms caused friction in the Cabinet, which only Liverpool could keep together. And his retirement in 1827 because of a stroke brought the first period to an end.

Canning succeeded him, and the Tory Party split, Wellington, Peel and many others refusing to join the Government. After Canning's death and a few months of drifting, Wellington became Prime Minister in January 1828 for two disastrous years. At the first Cabinet dinner one of its members noted that 'the courtesy was that of men who had just fought a duel',[11] and Wellington soon lost Huskisson and the Canningites. The following year Wellington and Peel correctly decided that O'Connell's election for County Clare had made Catholic emancipation inevitable. The trouble was that both of them had long opposed relief for Catholics, and so had many of their followers. In consequence the Tory Party was again broken.

Wellington remarked that England was never governed by 'extreme principles of any party whatever' and confessed that he did not have a 'clear idea' of what was meant by Whig or Tory principles.[12] By declining to learn the lesson taught by their opposition and then belated conversion to Catholic emancipation, Wellington and Peel did nothing about parliamentary reform. Indeed Wellington gratuitously suggested that the existing system of representation was of an 'excellence' rarely found in this world, and declared that he would always resist its alteration.[13] This doctrinaire refusal to contemplate reform swept the Whigs into office and the long Tory ascendancy was over.* By 1833 the Tories held 150 seats, less than a quarter of the House of Commons.

Peel's Tamworth Manifesto, his acceptance of the Reform Bill as a 'final and irrevocable settlement of a great constitutional question',[14] and his conduct of the opposition set the pattern for the future performance of the Tory Party. His object in opposition was to help the Whig Government to keep out of the clutches of the Radicals.

Though kind and generous in his private life, Peel was rigid and unimaginative over reform of the Poor Law and the Factory Acts. Yet he was no bigoted believer in *laissez-faire*. In 1818 he supported his father's bill to protect children in factories and he opposed the Radical Hume's defence of 'truck'.[15] In Glasgow in 1837 he told his audience that he did not want the great machine of government to stand still; he wanted to see it 'animating industry, encouraging production, rewarding toil, correcting what is irregular, purifying what is stagnant or corrupt'.[16] He urged them to join with him to defend 'the existing institutions of the country'. Peel was steadily winning back the support of the urban middle class, and in 1841 he was able to form a Government very much abler than any of its Whig predecessors.

Eleven years earlier Peel had thought the great evil of the times was a 'tendency to diminish the enjoyments of the poorer classes . . . and widen their separation from the upper classes'.[17] And as Prime Minister he was clear that whatever the financial difficulties he would not introduce measures which bore on 'the comforts of the labouring classes of society'.[18] His reintroduction of income tax showed his

*'Nought's permanent among the human race', Byron had written in *Don Juan*, 'Except the Whigs *not* getting into place?'[19]

determination to make the Conservatives a national party, pursuing a national not a class policy. He carried on Huskisson's work of twenty years before by greatly reducing tariffs while increasing colonial preferences. The economy was revived and the cost of living reduced. The most competent of British Prime Ministers, Peel did more than anybody else to prevent revolution or serious disorder in the 1840s.

Much earlier Wellington had said of him that he was 'afraid to place himself on high ground'.[20] A fairer judgement would be that he tended to place himself on high ground much too late. Thus he wrecked the party he had fashioned when the Irish potato famine led him to repeal the Corn Laws against the opposition of most of his followers. He had done little to prepare his party for a measure which, like Catholic emancipation, he had previously opposed and which offended his party's ideological susceptibilities and also its pockets. Proud and reserved, he had no fund of popularity to draw upon in the parliamentary party. Yet Greville was probably right in believing a year after his fall that in the country an overwhelming majority would vote for him as Prime Minister.[21]

The split left the Tories with its country gentlemen – and Disraeli. To many of the political nation, the Tories without Peel and his followers seemed to be both narrow and short of talent, and hence an unsuitable instrument of government. Except for three short periods of minority rule they were out of office from 1846 to 1874. They were the country party both in the sense of town and country, and in the sense of court and country. Their 'countryness' at least made them less ready than their opponents to accept as inevitable the appalling conditions in the factories. In one vote on Ashley's Ten Hours Bill, 81 Liberals voted against and 71 for, 73 Peelites out of 80 voted against, while 117 out of 168 Protectionists voted for it.[22] In the sixties the Tories were not 'noticeably different' from the Liberals 'on humanitarian and social matters',[23] but they did not inspire confidence in the country. And that remained true until almost the end of the second period.

In the first half of the nineteenth century, the British Empire was fostered and extended by Radicals and Liberals. Peel did not favour imperial expansion. He preferred consolidation and wrote disparagingly 'of the cravings of our army for more conquests and more glory'.[24] Similarly the Tories disapproved of Palmerston's aggressive and turbulent diplomacy. In 1857, for instance, they joined with

Gladstone in attacking Palmerston's China policy. 'I am an advocate,' Derby declared, 'for the feeble defencelessness of China against the overpowering might of Great Britain.'[25] At that time Disraeli had similar views and was not an imperialist.

It was only from Disraeli's 1874 Administration onwards that the Tory Party made a take-over bid for imperialism and began to adopt an assertive foreign policy. The Conservatives were no longer the Little-Englander Party, a role which was assumed by the Liberals. Even then party divisions were not clear-cut. The highly imperialist bombardment of Alexandria was ordered by Gladstone's Liberal Government and fiercely attacked by the Tory Lord Randolph Churchill.

Like Bismarck in Germany, Disraeli saw that a wider franchise might forge an electoral alliance between the urban masses and the landed classes, and his Reform Bill of 1867 enfranchised the urban artisan – the proletariat of his opponents. Disraeli had complained of Peel stealing the Whigs' clothes while they were bathing, and he and Derby were now doing the same, with the important difference, however, that their clothes-lifting was done in the interests of their party and did not split it. Disraeli was not content merely to terminate 'the monopoly of liberalism'[26] by enfranchising the urban artisans. The social legislation of his 1874 Government, which begins the third period, was on such matters as trade unions and public health far in advance of that of Gladstone's.

Unfortunately the impetus died with Disraeli. Lord Randolph Churchill tried to carry on the tradition, but his tactics were faulty, the old guard was strong, and his conception of Tory democracy lacked definition. Had it not been for Gladstone's miscalculation over Home Rule and the resulting Liberal split, the Tory Party might have returned to the wilderness out of which Disraeli had led it. Instead, 'Home Rule' gave it new allies, a cause to defend, and with one short interlude, twenty years in office.

The Conservatives had to pay for the continued support of Chamberlain and the Liberal Unionists by enacting parts of the Radical programme. The reforms were often extensive, but they were grudging. In contrast to Disraeli, the party now saw Conservatism as a rearguard action against social reform. As early as 1892 Chamberlain put old-age pensions among the most important reforms, but the Salisbury and Balfour Governments produced nothing but inquiries. It was left to the Liberals and Asquith to bring in the first Old-Age Pensions Bill in 1908; Bismarck's Germany had had old-age pensions since 1889. The Liberal split had brought the Conservatives the Whigs as well as Chamberlain, and between then and 1914 the Conservatives came nearer than at any time in their history to resembling a continental party of the Right, nearer to being dominated by a single interest, the rich, and to neglecting their wider responsibilities to the nation as a whole. The party was 'sodden with Whiggery'.[27]

'My uncle is a Tory,' said Balfour, 'and I am a Liberal,'[28] yet he bore a closer resemblance to Salisbury than to Lord Randolph Churchill. For an issue to revive the party after the Boer War Chamberlain was driven not to urgent social measures but to tariff reform without any of the trimmings that would have made it palatable to the working-class voter. Admittedly, tariff reform was intended to relieve unemployment and to provide money for further social advance. And Chamberlain was much more far-sighted than his opponents in his assessment of the future of British industry. But tariff reform was also part of a grand scheme of Empire unity, which most of the Colonies did not want and which necessitated taxes on food. The scheme as a whole was therefore both impracticable and unpopular. Stripped of its imperial grandeur it was fully viable and would have led to social reform; as presented, however, it merely succeeded in splitting the Conservatives into three and the party remained divided on the issue until the 1930s. Unable to keep his followers together, Balfour clung to office until the Committee of Imperial Defence was fully established and then went down to disastrous defeat in 1906.

A Liberal MP, Samuel Plimsoll, had said in 1875 that 'the interests of the working classes when at issue between themselves and the capitalists are safer with the Conservatives than with the Liberals'.[29] Despite the fact that the Conservatives drew increased support from the urban masses, this became less true after Lord Randolph's resignation.

Damaging in office, the doctrine and mentality of retreat was disastrous in opposition, leading all too logically to the taking up of a do-or-die position in the last ditch against the Lloyd George Budget and the reform of the House of Lords. Balfour tried to restrain his followers, but the Lords were beyond restraint, at least by Balfour. The lessons taught by Peel followed those of Disraeli into oblivion. Opposition was fractious, inflamed, and, under Balfour's

successor Bonar Law, unconstitutional. From 1906 to 1914 the
Conservative Party in opposition betrayed itself and came close to
betraying its country.

After taking part in Asquith's coalition, the Conservatives were
the preponderant part of Lloyd George's war and post-war Coalition
Governments. In 1922 the backbenchers revolted, Lloyd George
resigned and Bonar Law formed his Government of 'under-secretaries'
– most of the Conservative leaders electing to stay with Lloyd George
outside. Bonar Law once said that before the war the 'only two things
[he] really cared for' were tariff reform and Ulster, 'the rest was
mainly a game'[30] – a startling confession if seriously meant. Certainly
the condition of the people does not seem to have preoccupied him.
Fortunately the attitude of his successor, Baldwin, towards labour
was similar to that of Disraeli and Lord Randolph Churchill.
Baldwin's objective was to mitigate or avoid a class war in Britain.
In this he was strikingly successful. He did not prevent his party
passing the Trade Disputes Bill of 1927 after the General Strike, but
he kept its revenge down to little more than the minimum. Though
merciless to the Labour Party electorally, he was conciliatory to
labour politically. He treated its leaders with courtesy and its
aspirations with respect. He once said that Socialism and *laissez-
faire* are like the North and South Pole – they don't really exist.[31]
And he acted accordingly.

Schumpeter remarked that it was difficult for the first Labour
Government in 1924 to strike a distinctive note, because 'fiscal
radicalism had been (and continued to be) carried, quite as far as was
possible under the circumstances, by Conservative governments'.[32]
Much the same could be said of Conservative policies towards the
social services. Davidson, who was then Bonar Law's parliamentary
private secretary and was later a Conservative Minister or Chairman
of the party for most of the twenties and thirties, told Bonar Law that
he would like to fight his election in 1922 'on the programme of every
boy and girl entering industry being insured against old age, sickness,
and unemployment . . .' Bonar Law told him that it was a 'very fine
goal to aim at'. Looking back, Davidson regretted that the Tory
Party had not been more imaginative and reflected that 'it would have
been a wonderful thing' if his idea had been adopted by the party in
1922 or 1923.[33]

Nevertheless, in the twenties considerable progress was made
towards the welfare state.[34] Neville Chamberlain, with Churchill's

B

assistance, was the driving force. On becoming Minister of Health in 1924, he straightaway devised a massive programme of twenty-five Bills to be passed in four years, and succeeded in passing twenty-one of them before the end of the Government, the rest being enacted later.[35] In alliance with Winston Churchill, he passed the Widows, Orphans and Old-Age Pensions Act, which gave pensions without a means test to the widows, dependent children and orphans of those insured for health, and old-age pensions at sixty-five to insured men and their wives. His Rating and Valuation Act pointed the way to the end of the Poor Law.[36] He subsidized housing, and while he was Minister, 800000 houses were built, far more than under any previous Government. Further improvements were made in the thirties, and in that decade nearly three million houses were built. In consequence, by 1939, the social services in Britain were, in Dr Addison's view, 'the most advanced in the world . . . and the Social Democrats in Sweden, the Labour Party in New Zealand and the New Deal Democrats in the United States were trying to bring about many of the improvements which Conservatism took for granted'.[37]

In economic affairs, too, the Conservative Party did not, between the wars, always show that single-minded devotion to the virtues of the market and free competitive enterprise, which is sometimes held to be the only true hall-mark of Conservatism. In 1926, the Baldwin Government brought in two nationalization measures: in electricity and in broadcasting. The Racecourse Betting Control Board followed in 1928, and Labour's intended nationalization of London Transport was carried into law by the predominantly Conservative National Government of 1933. Coal deposits were nationalized in 1938. These were very small beer compared with what Socialist governments have done in the last thirty years, but they explain Churchill's remark in 1946 that the nationalization of the Bank of England did not 'raise any matter of principle'.[38]

In the twenties, admittedly, there was little in the financial field to worry those who were opposed to intervention by government. Having fought and lost an election in 1923 on the introduction of a tariff, Baldwin was disposed to be cautious about protection for the rest of the decade. He had moreover tied his hands by making Churchill Chancellor of the Exchequer. Churchill, like most of the Labour Party, was still a free-trader, which in a world where most other countries had imposed tariffs was rather like being a supporter of CND in the sixties. In 1925 Churchill, with considerable misgivings, returned to the gold standard fixing the pound at its pre-war value with the dollar. This was welcomed at the time except by Keynes, and vilified later. Probably it had less effect than was generally believed, but an overvalued pound favoured 'finance' and handicapped industry as Churchill had feared.[39] Although he helped industry by lowering its taxes, Churchill, with Baldwin's acquiescence, was able to thwart the attempt of the protectionists to safeguard British industries, and any chance of solving the problem of unemployment was lost.

The harsh verdict of L. S. Amery, a fervent protectionist, who sat in Baldwin's Cabinet with Churchill, was that the Chancellor's policies represented the 'rigid finance of the previous century . . . The combination of deflation and free imports which he stubbornly maintained bore its immediate fruit in wage reductions, long-drawn industrial conflict and continuous heavy unemployment; its long-term results in the conviction of the working class that Socialism alone could provide a remedy for unemployment. The chief author of a great Prime Minister's defeat in 1945 was the Chancellor of the Exchequer of twenty years before.'[40] Mr Macmillan, then a backbencher but a protectionist like Amery, takes a more balanced view. He believes Baldwin's second Government to have been 'on the whole successful'.[41]

The Chancellor of the Exchequer in the 1929–31 Labour Government, Philip Snowden, was even less inclined to protection than his predecessor, Churchill. Neville Chamberlain suggested in the Budget debate of 1931 that Snowden would be the last Chancellor to introduce a free-trade budget. It marked the end, he thought, of 'an obsolete and worn-out system'.[42] And after the economic crisis and formation of the National Government, Chamberlain, as Chancellor, based his policy instead on protection, imperial preference and cheap money. In 1932 he lowered the Bank Rate to 2 per cent where it remained till the war. Apart from its imperial aspects, Chamberlain saw a tariff as a 'lever . . . for inducing or, if you like, forcing industry to set its house in order',[43] and he used it as such. The Government was highly interventionist. Rationalization of industry, control of prices and output, subsidies, agricultural marketing boards – these were now the features of Conservative economic policy, not competition and free trade.

Either by luck or as a result of these measures, Britain recovered from the slump quicker than other industrial countries. Two million more people were in employment in 1937 than in 1932. Between 1931 and 1937 productivity in manufacturing industry rose by more than 20 per cent.[44] Real wages rose, as did Britain's share of world trade. With the important exceptions of the depressed areas, Britain was prosperous. In acting as he did, Chamberlain was in no sense imitating the Socialists. Up to 1931, Labour favoured free trade. Snowden did not believe that Socialism entailed interference with the laws of supply and demand.[45] It was only in the thirties under the stimulus of its failure in government, the Russian Five-Year Plan, Roosevelt's New Deal and the writings of Keynes, that Labour adopted the idea of economic planning.[46]

Chamberlain himself thought the National Government was 'continually introducing changes of a really revolutionary character'.[47] Harold Macmillan advocated much more drastic measures throughout the decade and published *The Middle Way* in 1938. But whether or not the Government's changes were revolutionary, they were radical enough to distress Professor Hayek. Britain, he gloomily noted in 1943, had 'in the short space of the inglorious years 1931 to 1939, transformed its economic system beyond recognition'.[48] The far from *avant-garde* Sir John Anderson viewed the same developments with relaxed if not cheerful detachment. 'I prefer,' he told the voters when seeking election to Parliament in 1938, 'the moderate forms of Socialism practised by the great majority of supporters of the National Government to the more extreme forms advocated in other quarters.'[49] In the twenties Chamberlain once described himself as a Socialist,[50] but his policies were collectivist, if collectivism is taken to mean in Dicey's words 'faith in the benefit to be derived by the mass of the people from the action or intervention of the state',[51] rather than Socialist. Above all, they were protectionist. In any event, the history of the National Government bears out R. A. Butler's remark in 1956 that 'Conservatives have always been ready to use the power of the State'.[52]

In the first period of the party's history, then, the Tories were in power virtually without a break. By and large the party moved with and occasionally ahead of the times. It was above all a governing instrument and saw itself as such. During the third period it was the normal governing party, never splitting except partially over tariff reform and over the ending of the Lloyd George coalition. It never looked eccentric, it was seldom extreme except between 1906 and 1914, and it knew that it had to attract moderates and opponents to stay in power. The Conservatives always remembered that the purpose of a political party in a two-party system is the gaining of power, not the accretion of dogma; and they were lucky.

In the second period, save for the first three years, the party only once had a majority in the House of Commons. It split in 1827, 1829 and, most disastrously, in 1846. These splits were caused by a dogmatic insistence by large sections of the party on opposing the inevitable. Too many of the party put dogma before power and concentrated on the party's own sectional interests instead of on the national interest. In consequence the Tory Party seemed cranky and irresponsible, and its opponents became the natural governing party of the country.

However the history of the party is divided or regarded, there is no discernible 'true-blue' golden age. The right wing was in the ascendant during part of the years 1827–74, but by sticking to what it thought were its principles, it ensured that the Tory Party stuck largely to opposition. Peel was partly responsible for the right-wing 'victories' of 1827–30, and Disraeli was partly responsible for bringing down Peel in 1846. Both then had to repair the damage they had done by sharply altering course. The two greatest Conservative leaders of the nineteenth century saw that the party must abandon its concentration on trying to please itself. If it was not to degenerate into a mere right-wing faction, dependent on a single interest, it must look at politics in national not in party terms. It must become a national party, and both Peel and Disraeli succeeded in making it one.

The only other era in which the right wing was largely in control were the years before the First World War, though the control was far from absolute because of Chamberlain and the Liberal Unionists. Yet that era saw in 1906 the greatest Conservative defeat since 1832, and a selfishness, shortsightedness and lack of scruple in the party which had never been seen before, and which fortunately has never been seen since. If that age was 'true-blue', it was very far from golden.

Socialists may look forward to some grim utopia. Conservatives have no such illusions about the future or the past. For them, there never has been a 'golden age', and there never will be. Similarly, there is no discernible fixed or 'golden' policy to which the Conservative Party could or should return. The history of the party, however instructive it may be in other respects, provides little help on particular issues of policy. No wonder Disraeli, in his last novel *Endymion*, mocked the idea of a Tory apostolic succession which he himself had once held!

'Is not the Tory Party,' Waldershare would exclaim, 'a succession of heroic spirits, beautiful and swift, ever in the van, and foremost of their age? – Hobbes and Bolingbroke, Hume and Adam Smith, Wyndham and Cobham, Pitt and Grenville, Canning and Huskisson? – Are not the principles of Toryism those popular rights which men like Shippen and Hynde Cotton flung in the face of an alien monarch and his mushroom aristocracy? – Place bills, triennial bills, opposition to standing armies, to peerage bills? – Are not the traditions of the Tory Party the noblest pedigree in the world? Are not its illustrations that glorious martyrology, that opens with the name of Falkland and closes with the name of Canning?'

'I believe it is all true,' whispered Lord Beaumaris to Sylvia, who had really never heard of any of these gentlemen before, but looked most sweet and sympathetic.

'He is a wonderful man – Mr Waldershare,' said Mr Vigo to Rodney, 'but I fear not practical.'[53]

And it is certainly neither practical nor sensible to seek consistency in Tory policy through the ages in the shallow sense of 'sameness'. For instance, the party has had the good sense to move from protection to free trade, back to protection, and then again towards free trade according to the economic circumstances of the time. Again, there can be no permanent attitude to the state or to the relations between it and the individual, since the state is continually changing. The state today is quite different from what it was one hundred years ago. 'To predicate one entity as the State,' Professor Burn has written, 'and another as the individual without allowing for changes in either...' treating them as though 'they were subject to unchanging rules, is an exercise in folly.'[54] In implying, therefore, in the remark quoted at the beginning of this book that conservatism is something static and unchanging, Hicks Beach was profoundly mistaken. Critics of the post-war Tory leadership have fallen into the same error. Nothing is static, and a brief look at Tory history has shown that Conservatism, not surprisingly, is no exception. That glance also refutes the view that the Conservative Party has somehow deserted its past and its principles since the war. There has been greater use of the Budget as a weapon of economic management since Kingsley Wood's Budget of 1941, and there has been a greater emphasis on the desirability of competition than there was in the years before 1939. But ample continuity has been demonstrated between pre-war and post-war Conservatism. All policies have their defects, and Tory policies after the war did not break that rule. Moreover, conditions change, and policies which once were suitable may be disastrous thirty years later. Yet if post-war Conservative Governments were sometimes wrong, they were not anti-Tory. Hence the third and greatest period of the party's history can certainly be extended to 1964. Whether the years since 1964 are a continuation of that period or the beginning of a new one, it is too soon to tell.

The variations in Conservative policy have been no greater in this century than in the last, and in any case they have probably been less spectacular than the gyrations performed by some American or French politicians. Daniel Webster voted originally against the Bank of the United States, was opposed to protection, and believed that individual States had the power to nullify Federal laws. Some ten years later Webster favoured protection, supported the Bank of the United States and strongly defended the Union against those who advocated nullification of Federal laws.[55] But even Webster would have had difficulty in keeping up with Sir Harold Wilson.

Nevertheless on such fundamental issues as the extension of the franchise, free trade and protection, and imperial and foreign policy, the Tory position has widely varied. What Macaulay called 'the ignominious pride of a fatal consistency' has never been a Tory virtue[56] – any more than it has in practice been a Socialist or Liberal virtue. But whereas there are theoretical reasons why Liberalism and Socialism should be consistent, there are no similar reasons enjoining consistency on Conservatism. The Tory aim is harmony, not unison. And the Conservative Party has been more concerned to preserve continuity in the state than continuity in its own policies.

Part Two

The public good . . . depends on the concurrence of a multitude of causes.
David Hume[1]

Manners are of more importance than laws. Upon them, in a great measure, the laws depend.
Edmund Burke[2]

Liberty is the mistress of mankind.
Halifax[3]

1. George Savile, Marquis of Halifax (1635–95)

Among the statesmen of those times Halifax was, in genius, the first.
Macaulay[1]

A glance at Tory history shows therefore that no unchanging infallible guidance on policy can be derived from the past practice of
the party. Conservatism is too subtle a matter to be uncovered by
any such crude procedure. Let us seek further assistance, then, from
what may be called the fathers and doctors of Conservatism. As
with the party's origins, there is no agreement as to which writers
should be included in the Conservative canon and which should be
relegated to the apocrypha. My principles of selection were to choose
only from those who were undoubtedly Tory or Conservative in their
views and to see that every century was represented. Within those
rules I have picked the writers who seem to me to be the most important and the best.

No doubt the correctness of a thinker's judgement of the political
events of his own time should not be the test of the merits of his
thought. The contemporary misjudgements of the constitutional
issues raised by the Ulster crisis of 1912–14, for instance, by such
leading constitutionalists as Anson and Dicey do not destroy the
value of the rest of their opinions. But much as the sight of an
historian being silly about the present day inevitably, if mistakenly,
raises doubts about his historical writings, so a thinker's sure touch
about the politics of his own times adds weight and attraction to his
general views. And Halifax, at least to the present-day eye, was
almost invariably right.

'The truth is,' Macaulay wrote,

. . . that the memory of Halifax is entitled in an especial manner to the
protection of history . . . He was called inconstant, because the relative
position in which he stood to the contending factions was perpetually

varying. As well might the pole star be called inconstant because it is sometimes to the east and sometimes to the west of the pointers. To have defended the ancient and legal constitution of the realm against a seditious populace at one conjuncture, and against a tyrannical government at another; to have been the foremost champion of order in the turbulent Parliament of 1680, and the foremost champion of liberty in the servile Parliament of 1685; to have been just and merciful to Roman Catholics in the days of the Popish plot, and to Exclusionists in the days of the Rye House Plot; to have done all in his power to save both the head of Stafford and the head of Russell; this was a course which contemporaries, heated by passion, and deluded by names and badges, might not unnaturally call fickle, but which deserves a very different name from the late justice of posterity.[2]

In any case Halifax's writings need no protection from history. Even without the support of his practice, his precepts would repay study. They provide almost a grammar of Conservatism. 'It must be more than an ordinary provocation', was his amiable beginning, 'that can tempt a man to write in an age over-run with scribblers, as Egypt was with flies and locusts . . . [But] when madmen, in two extremes, shall agree to make common sense treason, and join to fix an ill character upon the only men in the nation who deserve a good one; I am no longer master of my better resolution to let the world alone . . .'[3]

Attacked as 'a Trimmer', he proudly accepted the title. The word, he said, merely meant that 'if men are together in a boat, and one part of the company would weigh it down on one side, another would make it lean as much to the contrary; it happeneth there is a third opinion of those, who conceive it would do as well, if the boat went even, without endangering the passengers'.[4] Halifax's trimming was thus the opposite of what is normally meant by political trimming. In action Halifax was bold and decisive.[5] He trimmed to weaken the stronger side, not to join it. In Halifax's sense of the word, trimming has been an important element in Conservatism, though in modern politics balance can normally be achieved only by the party and not by individuals. The Conservative Party trims by leaning against the prevailing fashion; and by the manner of its opposition to the other main party it tries to maintain the balance of the nation.

But there was no 'trimming' in Halifax's patriotism. Halifax had no sympathy with Rome, and he had a clear understanding of the threat posed by Louis XIV. In words fully applicable to Moscow today, he marvelled that Rome 'so painted and yet so pretending' should 'after having abus'd, depos'd and murther'd so many of her lovers' still be able to find many others proud to put on her 'chains'. His remarks about the admirers of Louis XIV are no less applicable to those who now determinedly refuse to recognize the Russian danger. He mocked anyone who believed that of all men living the King of France was the least disposed 'to be a conqueror', that he was 'a sleepy, tame creature, void of all ambition', only anxious for a bit of peace and quiet, who could not conceivably do Britain any harm.[6] The British entertainers in 1975 of Mr Shelepin and other luminaries of the Russian secret police have credulous seventeenth-century ancestors. Halifax saw no place for trimming in foreign policy or in defence. To Englishmen who asked what they should 'do to be saved in this world', Halifax's answer was, 'look to your moat. The first article of an *Englishman's* political creed must be, that he believeth in the sea, etc., without that there needeth no General Council to pronounce him incapable of salvation here.'[7]

Halifax's trimming was thus confined to home politics. He owned 'a passion for liberty', which he took to be the foundation of all virtue, but his passion was too restrained to 'impair or taint his allegance' to his sovereign. The English constitution was admirable because it successfully reconciled liberty and authority. There was a just proportion in the Government, 'no tympany, no unnatural swelling either of power or liberty'. Law was the foundation of our constitution and of civilization. Laws are 'chains that tie up our unruly passions, which else, like wild beasts let loose, would reduce the world into its first state of barbarism and hostility'. However good the apparent reason or motive, the rule of law must never be broken.[8]

His admiration of the law did not extend to lawyers. He believed that if laws could speak, their first complaint would be against the lawyers.[9] And he thought lawyers should be elected to Parliament 'with so much circumspection, that probably it would not often happen'.[10]

Halifax was a forerunner of Lord Acton on power, and he was mindful of the need for consent. Men were apt to become corrupted by great power, and if princes wished to keep their power they should not try to grasp too much of it.[11] Parliaments had lately been guilty of excesses, yet however troublesome they were they strengthened a wise administration by bringing it the consent of the people. The alternative, which was government by force, produced only a 'sluggish and constrained' nation incapable of great things.[12]

Halifax was thought by many of his contemporaries to lack religion. Certainly his remarks on the subject are more witty than devout: 'The several sorts of religion in the world are little more than so many spiritual monopolies.' Or, 'Men pretend to serve God Almighty who doth not need it, but make use of him because they need him.'[13] Halifax maintained that 'he believed as much as he could, and he hoped that God would not lay it to his charge if he could not digest iron, as an ostrich did, nor take into his belief things that must burst him'.[14] In any case, like Napoleon, he had no doubts about religion's political uses. It was indispensable as a foundation of government; without it man was 'one of the worst beasts' produced by nature, 'and fit only for the society of wolves and bears . . .'[15]

Like most political writers before Burke, Halifax found parties difficult to accept; some of his remarks about them would find favour with many voters today. He thought nothing was more evident than that the good of the nation had 'been sacrificed to the animosities of the several contending parties'.[16] He believed the best party was but a kind of a conspiracy against the rest of the nation, and he thought that if there were two parties, a man should choose the one he least disliked, even 'though in the whole he doth not approve it'. It was ignorance that made most men join a party, and shame that kept them from leaving it.[17]

Halifax was free from many of the illusions of later political writers. The utilitarians could have studied him with advantage. Man was too frail to be always capable of discerning where his interest lies, let alone of pursuing it. 'If men must be supposed always to follow their true interest', he declared, 'it must be meant of a new manufactory of mankind by God Almighty; there must be some new clay, the old stuff never yet made any such infallible creature.'[18] He had no great faith in reason. 'Our pride', he wrote, anticipating Burke, 'maketh us over-value our stock of thought, so as to trade much beyond what it is able to make good.'[19] 'Most men', he believed, 'put their reason out to service to their will.'[20]

Empiricism and scepticism were at the roots of Halifax's thought. He had a Burkean distrust of abstract speculation, and like Burke he emphasized the importance of 'circumstances'. 'There is hardly a single proposition to be made,' he believed, 'which is not deceitful, and the tying our reason too close to it, may in many cases be destructive. Circumstances must come in, and are to be made a part of the matter of which we are to judge.'[21] Halifax was the precursor of Hume as well as Burke. Men were continually trying to find some immovable principle, a 'fundamental' to which they could hold fast. But the search was vain. History showed that the principles of divinity, philosophy, morals, astronomy, etc., had all changed. All things including 'fundamentals' were mortal.[22] Zeal might hold sway for a time, but fortunately 'flesh and blood' beat it in the end, and would continue to do so for as long as mankind remained as it was.[23] Hence 'to know when to let things alone' is a sign of good sense. Few things are certain, but extremism is always wrong: 'that which is good cannot live a moment with it'.[24] Halifax presumed that angry men railed against moderation, because they favoured 'some very scurvy extreme', which was 'too strong to be digested by the more considering part of mankind'.[25]

'Our climate', he concluded, was 'a Trimmer'; so too was our Church, our laws, and even 'God Almighty himself'. Having placed himself in good company, Halifax was content to leave 'to the bold champions of either extreme' the task of opposing 'no less adversaries, than nature, religion, liberty, prudence, humanity and common sense'.[26]

2. Henry St John, Lord Bolingbroke (1678–1751)

Bolingbroke . . . stands in history as the man who, by courses
however devious and questionable negotiated a peace [the Treaties
of Utrecht] which proved in the working more satisfactory than any
other that has ended a general European conflict in modern times.

G. M. Trevelyan[1]

Bolingbroke's political career, unlike Halifax's, was not in concord
with his political writings. The intriguer for a Stuart succession in
1714 and the one-time Secretary of State to the Pretender later
expended much energy in attempting to separate the Tories from
Jacobitism. The promoter of the Schism Act, an extreme measure
which entrusted the education of Dissenters' children to school-
masters licensed by the Bishops, in his writings acknowledged 'error'
and made overtures to those he had injured.[2] The eloquent critic of
'party' and 'faction' was himself highly partisan during his brief
years of power. As Bolingbroke himself later admitted, he had
'launched into the deep before I had loaded ballast enough'.[3]

During his life, Bolingbroke gained extravagant admiration.
Swift, writing in 1711, thought Mr St John 'the greatest young man
I ever knew'.[4] And Pope, writing to Swift twenty-five years later,
believed that nothing could 'depress his genius. Whatever befalls
him, he will still be the greatest man in the world, either in his own
time, or with posterity.'[5] Even Voltaire 'found in this eminent
Englishman all the learning of his country and all the politeness of
ours'.[6]

Yet Bolingbroke has not enjoyed 'the protection of history'.
Though his considerable achievement in making the Peace of
Utrecht has not been denied him, he has received the treatment
usually accorded to those on the losing side. The verdict of Dr

Johnson, 'Sir, he was a scoundrel, and a coward',[7] has been more typical than that of Pope. His writings, though they were influential at the time, have fared little better. 'Who now reads Bolingbroke,' Burke asked contemptuously in the *Reflections*, 'who ever read him through?' And the answer both then and later seems to have been: almost nobody except Disraeli. But Disraeli's eulogies were enough to install him in the Tory pantheon, and though Disraeli greatly exaggerated his debt,[8] Bolingbroke has not yet been dispatched from it. While not advocating 'ignorance' of preceding ages, Bolingbroke thought that 'to be learned about them' was 'a ridiculous affectation'. He allowed, however, 'a temperate curiosity'[9] in such matters; in that spirit a brief glance at his writings may be instructive.

In *The Idea of a Patriot King*, Bolingbroke was much influenced by Machiavelli both in form and in content, though with the important differences that he took a less black view of human nature than his master and he favoured a limited not an absolute monarchy. Whatever his conduct as a powerful statesman, he was now a believer in a balanced constitution, and dismissed divine right as nothing better than 'blasphemy'. Much as Halifax had claimed God Almighty to be a Trimmer, Bolingbroke made Him a limited monarch. 'God is a monarch, yet not an arbitrary but a limited monarch, limited by the rule which infinite wisdom prescribes to infinite power.'[10] On a similar but lower plane was the King of Great Britain. The House of Commons and the House of Lords each had their own rights and privileges. 'If the legislative as well as the executive power was wholly in the King, as in some countries, he would be absolute . . . It is this division of power, these distinct privileges attributed to the King, the Lords and the Commons, which constitute a limited monarchy.'[11]

Parliaments kept the people quiet, he believed, and the people kept Parliaments within bounds.[12] The balanced British constitution fostered liberty. The object of government is the good of the people, and 'the greatest good of a people is their liberty'.[13] But, for Boling-broke, liberty was not an abstract ideal, which could be enjoyed and secured by general measures. Liberty was the outcome of the complexity of the British constitution and of British history. While absolute monarchy spelled tyranny, absolute democracy spelled both tyranny and anarchy. In contrast, our unique constitution secured 'society against the miseries which are inseparable from simple forms of government . . .'[14]

In all this Bolingbroke was undoubtedly right. Liberty in Britain in the eighteenth century was the result of chance more than intention, and it was preserved by particular measures and habits not by high-sounding general declarations and theories. Bolingbroke was thus fully justified in scorning those who affected a great regard for liberty in general yet derided the liberty established in Britain.[15] In this, he anticipated Burke's strictures on the Jacobins and their sympathizers.

Those who profess great love for all liberty except that which actually exists are likely in the end to turn out to be admirers of tyranny. Critics of Western democracy tend to find little fault with Communist dictatorships.

Bolingbroke's attitude is similar to Tennyson's conception of freedom slowly broadening down from precedent to precedent.[16] And Bolingbroke did indeed have a strong feeling for the continuity of the state. Nations, he pointed out, are not 'mortal like the men who compose them', and Britain would not perish with her degenerate children.[17] Nevertheless bad governments did damage whose effects were not confined to their own day. Statesmen should therefore be restrained by the fear of setting a bad example to posterity as well as by the knowledge that their experience was 'doubly defective'. 'We are born too late to see the beginning, and we die too soon to see the end of many things.'[18]

A wise minister always looked to the future. He considered 'his administration as a single day in the great year of government; but as a day that is affected by those that went before, and that must affect those that follow'. In words that have contemporary echoes, Bolingbroke contrasted 'the cunning minister', who neither saw nor was concerned to see, 'any further than his personal interests and the support of his administration require. If such a man', he added, 'overcomes any actual difficulty, avoids any immediate distress, or, without doing either of these effectually, gains a little time, by all the little artifices which cunning is ready to suggest and baseness of mind to employ, he triumphs . . .'[19] But his country does not, as we have recently seen.

Bolingbroke admitted that in Queen Anne's reign 'the principal spring of our actions was to have the government of the state in our hands'.[20] And his writings had a similar objective. The aim of much of his journalism in *The Craftsman* was to drive out Walpole and take his place; and the aim of *The Idea of a Patriot King* was to ingratiate himself with 'Poor Fred', the Prince of Wales and the presumed future King.

The Patriot King, like Machiavelli's Prince, would deliver the state from corruption. 'He is the most powerful of all reformers, for he is himself a sort of standing miracle . . .' For Bolingbroke to suggest a solution which required a standing miracle for success might seem ridiculous until we remember that British politicians in our own time have pursued policies which required at least a miracle to give them plausibility. It was essential for the Patriot King 'to espouse no party, but to govern like the common father of his people . . . For Faction is to party what the superlative is to the positive: party is a political evil, and faction is the worst of all parties. The true image of a free people, governed by a *Patriot King*, is that of a patriarchal family, where the head and all the members are united by one common interest, and animated by one common spirit . . .' Bolingbroke cited Queen Elizabeth I as an example of a Patriot Queen. 'She united the great body of the people in her and their common interest, she inflamed them with one national spirit.' But in advocating an active monarchy above party Bolingbroke was idealizing what Harley tried to achieve under Queen Anne. And one of those who had done his best to frustrate Harley's efforts was Bolingbroke himself.

Had Bolingbroke and his friends come to power under George II, Frederick, or anybody else, they would presumably have been 'a faction' much like any other. Yet British government under Walpole was as corrupt as it has ever been, and Bolingbroke's outrage at the general corruption of political life and at the aggrandizement of 'the moneyed interest' at the expense of 'the landed interest' was almost certainly genuine. He wanted Walpole's place but would not have imitated his methods.

Bolingbroke was in his writings a conservative with a small 'c', who wished to preserve the traditional values and to return to a recent and better past. In a fine passage, he expressed the wish to restore 'the nation to its primitive temper and integrity, to its old good manners, its old good humour, and its old good nature (expressions of my Lord Chancellor Clarendon, which I could never read without being moved and softened) . . .'[21] But his ideal of a King above party was only attainable when the monarchy retired from politics which was neither possible nor desirable in the eighteenth century, and his ideal of a free country without parties was attainable neither then nor later. Yet his emphasis on the importance of the unity of the nation and on the strain that excessive partisanship places upon that unity is salutary. If there have to be parties, let them be as national as possible. Perhaps after all Bolingbroke does deserve his place in the Tory pantheon.

3. David Hume (1711–76)

All general maxims in politics ought to be established with great caution.
David Hume[1]

Unlike Halifax and Bolingbroke, David Hume's activity in politics was slight. After being companion to a mad marquis, he was at various times secretary to a general, secretary and, briefly, Chargé d'Affaires at the Paris Embassy, and finally for a year Under-Secretary of State to the Northern Department. These were 'the only interruptions' which his studies received during the course of his life.[2]

Hume, the greatest of British philosophers, was a philosophic revolutionary and so successful a one that Bertrand Russell thought the *ancien régime* had never been convincingly restored.[3] Presumably that is why he has rarely been given his rightful place in the Tory temple. How could a man whose scepticism demolished God, the soul, miracles, causation, natural law, matter, and induction, be a good conservative? According to Boswell, Dr Johnson 'would not allow Mr. David Hume any credit for his political principles, though similar to his own; saying of him, "Sir, he was a Tory by chance." '[4] Nevertheless Hume's Toryism has been an important strand in British Conservatism.

Hume dethroned reason. 'All probable reasoning', he wrote, 'is nothing but a species of sensation.' We should follow our taste and sentiment not only in poetry and music but also in philosophy.[5] It was wrong to talk of a struggle between passion and reason. 'Reason is, and ought only to be the slave of the passions, and can never pretend to any other office than to serve and obey them.'[6]

'The rules of equity or justice depend' not on reason, Hume believed, but 'entirely on the particular state and condition in which men are placed . . .'[7] Man's affection for his family outweighed his selfishness, but his natural benevolence extended little further. The human mind knew no such passion as 'the love of mankind' in general. At the same time, there were not enough goods to supply everyone with what they wanted and needed. Prosperity was the chief advantage conferred by the existence of society, and the 'instability' of the possession of property was the chief enemy to it. Fortunately nature provided a remedy by enabling men to see that it was in their common interest to agree to 'leave everyone in the peaceful enjoyment of what he may acquire by his fortune and industry'. This 'convention', which was gradually established like languages, was necessary both for the survival of society and the welfare of the individual. And from this convention arose the ideas of justice and injustice. If men were not selfish, or if there were an abundance of goods in the world, there would be no such convention and there would be no need for justice. But since men are as they are and the world is as it is, justice is necessary, and the right of private property is the first principle of justice.[8]

Certainly since Hume's day there has been no civilized society in which there has not been a right to private property. As well as that right there were for Hume two other fundamental laws of nature. There must be the right to alienate one's property if one wishes, and promises must be kept. The alienation of property by consent facilitated 'commerce and intercourse, which is so beneficial to human society'. And the keeping of contracts and promises secured 'mutual trust and confidence' which promotes 'the general interest of mankind'. On the observance of these laws of property, trade and contract, 'the peace and security of human society entirely depended'.[9]

Again, subsequent history has done nothing to disprove Hume's fundamental laws. In many of his ideas, Hume anticipated Adam Smith and influenced the classical economists. Natural economic competition between men, in his view, should not be abolished but sensibly regulated. And the only object of all laws and regulations was 'the good of mankind' or 'public utility'.[10]

Hume was a considerable historian as well as a philosopher and economist. Bentham called him 'that prince of historians',[11] and his *History of England* retained its popularity for over a century.[12] The study of English history demonstrated, Hume believed, that 'the only rule of government, which is intelligible or carries any authority with it, is the established practice of the age, and the maxims of administration, which are that time prevalent, and universally assented to'.[13] An acquaintance with the past was chiefly useful for showing the superiority of the present British constitution over what had existed before. But it also revealed to us 'the great mixture of accident which commonly concurs with a small ingredient of wisdom and foresight, in erecting the complicated fabric of the most perfect government'. However, people should be wary of regarding 'the maxims of uncultivated ages as certain rules for their present conduct'.[14] Those who wanted to return to 'the ancient, barbarous and feudal constitution' should set an example. 'Let them make court to be admitted as retainers to a neighbouring baron; and, by submitting to slavery under him, acquire some protection to themselves; together with the power of exercising rapine and oppression over their inferior slaves and villeins.' Such was in former times the condition of the commons.[15]

But recognition that the present was better than the past and greatly preferable to imaginary utopias did not lead Hume to enshrine it. Burke would have applauded Canning's remark on parliamentary reform, that he preferred 'the wisdom of six centuries' to that of Lord John Russell.[16] While sympathetic to Canning's general attitude, Hume would have replied that in this instance Russell was right and the wisdom of the centuries was wrong.* Still, most people were governed by authority, not reason, so an established government had 'an infinite advantage, by that very circumstance, of its being established'. A wise magistrate respected what was old and would not 'try experiments merely upon the credit of supposed argument and philosophy'.[17]

Yet innovations were of course necessary in every institution. But they must not be violent; they should be adjusted so far as possible to 'the ancient fabric'. And they should, above all, be adjusted to human nature as it is. 'All plans of government, which suppose great reformation in the manners of mankind, are plainly imaginary.'[18]

Somebody who did not know human nature might try to assign the largest possessions to the most virtuous, and 'give everyone the power of doing good, proportioned to his inclination'. In a perfect theocracy, governed by 'a being infinitely intelligent', this might work. But with mankind as it is, such a law, owing to man's inability to judge merit and 'the self-conceit of each individual', would quickly lead to 'the total dissolution of society'. Therefore while

*See, for example, 'Idea of a Perfect Commonwealth'.

'fanatics may suppose that dominion is founded on grace and that Saints alone inherit the earth', the ruler very properly 'puts these sublime theorists on the same footing with common robbers, and teaches them by the severest discipline, that a rule, which, in speculation, may seem the most advantageous to society, may yet be found, in practice, totally pernicious and destructive'.[19]

The pursuit of economic equality, Hume maintained, was as impracticable and pernicious as the division of property according to merit. He was opposed to 'a too great disproportion among the citizens'. Everybody should enjoy the fruits of his labour, and possess not only the necessities but many of the conveniences of life.[20] But if men's possessions were made equal, their 'different degrees of art, care, and industry' would 'immediately break that equality'. Alternatively those virtues would be restrained, in which case the whole community instead of a part of it would be reduced to 'want and beggary'. Moreover 'the most rigorous inquisition' would be needed 'to watch every inequality on its first appearance; and the most severe jurisdiction, to punish and redress it'. Such a degree of authority would 'soon degenerate into tyranny, and be exerted with great partialities . . .'[21] The attempt to bring about equality, therefore, would produce both poverty and dictatorship. Instead of seeking violent changes, rulers should 'comply with the common bent of mankind', making as many improvements as suited it. Caution was all the more necessary, because 'all political questions are infinitely complicated', and it is impossible to foresee all the consequences of any measure.[22]

As a man always 'more fond of promoting moderation than zeal',[23] Hume found little to admire in the parties of his day. 'Parties from principle,' he wrote, 'especially abstract speculative principle, are known only to modern times, and are, perhaps, the most extraordinary and unaccountable phenomenon that has yet appeared in human affairs.'[24] He was the forerunner of Namier in pointing out the difficulty in distinguishing between the parties of his time. 'We have seen the conduct of the two parties, during the course of 70 years . . . Yet are we at a loss to tell the nature, pretensions, and principles, of the different factions.'[25]

Yet Hume conceded that it was not possible to abolish parties in a free country, and he saw that the only dangerous ones were those which 'entertain opposite views with regard to the essentials of government . . . where there is no room for any compromise or accommodation . . .'[26] Even the rise of the Labour Party with a Socialist constitution did not produce the situation that Hume feared. There was not in practice a profound cleavage in domestic policy between Labour and the Conservative Party between the wars.[27] It is only in the last few years that the parties have become 'dangerous' in the sense Hume laid down.

Religion was an area where men found it especially difficult to compromise. Hence a wise legislator would bribe the clergy into 'indolence' by paying them salaries. Otherwise 'each ghostly practitioner' would inflame his devotees against all other sects, and no regard would 'be paid to truth, morals, or decency'.[28] The dangerous 'practitioners' today are not 'ghostly' but secular, and they are not bribable by our legislators either because they are genuine fanatics or because they have already been bribed by foreign governments. The new barbarism is secular messianism. It disregards 'truth, morals and decency', and it is commonly found among the sects of the extreme Left and in the Communist Party.

Fanaticism of any kind was repugnant to Hume, and he gave caustic expression to the anti-puritan strain in Toryism. 'Celibacy, fasting, penance, mortification, self-denial, humility, silence, solitude, and the whole train of monkish virtues' should be rejected, he believed, by sensible men since they served only to 'stupify the understanding and harden the heart, obscure the fancy and sour the temper'. He conceded that 'a gloomy, hair-brained enthusiast' might after his death win a day in the calendar of saints, but while such a man was alive he would be appreciated only by those who were 'as delirious and dismal as himself'. Hume preferred the social virtues of humanity, benevolence, generosity, moderation, and friendship, and the companionable virtues of gentleness, good manners, decency and wit. Priests and some philosophers had clothed virtue in 'dismal dress'. Hume on the contrary represented her as having 'genuine and most engaging charms', as wishing to make all mankind 'cheerful and happy', and emphatically not as demanding 'useless austerities and rigours, suffering and self-denial'.[29]

Hume thus had an instinct for pleasure and enjoyment, proper for a good Tory. Excessive luxury was wrong, but it was preferable to 'sloth and idleness'. Gratification of the senses was innocent, provided indulgence was not pursued to the detriment of family and friends or to the exclusion of any 'proper object of generosity or compassion'. The enjoyment of good food and drink, fine clothes and other pleasures could only be considered vicious by those whose heads had been 'disordered by the frenzies of enthusiasm'.[30]

Hume's scepticism was also thoroughly Tory, but his philosophy so far from providing satisfaction occasionally tortured him. 'Sceptical doubt' was 'a malady' which increased the further his reflections were carried. For that, 'carelessness and inattention' were the only remedy. The choice 'betwixt a false reason and none at all' was a difficult one. We are scarcely if at all influenced by 'very refin'd reflections', but we 'can not establish it for a rule, that they ought not to have any influence'. The many 'contradictions and imperfections in human reason' sometimes made Hume 'ready to reject all belief and reasoning' and to embrace apathy and despair. Reason could not dispel 'these clouds'; only nature could cure him of 'this philosophical melancholy and delirium . . . I dine, I play a game of backgammon, I converse, and am merry with my friends.' And this amusement made his speculations when he returned to them appear 'so cold, and strain'd, and ridiculous'[31] that he could not continue them.

'A true sceptic', he concluded, 'will be diffident of his philosophical doubts, as well as of his philosophical conviction.'[32] If only later philosophers and their devotees had been as sceptical of their convictions as Hume was of his doubts!

4. Edmund Burke (1729–97)

In Mr Burke's writings indeed the germs of almost all political truths
may be found.
Coleridge[1]

Burke's 'stream of mind', said Dr Johnson, was 'perpetual'.[2] And
partly for that reason it is especially difficult to summarize his
thought – at least in prose.

Much as Goldsmith's famous lines,

> 'Who, born for the universe, narrow'd his mind,
> And to party gave up what was meant for mankind;
> Though fraught with all learning, yet straining his throat
> To persuade Tommy Townshend to lend him a vote;
> Who, too deep for his listeners, still went on refining,
> And thought of convincing, while they thought of dining . . .'[3]

best catch Burke's dual role of party propagandist and deep political
thinker, so Wordsworth best caught the tenor of his thought in lines
that appeared in the 1850, but not in the 1805, version of *The
Prelude*:

> 'I see him – old, but vigorous in age, –
> Stand like an oak . . .
> While he forewarns, denounces, launches forth,
> Against all systems built on abstract rights,
> Keen ridicule; the majesty proclaims
> Of Institutes and Laws, hallowed by time;
> Declares the vital power of social ties
> Endeared by custom; and with high disdain,
> Exploding upstart Theory, insists
> Upon the allegiance to which men are born . . .'[4]

The difficulty of summarizing Burke stems not merely from the
volume and quality of his writings. Still less does it stem from a

contradiction which some have seen between his attitude to George III, America, India, Ireland, and his opposition to the French Revolution. Burke was in fact consistent in the essentials of his thought.* Nor does the difficulty come from Burke having quite rightly not tried to erect a complete philosophical system. It comes from his marvellous style and the powerful sweep of his writing. Like Capability Brown, Burke needed space. Hazlitt thought, indeed, that to do Burke 'justice, it would be necessary to quote all his works; the only specimen of Burke is, *all that he wrote*'.[5]

Halifax distrusted parties and 'trimmed' against them; Bolingbroke was excluded from active politics by the ruling clique and sought a non-party kingdom; Hume found in parties intolerance, selfishness and zeal; with Burke, the trumpeter of the Rockingham Whigs, party came into its own. What Burke said of parties was doubtful constitutional doctrine in 1769–70, but it has proved true ever since. 'Party divisions', he wrote, 'whether on the whole operating for good or evil are things inseparable from free government.'[6] In the last 200 years, one-party states and no-party states alike have been uniformly unfree.

Burke's view of how parties should behave would have gained the qualified approval of Hume, though he did not always follow his own advice. This was to act 'with all the moderation which does not absolutely enervate that vigour, and quench that fervency of spirit, without which the best wishes for the public good must evaporate in empty speculation'.[7] Burke had no time for those 'detached gentlemen', who claimed to be above party, and other, battles. He was 'fully persuaded, that all virtue which is impracticable is spurious'; it was better 'to run the risk of falling into faults in a course which leads us to act with effect and energy, than to loiter out our days without blame, and without use'.[8]

If Burke was far away from Hume on party, he was close to him on political theorizing. Burke was not opposed to theory as such. When he spoke against theory, he said, 'I mean always a weak,

---

*Coleridge maintained that any scholar who compared Burke's speeches and writings on the American War with those on the French Revolution would 'find the principles exactly the same and the deductions the same; but the practical inferences almost opposite in the one case from those drawn in the other; yet in both equally legitimate and in both equally confirmed by the results'.[9] Burke himself effectively refuted the charge of inconsistency in *An Appeal from the New to the Old Whigs*.

erroneous, fallacious, unfounded or imperfect theory; and one of the ways of discovering that it is a false theory is by comparing it with practice.'[10] Hence 'the hocus-pocus of abstraction'[11] is continually denounced. Burke pointed out that no rational man governs himself 'by abstractions and universals'. A university professor could take a general view of society. But 'a statesman has a number of circumstances to combine with those general ideas and to take into his consideration'. If he did not take circumstances into consideration, he was 'not erroneous, but stark mad . . . metaphysically mad'.[12] It followed that 'nothing universal can be rationally affirmed on any moral or any political subject. Pure metaphysical abstraction does not belong to these matters.'[13]

This belief that politics like medicine and physiology was 'not to be taught *a priori*'[14] placed Burke at the opposite pole to Rousseau and the French revolutionaries. Burke thought it inconceivably presumptuous for any man 'to consider his country as nothing but *carte blanche*, upon which he may scribble whatever he pleases'. Rousseauism, he believed, was characterized by 'benevolence to the whole species and want of feeling for every individual'.[15] Written in 1791, that showed foresight.

While hostile to metaphysical speculation in politics, Burke had profound religious convictions. He is the most intensely religious of all British political writers. 'In a Christian Commonwealth', he said, echoing Hooker, 'the Church and the State are one and the same thing, being different integral parts of the same whole.'[16] He was much more tolerant to Roman Catholics and Dissenters than most of his contemporaries, but he excluded atheists. God 'willed the state', and 'all persons possessing any portion of power', he believed, 'ought to be strongly and awfully impressed with an idea that they act in trust; and that they are to account for their conduct in that trust to the one great Master, Author, and Founder of Society'.[17] Not surprisingly, Rousseau went further and made his 'civil religion' compulsory. Disbelievers would be banished or executed.[18]

But though 'we know, and what is better, we feel inwardly that religion is the basis of civil society, and the source of all good and of all comfort',[19] religion does not provide us with infallible rules for conducting our political affairs. Nor does history. From history 'much political wisdom may be learned'; but 'as habit not as precept, and . . . not as a repertory of cases and precedents for a lawyer'.[20] So while the object of government can be simply stated – it was '(so far as may be) the happiness of the whole'[21] – there is no easy way of achieving it.

There is no short cut. Human nature is our only guide. 'Politics ought to be adjusted, not to human reasonings, but to human nature; of which the reason is but a part, and by no means the greatest part.'[22] The foundations of government are 'laid not in imaginary rights of men (which at best is a confusion of judicial with civil principles) but in political convenience, and in human nature . . .'[23]

This leads to Burke's ideas of prejudice and prescription. Our reason is inadequate. Each man's 'stock' of it is small, and men 'do better to avail themselves of the general bank and capital of nations and ages'.[24] Wisdom lies therefore in combining reason with experience and prejudice. Prejudice is an opinion which has stood the test of time, and is far preferable to abstract thought. It 'renders a man's duty his habit; and not a series of unconnected acts'.[25] We cannot know or foresee the future, but we know the present and the past is all around us. The idea behind prescription is that our politics should be based on what we know rather than on what we do not know. Accordingly if a nation has long flourished under a system of government, that raises for Burke, as for Hume, 'a presumption'[26] in favour of that system and against any untried project. Government is a practical business; and so any sensible man will pause before knocking down a regime and seeking to replace it with something that he cannot be sure will work. The 'sole authority' of the British prescriptive constitution, Burke said, 'is that it has existed time out of mind . . . Prescription is the most solid of all titles, not only to property, but which is to secure that property, to government.'[27] Most of our institutions are indeed the creatures of the past and of habit, and in that sense prescription is undeniable. Prescription recognizes the value of continuity and seeks to ensure it.

'A nation', Burke said in the same speech on representation in 1782, 'is not an idea only of local extent and individual momentary aggregation, but it is an idea of continuity which extends in time as well as in numbers and in space.'[28] The same thing naturally applied to the state, of which Burke took an elevated view. 'It is a partnership in all science,' ran his famous dithyramb, 'a partnership in all art, a partnership in every virtue and in all perfection. As the ends of such a partnership cannot be obtained in many generations, it becomes a partnership not only between those who are living, but between those who are living, those who are dead, and those who are to be born.'[29] Regrettably, this is not a recognizable picture of any state that has ever existed, and bears no resemblance whatever to the Britain of George III. Yet for the state to be in some sense a partnership is a proper aim and, for all his exaggeration, Burke was far ahead of his contemporaries in seeing that a state and a nation were more than a mere aggregate of the people who happened to be living and governing within a particular area of territory at a particular moment.

Such a conception of the nation and the state should humble the pretensions of our legislators and our rulers, though in our day it does not. The votes of a majority, Burke pointed out, cannot 'alter the moral any more than they can alter the physical essence of things'.[30] Besides, however anxious the people may be to elect good representatives, their choice does not necessarily confer 'virtue and wisdom . . . upon whom they lay their ordaining hands'.[31] Mr Michael Foot and much of the Labour Party evidently do feel that they have been ordained by the process of election. And they believe that a temporary majority of the House of Commons, provided it is a Labour majority, is entitled to do what it likes, unhindered by a second Chamber, the rule of law, constitutional conventions, the rules of the House of Commons or anything else. This 'Jacobinical' belief, which is more than usually untenable when the parliamentary majority represents only a minority of the nation, subjects the destinies and freedom of the country, in Burke's words, 'to the caprices of weak and giddy men',[32] and is the route to dictatorship. 'The tyranny of the multitude', Burke said in a famous phrase, 'is but a multiplied tyranny',[33] and the tyranny becomes no more palatable when the multitude is in fact a minority.

Society, then, is much more than a collection of random individuals and is in some ways like an organism, but Burke did not believe that it is an organism. 'By *nature*', he said, 'there is no such thing as politic or corporate personality: all these ideas are mere fictions of law, they are creatures of voluntary institution; men as men are individuals and nothing else.'[34]

Nevertheless both man and society were highly complex. Therefore 'no simple disposition or direction of power can be suitable either to man's nature or to the quality of his affairs'.[35] And it certainly will not produce liberty. In seeking simplicity and in relying on reason and abstract ideas, the French revolutionaries had made fatal mistakes. 'The perennial existence of bodies corporate and their fortunes', Burke wrote in 1790, 'are particularly suited to a man who has long views', but the French had rashly destroyed them.[36]

Liberty was what distinguished the British constitution. But it was 'liberty connected with order', and it was the outcome of 'good and steady government'.[37] Liberty meant 'a constitution of things in which the liberty of no one man, and no body of men, can find means to trespass on the liberty' of anybody else. Liberty must 'be ascertained by wise laws, and secured by well constructed institutions'. Whenever liberty and justice were separated, neither was safe.[38]

Thus there is nothing simple about the foundations of liberty. They are not to be found merely in the individual or in the state, but in a complex assortment of historic rights, laws, traditions, political institutions and corporations. It is these buffers between the individual and the state which preserve liberty by preventing a direct confrontation between them. When they are swept away, tyranny or anarchy follows.

High-sounding declarations of rights, so far from leading to liberty, were likely to lead to its perversion or to absurdity. Because 'liberty in the abstract may be classed among the blessings of mankind', Burke asked if he was supposed to congratulate a madman on escaping from his cell.[39] Hence political ideas should be judged not by their speculative attractions but by their 'practical consequences'. Political problems do not 'primarily concern truth or falsehood. They relate to good or evil. What in the result is likely to produce evil is politically false; that which is productive of good, politically true.'[40] Thus for Burke 'expediency' is not in opposition to 'right'. What is expedient is right. 'Expedience is that which is good for the community and good for every individual in it . . . If we are to judge of a Commonwealth actually existing, the first thing I enquire is what has been *found* expedient or inexpedient.'[41]

The test is a practical one: does it work? Nothing can be judged in isolation 'in all the nakedness and solitude of metaphysical abstraction. Circumstances (which with some gentlemen pass for nothing) give in reality to every political principle its distinguishing colour and discriminating effect. The circumstances are what render every civil and political scheme beneficial or noxious to mankind.'[42]

And in judging the circumstances and making decisions, 'Prudence is not only the first in rank of the virtues, political and moral, but she is the director, the regulator, the standard of them all.'[43] Prudence will stop us making the best the enemy of the good. It is much the same thing as moderation. 'In all changes in the state, moderation is a virtue, not only amiable, but powerful. It is a disposing, arranging, conciliating, cementing, virtue . . . Moderation . . . is the virtue only of superior minds.'[44]

Despite Senator Goldwater and a few other eccentrics, moderation and prudence are still generally numbered among the political virtues. And most people probably agree with Burke that there is no one form of government that is suitable for all peoples at all times. Probably, too, many people still attach value to old institutions. The twentieth century is, with good cause, less confident than the eighteenth that a grand new constitution which looks good on paper will be an improvement on the old or will have any existence except on paper.

Yet Burke was generally both in theory and practice a reformer. He did not, as is well known, support the American War. He thought both the Americans and the Irish should be given 'an interest in the constitution'.[45] Their nationality should be recognized, and they should be given local independence under the Crown. Burke's view of the Empire was similar to that enshrined in the Statute of Westminster 150 years later. He favoured relief for Roman Catholics and Dissenters. He wanted to liberalize the penal code and to reduce the excessive power of the judges in criminal libel cases. He attacked the slave trade, and he proposed and enacted some important measures of financial reform.

He was a believer in compromise. 'All government, indeed every human benefit and enjoyment, every virtue and every prudent act, is founded on compromise and barter. We balance inconveniences; we give and take; we remit some rights, that we may enjoy others; and we choose rather to be happy citizens than subtle disputants . . .'[46] Peace was much more important than legal niceties. 'I am not determining a point of law,' he said in a speech on America in 1775, 'I am restoring tranquillity . . .'[47] And tranquillity and the general welfare could often be preserved only by concessions. 'If there is any one eminent criterion which above all the rest distinguishes a wise government', he said in 1780, 'from an administration weak and improvident, it is this: "Well to know the best time and manner of yielding what it is impossible to keep." '[48]

The impact of the French Revolution did not cause him to change his mind. 'A state without the means of some change', he wrote in the

C

Reflections, 'is without the means of its conservation.' And again, 'a disposition to preserve and an ability to improve, taken together, would be my standard of a statesman. Everything else is vulgar in the conception, perilous in the execution.'[49]

Thus Burke's belief in prescription did not as a rule lead him into its obvious danger: that of sanctifying the present and the past and of shackling the future. But on two issues he did not altogether escape the trap. Pitt's mild and fitful attempts to cut out a few rotten boroughs were opposed by Burke with a vehemence that might have been justified, had Pitt been trying to abolish the monarchy, the judiciary, and the House of Commons itself. Just as Burke's abhorrence of the French Revolution led him to ignore the abuses of the *ancien régime*, so his veneration for the British constitution and the Revolution of 1688 banished from his mind the many blemishes and deformities which tarnished the representative system. In 1780 Manchester and Birmingham were not represented in the House of Commons, and Cornwall had forty-four members. Yet Burke could describe our 'representation' as 'nearly perfect'.[50]

The same dogmatism is occasionally apparent in Burke's attitude to economics. In 1766, anticipating Carlyle, he wrote of Ireland: 'I am sure the people ought to eat, whether they have septennial Parliaments or not.'[51] Yet thirty years later, shortly before his death, he could ask: 'In the name of God, what is the meaning of this project of Mr. Pitt concerning the further relief of the Poor? What relief do they want, except that which it will be difficult indeed to give, to make them more frugal or more industrious?'[52]

And a year earlier in his 'Thoughts and Details on Scarcity', he asked, 'When a man can not live and maintain his family by the natural hire of his labour, ought it not to be raised by authority?' Burke's answer was a firm 'No'. 'To provide for us in our necessities', he wrote, 'is not in the power of government . . . The labouring people are only poor because they are numerous . . . Patience, labour, sobriety, frugality, and religion should be recommended to them. All the rest is downright fraud.' 'The laws of commerce . . .' he added, 'are the laws of nature and consequently the laws of God.'* But charity to the poor was a duty on all Christians.[53]

Burke was the friend of Adam Smith who paid him the compliment of saying that Burke was the only man who thought on economics

---

*'No wonder', Marx commented unfairly on this passage, 'that, true to the laws of God and of Nature, Burke always sold himself in the best market.'[54]

exactly as he did himself; and there was economic sense in what Burke said. Burke was also the friend of Arthur Young, the agriculturalist, and as owner of a farm he had practical experience of what he was discussing. Yet here Burke argued in the abstract and general manner that he condemned in his opponents. Should not 'the circumstances' of starvation influence economic theory? Could it really be 'prudent' for the government and the magistrates to stand back and permit widespread destitution? Surely the laws of supply and demand should also apply, as Nassau Senior maintained, to the relief of the poor?[55] Above all, in what conceivable sense could a state, which decided as a matter of principle not to interfere with economic conditions that condemned some of its people to starve to death, be described as 'a partnership in all art, in all science, in all perfection'?

But Burke was not a professional political philosopher working in cloistered seclusion and seeking to erect a wholly coherent system of thought in three or four volumes. He was a ceaselessly busy politician. The only cause for astonishment is not that there is the occasional incongruity in his thought but that the enormous quantity of his writings and speeches, produced over a long period of years on a multitude of issues, live so well together with each other. Burke's inconsistency over party was only apparent. His quarrel with Fox was inevitable: the challenge of the French Revolution made the preservation of old party connections impossible. So the foremost apologist of party, the man who refused to join the Fox–North coalition because he regarded it as a betrayal of Whig principles, crossed the floor of the House near the end of his life to support the Younger Pitt. At the time of crisis the greatest Conservative thinker put his country and the constitution above his party.

5. Samuel Taylor Coleridge (1772–1834)

By wholesome laws to embank the sovereign power;
To deepen by restraint; and by prevention
Of lawless will to amass and guide the flood
In its majestic channel, is man's task
And the true patriot's glory!
Coleridge[1]

When Coleridge sent Lord Liverpool a copy of his *Lay Sermons*, the Prime Minister complained that he 'did not well understand them'.[2] The fault was not all Liverpool's; he was merely the first of many. Coleridge's prose is often obscure. Some lines in his poem 'Talleyrand to Lord Grenville' well describe it:

> 'The tortoise crawls straight, the hare doubles about;
> And the true line of beauty still winds in and out.
> It argues, my Lord! of fine thoughts such a brood in us
> To split and divide into heads multitudinous, . . .
> Were a genius of rank, like a commonplace dunce,
> Compell'd to drive on to the main point at once, . . .'

If only Coleridge would, like a commonplace dunce, drive on to the main point at once! Instead, genius exacts a heavy price, and it is often not beauty but a tortoise that seems to be winding in and out.*

Like Wordsworth and Southey, Coleridge was an enthusiastic supporter of the French Revolution. Pitt was denounced as one:

> 'Who with proud words of dear-lov'd Freedom came –
> More blasting than the mildew from the South!
> And kiss'd his country with Iscariot mouth
> (Ah! foul apostate from his Father's fame!)'[3]

---

*Coleridge himself admitted that his prose writings had been 'charged with a disproportionate demand on the attention; with an excess of refinement on the mode of arriving at truths; with beating the ground for that which might have been run down by the eye; with the length and laborious construction of my periods; in short with obscurity and the love of paradox'.[4]

The course of the revolution together with the development of Coleridge's own ideas brought disillusionment, which the French invasion of Switzerland turned into outright hostility. Coleridge depicted the evolution of his attitude in his 'Ode to France' of 1798. And the last stanza of that poem finely states his belief that liberty cannot be achieved by any form of government but only by individual man through his worship of God in Nature. Coleridge then, as he put it, 'snapped my squeaking baby-trumpet of sedition, and the fragments lie scattered in the lumber-room of penitence'.[5] Four years earlier Coleridge had savagely attacked Burke for crossing the floor of the House:

> 'Great Son of Genius! sweet to me thy name,
> Ere in an evil hour with alter'd voice
> Thou bad'st Oppression's hireling crew rejoice'[6]

Now in effect Coleridge did the same thing, and became indeed the greatest of Burke's followers. Like Burke, he was intensely religious. Religion, he believed, was always 'the centre of gravity in a realm, to which all other things must and will accommodate themselves'.[7] Though a metaphysician, he thought metaphysics had no place in politics; and he was as hostile as Burke to abstract political systems allegedly based on pure reason. He scoffed at 'the Mechanico-Corpuscular Theory',[8] and wrote that 'the moral laws of the intellectual world, as far as they are deducible from pure intellect are never perfectly applicable to our mixed and sensitive nature, because man is something beside reason . . .'[9] Hence for Coleridge Jacobinism was a monstrous hybrid, 'made up in part of despotism and in part of abstract reason misapplied to objects that belong entirely to experience and the understanding'. Jacobinism pandered to the brute passions of the mob in order to erect a society and government based on abstract reason instead of on established institutions and experience.[10] England, in contrast, had the good fortune to possess social institutions that had 'formed themselves out of our proper needs and interests . . .'[11]

Writing about the idea of a constitution, Coleridge defined an idea as 'that conception of a thing, which is not abstracted from any particular state, form, or mode, in which the thing may happen to exist at this or at that time; nor yet generalised from any number or succession of such forms or modes; but which is given by the knowledge of *its ultimate aim*'.[12] And a constitution was 'an idea arising out of the idea of a state; and because our whole history from Alfred onward demonstrates the continued influence of such an idea, or ultimate aim, on the minds of our forefathers, in their characters and functions as public men; alike in what they resisted and in what they claimed; in the institutions and forms of polity which they established . . . we speak . . . of the idea itself, as actually existing i.e., as a principle, existing in the only way in which a principle can exist – in the minds and consciences of the persons, whose duties it prescribes, and whose rights it determines'.[13]

This seems fully acceptable. We have had more experience than Coleridge of constitutions remaining mere scraps of paper, of institutions, like bad wine, not travelling well. Successful constitutions and institutions are not mere pieces of machinery. If they work, it is because of the ideas and beliefs of those who try to work them. Whether the constitution is written or unwritten, a great deal will always depend upon convention and sensible adaption. In Britain, at least, the idea of the constitution, in the sense that Coleridge used the words, is certainly more important than the constitution itself. The British constitution depends upon the attitudes, ideas, scruples and practices of those who operate it. Once 'the idea' is rejected, the constitution breaks down.

For Coleridge, the principle of the British constitution was the harmonious balance between permanence and progression or law and liberty. The landed interest and the House of Lords provided permanence and stability, the mercantile classes and the House of Commons ensured progression and personal freedom, and the Monarch supplied unity and cohesion. But all this depended upon a continuing improvement in civilization which was the responsibility of the national Church, 'the third great venerable estate of the realm'.[14] The Church had a vital educational duty and function. It should through education provide everyone with the chance of bettering their children and impart the knowledge necessary to qualify 'every nature' to be 'the free subject of a civilised realm'.[15]

Coleridge pointed out that for nearly 150 years Englishmen had been freer than the citizens of any other known country. This was due to our 'insular privilege of a self-evolving constitution'. Whereas in both a democratic republic and an absolute monarchy the people delegated their whole power, 'in the constitution of England according to the Idea' no such delegation had taken place. In England the delegation has been partial and circumscribed both 'in respect of the duration of the Trust [and] of the particular interests entrusted'.[16] Not for Coleridge any nonsense about sovereignty.

In conformity with his dislike of abstraction, Coleridge dismissed the theory of the original social contract, which he thought 'at once false and foolish'. But 'the idea of an ever-originating social contract' was something very different. That was indispensable; without it subjects would be serfs, and a commonwealth would be a slave plantation. 'All social laws and justice [are] grounded on the principle, that a person can never, but by his own fault, become a thing, or, without grievous wrong, be treated as such: and the distinction consisting in this, that a thing may be used altogether and merely as the means to an end; but the person must always be included in the end . . .'[17] This principle, derived from Kant, is one of the bases of Conservative philosophy and distinguishes free states from tyrannies. Kulaks, Jews, Poles, Cambodians are starved or murdered wholesale by tyrants, because they are regarded as things or types or as obstructions to some desired end. They are sacrificed to an idea and treated as 'a thing'. In a state free from tyrants and not demented by ideology, individuals have their own intrinsic worth and cannot be degraded into being a mere means to an end – partly because they are respected in themselves and partly because such a state does not, or should not, have in that sense 'an end'.

Coleridge's idealism avoided the excesses of some idealist philosophers on the Continent. It also enabled him to avoid two of Burke's failings. Like Wordsworth and Burke, he had an elevated idea of the nation, and rejected the eighteenth-century idea that it was merely a random collection of atomized individuals. But he drew a clear distinction between the ideal and the actual, and there was much in the actual that he strongly disliked. This stricture on the world around him could not have been penned by Burke:

State-policy, a cyclops with one eye, and that in the back of the head! Our measures of policy, either a series of anachronisms, or a truckling to events substituted for the science, that should command them; for all true insight is foresight . . . Mean time, the true historical feeling, the immortal life of an historical Nation, generation linked to generation by faith, freedom, heraldry, and ancestral fame, languishing, and giving place to the superstitions of wealth, and newspaper reputation. Talents without genius: a swarm of clever, well informed men: an anarchy of minds, a despotism of maxims. Despotism of finance in government and legislation . . . of presumption, temerity, and hardness of heart, in political economy

. . . the wealth of the nation (i.e., of the wealthy individuals thereof, and the magnitude of the Revenue) [substituted] for the well-being of the people. Gin consumed by paupers to the value of about eighteen millions yearly . . . Lastly, crimes quadrupled for the whole country, and in some counties decupled.[18]

This realization of how far the real fell below the ideal made Coleridge more sensitive than his contemporaries not only to the evils of the Industrial Revolution but also to the need to do something to cure them. Not for him the easy assumption of Burke that the laws of commerce were the laws of God. 'Upstart theory' did not get the better of Coleridge. He described political economy as 'solemn humbug'.[19] And in his eyes, the economic system was 'Game laws, Corn Laws, Cotton Factories, Spitalfields, the tillers of the land paid by poor-rates, and the remainder of the population mechanized into engines for the manufactory of new rich men – yea, the machinery of the wealth of the nation made up of the wretchedness, disease and depravity of those who should constitute the strength of the nation'.[20]

A reformation was clearly essential. Supporting Peel's Factory Children Bill of 1818, Coleridge asked a friend for 'any other instances in which the legislature has . . . interfered with what is ironically called "free labour"? (i.e., DARED to prohibit soul-murder and infanticide on the part of the rich, and self-slaughter on that of the poor!)'[21] He believed the chief object of the 'social bond' and the state was the protection of property.[22] But property was a sacred trust which imposed duties. Manufacturers should therefore consent to adequate regulation of factory conditions, and the gentry should concern themselves with the education of their dependents and those who lived on their land. 'National education', he consistently believed, 'and a concurring spread of the gospel were the indispensable conditions of any true political amelioration.'[23]

Despite his idealism, Coleridge had a Burkean attitude to expediency and prudence. Forms of government, he believed, should be derived 'from human prudence', and he thought what 'experience has proved to be expedient' should be deemed just. He held the conservative view that something which had existed successfully for a long time had proved its merit and must be 'founded either in the nature of things or in the necessities of our nature'.[24] Equally it was only to a limited extent that laws could 'be wiser than the nation for which they are enacted'.[25]

Coleridge's Toryism did not, however, extend to an admiration of Tory statesmen. He thought Peel 'rather remarkable for groundless and unlucky concessions'.[26] And wherever he looked in religion or in politics, he seemed to see 'a world of power and talent wasted on the support of half truths . . .'[27] Notwithstanding his difficulty in understanding Coleridge, Liverpool had been induced to promise a sinecure for the poet, but he suffered a stroke before he could provide it.[28] Still Coleridge could fairly claim that he did not write out of 'hope, or fear, of expectation or wish'.[29] In his late poem 'A Character' he wrote:

> 'Alas, poor Bard! no gold had he;
> Behind another's team he stept,
> And plough'd and sow'd, while others reapt; . . .
> Besides, whate'er he wrote or said
> Came from his heart as well as head;
> And though he never left in lurch
> His king, his country, or his church,
> 'Twas but to humour his own cynical
> Contempt of doctrines Jacobinical;
> To his conscience only hearty,
> 'Twas but by chance he serv'd the party; . . .
> The self-same things had said and writ,
> Had Pitt been Fox, and Fox been Pitt; . . .
> Who swore it vex'd his soul to see
> So grand a cause, so proud a realm,
> With Goose and Goody at the helm;
> Who long ago had fall'n asunder
> But for their rivals' baser blunder.

There is nothing sycophantic about that.

6. Benjamin Disraeli (1804–81)

Toryism, or the policy of the Tories, being the proposed or practised embodification, as the case may be, of the national will and character it follows that Toryism must occasionally represent and reflect the passions and prejudices of the nation, as well as its purer energies, and its more enlarged and philosophic views.

Disraeli[1]

'The Bishop of London', Disraeli told Queen Victoria in 1868, 'sympathises with everything that is earnest; but what is earnest is not always true; on the contrary, error is often more earnest than truth.'[2] The truth of this observation has not always been instinctively accepted in Anglo-Saxon countries. And because Disraeli often was not earnest, it was commonly thought that what he said was not true. He might have done better to follow the advice of the contemporary American politician, which has become known as Corwin's law: 'If you would succeed in life, you must be solemn, solemn as an ass. All the great monuments of earth have been built over solemn asses.'[3] In Disraeli's novel, *Sybil*, Mr Tadpole makes a similar point: 'We must go with the times, my Lord. A virtuous middle class shrinks with horror from French actresses; and the Wesleyans, the Wesleyans must be considered, Lord Marney.'[4] Disraeli did not sufficiently consider the Wesleyans.

In any case, Disraeli's frequent lack of gravity combined with the flexibility of his political tactics gave him for some time the reputation of a charlatan. Yet in fact his political opinions, as opposed to his political manoeuvrings, were remarkably consistent. Writing a general preface to a re-issue of his novels in 1870, Disraeli reaffirmed the views he had expressed in them and in his *Vindication of the English Constitution* many years before. 'The origin and character of our political parties,' he wrote, 'their influence on the condition of the people of this country, some picture of the moral and physical condition of that people, and some intimation of the means by which it might be elevated and improved, were themes which had long engaged my meditation . . .' Disraeli justifiably added that 'the general spirit' of his novels 'ran counter to the views which had long been prevalent in England . . .'[5]

Like Burke, Disraeli had a sense of the limitations of human reason. Reason was not responsible for any of the great achievements of mankind.[6] Sensible men studied the national history, since 'nations have characters, as well as individuals'; and through this study, statesmen separated the essential from the adventitious in their history and discovered the principles of national conduct. These principles became 'their guides and their instructors', and that should be the limit of theory in politics.[7]

Disraeli also shared Burke's hatred of abstract ideas in politics, though his principal enemy was Benthamism,* while Burke's had been Jacobinism. And he held the accompanying belief that political rights and institutions, if they were to be effective, must be based on law and on the habits and opinions of the people concerned. 'The Good Louis', he mocked, 'presented his countrymen with a free constitution . . . drawn up in a morning. . . Louis XVIII achieved that in one morning which in less favoured England has required nearly a thousand years for its accomplishment.'[8] In England, in contrast, he wrote in 1835, 'the leading men have invariably agreed to eschew abstractions'. This was the distinguishing feature of English statesmanship and the principal cause of the duration of the English State.[9]

Disraeli shared, too, Burke's attitude to law and prescription. All our struggles for freedom smacked of law. And 'this respect for Precedent, this clinging to Prescription, this reverence for Antiquity, which are so often ridiculed by conceited and superficial minds, and

---

*His early novel *Popanilla* has some satirical passages on the utilitarians and political economy: 'The object of all mechanism is the attainment of utility; the object of man, who is the most perfect machine, is utility in the highest degree. Can we believe, therefore, that this machine was ever intended for a State which never could have called forth its powers, a State in which no utility could ever be attained, a State in which there are no wants; consequently, no demand; consequently, no supply; consequently, no competition; consequently, no invention; consequently no profits; only one great pernicious monopoly of comfort and ease? . . . that which is most useful is most natural, because utility is the test of nature; therefore a steam-engine is in fact a much more natural production than a mountain.'[10]

move the especial contempt of the gentlemen who admire abstract principles, appear to me . . . satisfactorily to account for the permanent character of our liberties . . .' Society was an artificial creation; the subject could not exist without the state. Man was therefore born with filial duties to the state. Our ancestors would not allow theory to dislodge habit. 'Hence their reverence for prescription, which they placed above law, and held superior to reason.'[11]

Nevertheless Disraeli's view of history was profoundly different from that of Burke. For Burke, the present was the outcome of the Glorious Revolution of 1688, which had given England a nearly perfect constitution and conferred liberties on Englishmen which were not enjoyed by any other European nation. Disraeli agreed about the liberties of Englishmen; he shared Burke's reverence for the institutions of the country. But for him, the present was the England of the Industrial Revolution. This had, admittedly, brought a rapid advance in material civilization. But in a passage which seems to echo Coleridge, Disraeli lamented that 'in the hurry-skurry of money-making, men-making, and machine-making' there had been 'no proportionate advance in our moral civilisation'.[12]

As a result much of the population lived in appalling conditions, of which their more favoured countrymen were wholly unaware. The Queen reigned over 'two nations; between whom there is no intercourse and no sympathy; who are as ignorant of each other's habits, thoughts, and feelings, as if they were dwellers in different zones, or inhabitants of different planets; who are formed by a different breeding, are fed by a different food, are ordered by different manners, and are not governed by the same laws . . . THE RICH AND THE POOR.'[13] Disraeli described the living conditions of the second of the two nations. 'About a fortnight after his mother had introduced him into the world, she returned to her factory, and put her infant out to nurse . . . The expense is not great; laudanum and treacle, administered in the shape of some popular elixir, affords these innocents a brief taste of the sweets of existence, and, keeping them quiet, prepares them for the silence of their impending grave. Infanticide is practised as extensively and as legally in England as it is on the banks of the Ganges; a circumstance which apparently has not yet engaged the attention of the Society for the Propagation of the Gospel in Foreign Parts.'[14]*

*Dickens a few years later made a similar point through Mrs Jellyby in *Bleak House*. That lady neglected her family and everything else, while she concentrated

Plainly a present containing such horrors could not be the outcome of a perfect past. Accordingly Disraeli, in the *Vindication* published in 1835 and in *Coningsby* and *Sybil* written in 1844 and 1845, turned Whig history on its head. Where the Whigs saw the history of England as the evolution of liberty under their auspices culminating in God's greatest work, early Victorian England, Disraeli saw the last two centuries of English history as usurpation by the Whig oligarchy leading to the creation of the Two Nations.

The written history of the country had been so distorted, he believed, that for an Englishman to read it was about as profitable 'as reading the Republic of Plato or the Utopia of More, the pages of Gaudentio di Lucca or the adventures of Peter Wilkins'.[15] Disraeli set out to remedy this. It was the plundering of the Church at the Reformation which set England on the wrong course, since it had 'created a factitious aristocracy'.[16] The great Whig families had 'in one century plundered the Church to gain the property of the people and in another century changed the dynasty to gain the power of the Crown . . .'[17]

When George I became King of England, the Whig peers obtained much of the executive power of the state through the establishment of the Cabinet. They also tried to extend their legislative power and to entrench the oligarchy by proposing the Peerage Bill, which would have prevented the King from making any more peers. The Venetian party, which was composed of the great Whig families, the Non-conformists, and the money interest, alienated the rest of the nation during 'more than sixty years of a government of singular corruption'.[18] The Whigs were an anti-national party, and 'in the long run, the English nation declares against them'.[19]

In contrast to the Whigs, the Tory Party 'is the national party', which 'supports the institutions of the country, because they have been established for the common good, and because they secure the equality of civil rights'.[20] Pitt wished to widen the electoral system, to facilitate commerce, and to free the Roman Catholics from the fetters which had been 'fastened on them by English Parliaments in

---

on trying to get 'two hundred healthy families cultivating coffee and educating the natives of Borrioboola-gha, on the left bank of the Niger'.[21] But as R. J. Cruickshank remarked, 'Disraeli's account of the boy Devilsdust in *Sybil* contains a far deeper sympathy with the proletariat than is to be found' in *Bleak House* or even *Hard Times*.[22]

spite of the protests and exertions of English Sovereigns'.[23] Unfortunately, after 1789, things were little better under the Tories than under the Whigs. Pitt's ability was vast and 'his spirit lofty', but he was unfitted for an age of revolution. In consequence he acted contrary to his system. 'He appealed to the fears, the prejudices, and the passions of a privileged class, [and] revived the old policy of the oligarchy he had extinguished . . .'[24]

The years from Pitt's death to 1825 were 'a history of great events and little men'.[25] Pitt's successors called themselves Tories, but their policy was based either on no principle at all or on principles that were anti-Tory. By 1820 the Tories had become as successful as the Whigs had been in the previous century in managing elections; and the Whigs realized that they would never regain power under the existing parliamentary system. They therefore became parliamentary reformers.[26]

Originally, the Cabinet of Liverpool, 'the Arch-Mediocrity', was composed of mediocrities. They were practical men, 'a practical man [being] a man who practises the blunders of his predecessors . . . Like all weak men, they had recourse to what they called strong measures. They determined to put down the multitude.'[27] The Arch-Mediocrity gradually realized, however, that talent and knowledge were needed, and in turn Wellington, Peel, Canning and Huskisson were brought into the Cabinet. Unfortunately this Cabinet, with all its talents, did not attain to principles; expediency was its guide. In consequence, it did not take the opportunity to organize the Tory Party on a broad and national basis, to settle Ireland, to introduce parliamentary reform gradually, or to deal with industrial misery. In the event, therefore, that brilliant Cabinet was 'the real parent of the Roman Catholic Association, the Political Unions, the Anti-Corn Law League'.[28]

Canning's death disorganized both parties even more than had his rise. 'The distinctive principles of these connections were now difficult to trace.'[29] With 'an exhausted sensualist on the throne', 'a voluptuous aristocracy, and a listless people', the government was consigned to a great man, the Duke of Wellington. But Wellington knew nothing of England, and hence broke 'up his government [and] wrecked his party'.[30] The growl of reform was not very fierce. Wellington could have saved himself. Instead, he panicked and 'precipitated a revolution which might have been delayed for half a century, and never need have occurred in so aggravated a form'.[31]

In 1844, Peel could not be said to be the leader of the Tory Party, since the party had virtually ceased to exist. Yet it was not dead; it was asleep. And, 'in an age of political materialism . . . that aspires only to wealth because it has faith in no other accomplishment, as men rifle cargoes on the verge of shipwreck', Toryism would in time rise again 'to bring back strength to the Crown, liberty to the subject, and to announce that power has only one duty: to secure the Social Welfare of the PEOPLE'.[32]

Disraeli was not writing as an academic historian with Namierite standards of scholarship. He wrote as a novelist and politician, who believed that 'it is the past alone that can explain the present'.[33] Of course the novels are exotic and occasionally fantastic. There is much exaggeration in his history, a good deal of party propaganda, and a lot that present-day historians do not accept. Yet Disraeli's history made an attempt to explain the ugly reality of early Victorian England – a reality which Whig history ignored. Stripped of the fripperies and absurdities of 'Young England', with its medieval tournaments and its maypoles, Disraeli's political views are clearly visible in his novels, and in his political career he tried to carry them out. Nature copied art only in broad outline, but it was a surprisingly faithful imitation. All depended, in his view, upon the creation of a new and revived Tory party which would be truly national and which would be a party of principle. This party composed of the gentry and the people would, in alliance with the Crown and the Church, transform England by dealing with the condition of the people. It would thus create one nation where two at present existed. Disraeli's objective was to show that 'Toryism was not a phrase, but a fact'.[34]

'The liberty of England', said Disraeli in 1872, 'depends much upon the landed tenure of England – upon the fact that there is a class which can alike defy despots and mobs, around which the people may always rally, and which must be patriotic from its intimate connection with the soil.'[35] He said the same thing in the thirties and forties. The landed interest, he believed, was the bulwark of liberty. This was a fully tenable view.* 'In a territorial constitution', he said in 1846, 'you and those whom you have succeeded have

---

*As late as 1885 Gladstone wrote that he regarded it 'as a very high duty to labour for the conservation of estates, and the permanence of the families in possession of them, as a principal source of our social strength, and as a large part of true Conservatism'.[36]

found the only security for self-government, the only barrier against that centralizing system which has taken root in other countries.'[37]

Shortly after there had been, in 1848, revolutions in most continental countries and then violent reaction, Disraeli wrote in his life of Bentinck: the people of England 'will perhaps after due reflection discover that ancient communities like the European must be governed either by traditionary influences or by military force'. England was the only important European country still governed by traditionary influences, and the only one that had preserved her liberty.[38]*

For Disraeli, the great virtue of landed property was that it produced obligations as well as rights. Liberty was not secured in England by abstract rights, but by law, by traditional rights, by England's independent corporations and institutions, and by the territorial constitution. It was these things which were the barrier to Jacobinism, to Benthamism, or to an all-powerful House of Commons. Like Burke, Disraeli was something of a corporatist. It was our natural institutions, he wrote, which made us a nation. 'Without our Crown, our Church, our Universities, our great municipal and commercial corporations, our Magistracy, and its dependent scheme of provincial polity, the inhabitants of England, instead of being a nation, would present only a mass of individuals governed by a metropolis, whence an arbitrary senate would issue the stern decrees of its harsh and heartless despotism.'[39]

The Kings and Queens of England, in Disraeli's eyes, had always been the protectors of the English people; and a strong Crown was still necessary to withstand oligarchy and to unite and strengthen the nation. Disraeli may have been saying little more than that executive government in England was too weak. In the largely *laissez-faire* age of the 1830s, 40s and 50s, that was certainly true, and Disraeli may merely have been expressing the thought in colourful language. Or he may have been speaking of the wearers of the Crown. In any case, the monarchy was still powerful. The two-party system removed the British monarch from politics. Disraeli was writing at a time when

*Nearly a century later, Sir Lewis Namier expressed a not dissimilar view: 'The British system of representative and responsible government, carried on through parliamentary institutions, seemed to [the Continental middle-class revolutionaries of 1848] to secure in practice the basic maxims of the French Revolution; and they did not realise how deeply ingrained the proprietary principle is in the public life of this country . . .'[40]

that system was scarcely in embryo; and at least until the death of Prince Albert the monarchy retained considerable political import- ance. In looking to an active monarch, therefore, Disraeli was not out of tune with the times. Besides, while there is dispute as to the exact nature and extent of the monarch's powers today, she remains the guardian of the constitution. If a Government behaved uncon- stitutionally, the Queen would be under no compulsion to behave like King Victor Emmanuel with Mussolini and meekly acquiesce in the establishment of a dictatorship.* By the time Disraeli became Prime Minister, Albert was dead and the two-party system had begun its sway. There was little scope for political action by Queen Victoria. But by making her Empress of India and drawing her out of retirement, Disraeli began that process which has ended with the monarch sitting securely at the top of the English state and society and enjoying unrivalled popularity and prestige.

'I am', Disraeli once probably said, 'the blank page between the Old and the New Testament.'[41] And he occasionally used odd expressions about the Church as when he described it as 'a sacred corporation for the promulgation . . . of certain Asian principles, which, although local in their birth, are of divine origin, and of universal and eternal application'.[42] In his Hughenden preface he said the Church was in theory and once had been in practice 'the spiritual and intellectual trainer of the people'. This has overtones of Newmarket and was perhaps a throw-back to Lord George Bentinck. And his friend, George Smythe, thought that 'Dizzy's conversion to moderate Oxfordism is something like Bonaparte's to modern Mohammedanism'.[43] But while there are passages in *Tancred* which point otherwise, Disraeli was a good churchman and a regular worshipper, who believed that 'no practical religion' could exist without 'the maintenance of formularies and the belief in dogmas'.[44]

'The Church,' he wrote in 1835, 'is part of our constitution, and its character has changed in unison with that constitution.' The Establishment, which under Laud had tried to obtain conformity by persecution, was now our best guarantee of toleration.[45] And speaking in Manchester nearly forty years later he maintained that the combination of a national Church with the free enjoyment of private judgement in religion was 'one of the triumphs of civili- sation'.[46]

*This subject is discussed in Gilmour, *The Body Politic*, pp. 318–22.

Disraeli was a consistent supporter of religious education. In a speech in 1839 he was an advocate of national, but not of state, education. The latter was only suitable for tyrannies like China, Persia, Austria and Russia.[47]* In his Manchester speech in 1872, having said that next to being 'the stewards of Divine mysteries' the clergy's greatest distinction was the devotion of their lives and fortunes to education, he went on to express his 'mortification that, from a feeling of envy or of pique, the Nonconformist body, rather than assist the Church in their great enterprise, should absolutely have become the partisans of a merely secular education'.[48]

Writing in 1870 Disraeli said that amongst the ideas in his novels were the need 'to change back the oligarchy into a generous aristocracy round a real throne; . . . to emancipate the political constituency of 1832 from its sectarian bondage and contracted sympathies; to elevate the physical as well as the moral condition of the people, by establishing that labour required regulation as much as property; and all this . . . could only, with all their faults and backslidings, be undertaken and accomplished by a reconstructed Tory Party'.[49] The Whigs were the classical oligarchs, but the Tories also had oligarchic leanings. To prevent oligarchy and to preserve the Tories as a national party, Toryism had from time to time to be divested of those aspects which in the course of time had become obsolete and open to misrepresentation by its opponents, just as Bolingbroke had divested it of Jacobitism in the eighteenth century.[50]

In early Victorian England that primarily meant widening the party's basis of support and improving 'the condition of the people'. The people must be brought within both the constitutional and the economic pale. Disraeli, unlike many economists, was not one of those who believed that liberty would be infringed or the prosperity of the country threatened, if the state intervened to shorten the hours women and young persons worked in factories from twelve to ten. In 1873 he said that supporting the Ten Hours Act in 1847 was 'one of the most satisfactory incidents' in his career.[51]

In 1836 he wrote that 'the wider the popular suffrage the more powerful would be the natural aristocracy',[52] and in 1867 he passed

---

*J. S. Mill later said much the same thing: 'A general state education is a mere contrivance for moulding people to be exactly like one another.' In so far as it was efficient, it established 'a despotism over the mind'. Mill thought that if there had to be state education, it should be only 'one among many competing experiments'.[53]

the Second Reform Bill. No doubt there was much opportunism in the Tory manoeuvrings over that Reform Bill as there had been over previous projects for reform. The fact remains that Disraeli was almost the only statesman who had seen and said many years before that a wider franchise could forge an electoral alliance between the masses and the landed classes, and who then carried his belief into law. That Act, Disraeli said at Crystal Palace five years later, 'was founded on a confidence that the great body of the people of this country were "Conservative" . . . I mean that the people of England, and especially the working classes of England, are proud of belonging to a great country, and wish to maintain its greatness . . . [and] the ancient institutions of the land.'[54]

In the same speech Disraeli laid down that one 'great object of the Tory Party' was 'the elevation of the condition of the people' – the other two being the maintenance of the institutions of the country and the upholding of the British Empire. 'No important step', he said, could be gained in improving 'the condition of the multitude . . . unless you can effect some reduction of their hours of labour and humanise their toil'. He went on to recall how, many years ago, the Tories believed that these results could be obtained without inflicting 'injury on the wealth of the nation', and that despite the opposition and forebodings of their Liberal opponents they had been proved right.[55]

Disraeli's advocacy of social reform and his insistence that the people's economic conditions must be improved was consistent from his opposition to the new Poor Law of 1834 down to the legislation passed by his government forty years on. In his speech in Edinburgh after the 1867 Reform Act he could say that he had supported all of the thirty-two measures that had been passed in three decades on 'the condition of the people' and that the party had opposed none of them.[56] Disraeli's 1874 government, which was the first majority Tory government for thirty years, did not pass thirty-two measures to improve the conditions of the people, but it passed an impressive number. Disraeli told Lady Bradford that the reforms were 'a policy round which the country can rally',[57] and he told Lady Chesterfield that Cross's two labour measures would 'gain and retain for the Conservatives the lasting affection of the working classes'.[58] Disraeli did not concern himself with the details; he left those to Cross, the Home Secretary. But his government carried through more social reform than any other government in the nineteenth century.[59] Much remained to be done, but Disraeli surely vindicated his claim that the Tory Party was the national party, that the Tory Party would improve the condition of the people, and that the masses would support its defence of England's institutions.

For Disraeli there were two sorts of equality: 'the equality that levels and destroys, and the equality that elevates and creates. It is this last, this sublime, this celestial equality, that animates the laws of England. The principle of the first equality, base, terrestrial, gallic and grovelling,' he wrote in the *Vindication*, 'is that no one should be privileged; the principle of English equality is that everyone should be privileged.' Every Englishman enjoyed equality of civil rights, freedom, justice, and the right to acquire property and to aspire to any position to which his talents were suited.[60]

To be national, therefore, was not to be egalitarian. The Tory Party was the national party of England. It was formed, he said in 1867, 'of all classes from the highest to the most homely, and it upholds a series of institutions that are in theory, and ought to be in practice, an embodiment of the national requirements and the security of the national rights'. Whenever the Tory Party degenerated into an oligarchy it became unpopular; whenever the national institutions did not fulfil their original intention, it became odious. 'But when the people are led by their natural leaders, and when, by their united influence, the national institutions fulfil their original intention, the Tory party is triumphant, and then under Providence will secure the prosperity and the power of the country.'[61]

Disraeli's remarks about oligarchy had application to the future as well as the past. All government is oligarchical, but the extent obviously varies. The Labour Party enshrined oligarchy in its constitution when it gave the block vote to trade unions at the Labour Conference. And the 'Venetian' oligarchy of today are the leaders of the TUC, who sometimes reduce the Leader of the Labour Party to a mere Doge. They, more than anybody else in the country, seek to practise the principles of what Disraeli called 'exclusion' – the exclusion from power of everybody else.

Equally the Tory Party has more than once since Disraeli's death forsaken its national task and become oligarchic and exclusive. The most glaring example was the Balfour Government's shirking of social reform and its failure to bring in legislation to overrule the Taff Vale and other judgments, which deprived the trade unions of rights that Disraeli's 1875 Act had given them. The Arch-Mediocrity himself could scarcely have been as obtuse in ignoring both the duty and the interest of Toryism.

The middle classes have been gravely injured by the Labour Government, and the Tory Party must ensure their recovery as part of the national recovery. That is plainly in the national interest. But any concentration, today, on the interests of business and the needs of the middle classes, to the exclusion of the needs and interests of the rest of the country, would similarly be a degeneration into oligarchy and a departure from those national principles essential to the party's true character. The Tory Party can claim to be representative of all the people and to be truly national only when it is the defender of all the people. If it becomes exclusive, it becomes oligarchic – and it excludes itself from power.

The *Vindication* and the political novels did not attempt to put forward a blueprint for future policies. They provided sketches, insights and pointers. Disraeli had therefore no rigid programme to follow. In any case he was not a doctrinaire; like Burke, he was implacably opposed to doctrinaires. Alone or with Derby, he was the leader of his party for thirty years, and undeviating sameness is in a party leader neither possible nor desirable – least of all in a period when party divisions were less clearly marked than usual. Opportunism, dexterity and contrivance are, within limits, the necessary tools of a parliamentary leader. He cannot just impose his own views; he must often defer to the views or prejudices of others. There can be no uniformity in his professions or conduct. Certainly Disraeli's remark, for example, about 'these colonial deadweights which *we do not govern*' and his wish to withdraw from Canada and West Africa do not square with his later imperialism.[62] Certainly his defence of the Corn Laws in the 1840s is in marked contrast to his refusal to protect agriculture thirty years later. Certainly when he told the House of Commons that he had never asked for office, he lied. Yet, when all is said, within the limits imposed by the nature of the political trade, his political views and his political career were strikingly harmonious.

Disraeli greatly broadened the base of Toryism and made the Tory Party national; he strengthened England's political institutions by enfranchising without upheaval the artisan class in the towns; he acted to improve the social and economic conditions of the poor. Many years before he had criticized the oligarchic tendencies of his party and demanded that it revert to its true nature; he had advocated a wider suffrage; and he had publicized the shocking conditions under which many people lived, with 'some intimation', as he later said, how they might be 'elevated'.

To deny a connection between those concerns and his subsequent actions is surely to give coincidence an unreasonably long arm. Rather similarly, it has been argued that, although Hitler frequently stated that he would go to war and then actually started a war, he somehow did not intend it. [63]But if a man states a wish or an intention and then carries it out, the safer assumption surely is that there is a link between that wish or intention and the subsequent action. Of course Disraeli's translation of his ideas into action does not prove them to be valid, but it does dispose of the allegation that he was a charlatan. It also gives substance to the Disraelian 'myths' that are important to the Conservative Party. Disraeli was one of the few Tory leaders who has been able to bring warmth to Conservatism and to add to its basic common sense a degree of romance, generosity and excitement, which is present in many Conservatives but which, unless they are a Baldwin or a Churchill, they are usually unable to express. It is therefore just as well that Disraeli's 'intimations' were genuine and not meretricious.

Disraeli believed profoundly that England should be one nation, not two. He thought this aim could only be achieved if the Tory Party were true to its traditions, avoided oligarchy, and became a truly national party. Such a party should not be egalitarian, or classless. It should be composed of all segments and all classes, and it should act in the interests of all segments and all classes. But it could only act in the interests of all if it avoided dogma. Plainly *laissez-faire* could not bring it the support of the working classes, since it denied those classes the protection they needed and were entitled to expect. *Laissez-faire* was the doctrine of oligarchy and exclusion. 'Liberal opinions', he said, 'are the opinions of those who would be free from certain constraints and regulations, from a certain dependence and duty which are deemed necessary for the general or popular welfare. Liberal opinions are very convenient opinions for the rich and powerful. They ensure enjoyment and are opposed to self-sacrifice.'[64] By abstaining from such comfortable opinions, the Tory Party could properly defend the national institutions and enlist in their support the bulk of the nation. The nation would then support the national party, and the national party would represent and protect the nation.

7. Lord Hugh Cecil (1869–1956)

The distrust of the unknown and the love of the familiar are motives
to which no mind is a stranger . . . it is possible that the recent ill-
success of the Conservative Party has been in some degree due to
neglect of these unsensational but omnipresent allies in favour of
appeals to more sublime but less potent emotions.

Lord Hugh Cecil in 1912[1]

Disraeli's successor, Salisbury, produced much polemical journalism
of high quality in the *Quarterly* and other reviews, but he wrote
nothing of greater length. His son, Lord Hugh Cecil, however, who
was a fellow of Hertford College, Oxford, for forty-five years and a
Tory MP for nearly as long, put his thoughts on Conservatism into a
book published in 1912.

Throughout his life, Cecil was an ardent High Churchman. An
opponent at Oxford in 1909 complained of 'his reactionary sacer-
dotal views',[2] and some years earlier his attitude to his Nonconformist supporters at Greenwich had caused his mother to lament
that 'that young man's theology is terrible'.[3] Certainly his opinion
that a marriage between a man and his deceased wife's sister was 'as
immoral as concubinage or bigamy . . . [and] an act of sexual vice'[4]
was far from permissive.*

For Cecil, 'the championship of religion' was the most important
of the Conservative tasks. If Conservatism properly performed this
function, it would be able to ward off the two dangers that beset it:
'the danger of sinking into a mere factious variation of Liberalism,
supporting the claims of another set of politicians, but propounding
measures not distinguished by any pervading principle: or the other
danger of standing only for the defence of those who are well off,
without any sincere endeavour to consider the interests of the whole
people, or any higher object than the triumph of the sagacious sel-

---

*After Cecil had strongly opposed the conscription of Irish priests in 1918,
Bonar Law commented that 'he considers religion an essential occupation'.[5]

fishness of the prosperous'. A religious purpose was needed to 'purify' the aims and methods of politicians.[6] In fact, if the Conservative Party succumbs to the first danger, it avoids the second. If it becomes a factious variation of Liberalism, or today of Socialism, it is compelled to do more than stand only for the well off, who are bound to be a minority. The first danger, of competing unscrupulously for electoral support, is perhaps less easily avoided. And with the decline of religion some other means of purification is evidently needed.

'Virtue,' Cecil said at Edinburgh University in 1909, 'is attained in proportion as liberty is attained: for virtue does not consist in doing right, but in choosing to do right. This is the great distinction, surely, between the animal and man.'[7] Since there was a clear distinction between vice and crime, the state should not try to act as a moral censor.[8] In Cecil's view the prohibitionist destroyed 'true temperance', since temperance consisted 'not merely in abstaining from getting drunk, but in choosing to abstain from getting drunk'.[9]* The occasionally bigoted Churchman was thus more level-headed about the state and morals than many of today's neo-puritans.

Cecil combined reverence for the British constitution with advocacy of unconstitutional courses and with behaviour that caused him and his followers to be called the 'Hughligans'. The man who wrote that 'the constitution is the greatest contribution that the English people have made to human progress'[10] wanted the King in 1909 to dismiss Asquith and to make Rosebery Prime Minister. In 1911, Cecil led the shouting down of Asquith in the House of Commons. A few years earlier he had prevented the passage of a Bill he disliked by lingering in the division lobby until after its time had run out.[11] Labour's business managers would have had nothing to teach him in parliamentary chicanery.

Cecil, a fierce free-trader, lost his seat at Greenwich in 1906, because a tariff reformer split the Conservative vote; and for a time he hoped for the formation of a new centre party, composed of Conservative free-traders and moderate Liberals, and led by Rosebery.[12] Back in the Commons four years later as Conservative Member for Oxford University, Cecil's own partisanship was unabated, but his experience over tariff reform had given him a strong distaste for that of lesser men. It was only a 'pretence', he had

*H. L. Mencken put the point rather differently. He defined a prohibitionist as 'the sort of man one would not care to drink with even if he drank'.

discovered, that the House of Commons represented the people. It represented the ardent partisans and the party machines. Independents were being squeezed out, and public opinion had limited influence. As a result, 'the highest authority of our immense and unequalled Empire lies alternately in the hands of one of two knots of vehement, uncompromising and unbalanced men'. As a remedy, Cecil advocated the referendum. This would be the most effective brake upon the 'vigorous Radical partisans', since the English people's strong leaning towards Conservatism would probably cause them to reject 'any very revolutionary measure . . .'[13]

For Cecil there were three elements in modern Conservatism: pure or natural Conservatism, 'that is the distrust of the unknown and the love of the familiar . . .; Toryism, or the defence of Church and King, the reverence for religion and authority; and . . . imperialism, a feeling for the greatness of the country and for that unity which makes its greatness'.[14] Conservatism was brought into existence by the French Revolution, and Burke had outlined its main principles which were still valid. Conservative imperialism also stemmed from opposition to the French Revolution. The great wars against France 'identified the Conservative Party with upholding the greatness and power of England in external affairs', since the Whig Party first opposed the war and then became dissatisfied critics of it.[15]*

Reviewing the party struggle of the last 100 years, Cecil discussed four great events, all of them, in his view, disastrous to the Conservative Party: Roman Catholic emancipation, the Reform Bill of 1832, the repeal of the Corn Laws, and the Second Reform Bill. The first three were caused by the Conservative leaders failing to bring about gradual change. If the Roman Catholics had been emancipated before the agitation of O'Connell, 'we should not have heard of Home Rule'. Had the more scandalous features of the representative system been removed piecemeal, the dangerous crisis of 1832 and the lasting injury to the Conservative Party could have been avoided. Similarly, the duties on corn and the powers of the landowners should have been reduced gradually over the years, 'before the crisis of 1845 made the question dangerously acute'.[16] Cecil's analysis of these crises was therefore very similar to Disraeli's.†

*Fox said of the Peace of Amiens that 'the triumph of the French Government over the English does in fact afford me a degree of pleasure which it is very difficult to disguise'.[17]

†See *Coningsby*, Book II, ch. I.

In the fourth great Conservative disaster, the passing of the 1867 Reform Act, Disraeli's error was the opposite of Peel's. 'He was too quick where Peel had been too slow.' In consequence Conservative sentiment was scandalized.[18] On the face of it, therefore, Cecil demanded split-second timing from Conservative leaders – an exacting requirement. Yet his father, Salisbury, had resigned on the franchise issue in 1867, and later described the Second Reform Bill as 'a headlong rout' and 'this great surrender'. And it was presumably loyalty to his father that led Cecil to censure Disraeli as well as Peel. Salisbury himself was more consistent, or less hard to please, than his son: he praised Peel for his 'tenacity' in 1832.[19]

In Cecil's view, one of the principal purposes of Conservatism ever since its inception had been the defence of property. The urge to own property was one of the strongest of human instincts, and it had many highly beneficial effects. But the right of property was not founded on justice 'derived from the circumstances of its acquisition'. There was no element of 'desert' in either earning or ownership. A man's right to the property he owned lay in the simple consideration that it is wrong to inflict an injury upon any man and that to deprive him of his property clearly injures him.[20]

It was plain to Cecil that 'to deprive a person of half his income is not to tax him, but to inflict on him a very heavy fine'. And he believed that 'most men would prefer to incur a substantial term of imprisonment than to pay such a tax'. Had that been true, the House of Lords would long since have been transferred from Westminster to Wormwood Scrubs. But with taxation on earned income now at a top rate of 83 per cent and of unearned at 98 per cent, Cecil's belief that without a limit upon it 'taxation may develop into robbery'[21] was rather nearer the mark. Even at a time of ever-rising crime, many taxpayers find the Inland Revenue even more predatory than thieves and robbers.

Like Burke, Cecil was certain that 'the paths of justice and ultimate expediency always lie side by side'. The idea that measures of social reform could be founded on 'wrong' was mistaken and immoral.[22] Yet Christians had cause to censure the economic system which was certainly not Christian. Self-interest, not love, was the governing motive in industry and commerce, 'and Christianity indisputably requires that the mutual relations of all men shall be controlled by love'. But the social system would only be transformed by an improvement in human nature which substituted love for self-interest.

Socialism could not transform the social system, since it did not pretend to change human nature. Indeed Socialism 'claims only to substitute the action of a regulating State for the working of competition'. Hence, as human nature would always inflict suffering on the weak, 'Christianity was not concerned with any political change which left the moral nature of men as it was'.[23]

There was 'no antithesis', Cecil declared, 'between Conservatism and Socialism, or even between Conservatism and Liberalism'. Conservatives could not give a general answer about the respective spheres of the state and the individual. The only certain proposition was that the state must not be unjust to individuals. Otherwise any proposals to increase the functions of the state had to be judged on their merits. Conservatism had achieved 'a compromise between liberty and authority'. And defence of the British constitution, to which Conservatives were dedicated, necessarily included the defence of liberty.[24]

Similarly in pursuing social reform to improve the conditions of the poor, Conservatism 'must often itself be in sympathy at least with some of the objects of Socialism'. Conservatism had inherited the Tory traditions which favoured the activity and authority of the state. Indeed Mr Herbert Spencer attacked Socialism as being in fact the revival of Toryism; he called it 'the New Toryism'. Yet to Cecil there seemed to be an element of Jacobinism in the Socialist movement. Socialists wanted to abolish competition and at the same time to reward everybody according to his worth. Like Hume, Cecil saw this was impossible. In any case, he was convinced that better economic arguments than any so far advanced would be needed to persuade any Conservative of the possibility of considerably reducing, let alone abolishing, the role of competition in the production and distribution of wealth.[25]

Conservatism, Cecil concluded, formed 'a political creed constructive, balanced and prudent, drawing its inspiration from the elevating sentiments of patriotic enthusiasm and religious truth; tender to the sufferings of humanity, but scrupulous of the obligations of justice; sobering activity by a prudent veneration for experience, and securing the efficiency of progress by basing it on what time has tried and tradition has cemented'.[26]

8. Michael Oakeshott

To be Conservative is not merely to be averse from change (which may be an idiosyncrasy); it is also a manner of accommodating ourselves to changes, an activity imposed upon all men. For, change is a threat to identity, and every change is an emblem of extinction.
Michael Oakeshott[1]

Apart from Hume, Michael Oakeshott is the only man considered here whose primary concern has been philosophy, and like Hume his studies were interrupted by military service. He has been almost the only practising academic Conservative philosopher during a period when it has usually been unfashionable to be a Conservative intellectual. Regrettably, he is not a prolific writer. Leaving aside his *Guide to the Classics*, which before the war gave valuable hints on the picking of Derby winners, his high reputation rests largely on a collection of essays, written between 1947 and 1961, entitled *Rationalism in Politics*, and on three long connected essays in his book *On Human Conduct* published in 1975. If the difficulty of interpreting Burke is that he wrote so much, the difficulty with Oakeshott is that he has written too little. His full meaning is sometimes hard to discern.

This is not through any fault in Oakeshott's highly individual writing. His style is rich, aphoristic and elegant, but never vulgar or affected. The occasional obscurity stems from a combination of intellectual radicalism and intellectual diffidence. This compound is integral to his thinking. Yet his originality, the subtlety of his reasoning, and his assault on common modes of thought require a more extended account of his views than we have yet been given to make his meaning entirely plain.

Oakeshott's scepticism is as far-reaching as that of Hume. This marvellous passage in his inaugural lecture at the London School of Economics, 'Political Education', sets the tone: 'In political activity, then, men sail a boundless and bottomless sea; there is neither harbour for shelter nor floor for anchorage, neither starting-place nor appointed destination. The enterprise is to keep afloat on an even keel; the sea is both friend and enemy; and the seamanship consists in using the resources of a traditional manner of behaviour in order to make a friend of every hostile occasion.'[2] And the point here is not merely that politics is an ever-unfinished activity but that it is a secondary activity concerned with rules, procedures and arrangements and not with substantive satisfactions and delights, and is therefore something about which it is appropriate to be conservative.

For Oakeshott, politics is 'the activity of attending to the general arrangements of a set of people whom chance or choice have brought together'. Now to understand this or any other activity we must 'know it as a concrete whole', and we must 'recognise [it] as having the source of its movement within itself', since an understanding 'which leaves the activity in debt to something outside itself is, for that reason, an inadequate understanding'. It follows that politics is not a purely empirical activity. Empiricism has always to be joined with something else before it can be recognized as a concrete manner of activity. An even greater error is to see politics as the activity of bringing the arrangements of a society into conformity with an ideology or a single abstract idea. A political ideology is not 'the quasi-divine parent of political activity' but 'its earthly step-child'. It is the political activity which comes first, and which is then followed by a political ideology. Systems of abstract ideas or ideologies are mere 'abstracts of some kind of concrete activity'.[3]

In politics, therefore, both empiricism and the ends to be pursued are dependent upon a traditional manner of behaviour. Any collection of people which did not have recognized traditions of behaviour would be incapable of politics. Taking the legal status of women as an example, Oakeshott argued that the only cogent reason for 'the technical "enfranchisement" of women was that they were already effectively enfranchised'. Abstract general arguments were irrelevant; there was 'an incoherence' between their status in current moral belief and their status in constitutional law which called for removal.[4]

It is an illusion to believe that 'politics is ever anything more than the pursuit of intimations'; it is 'a conversation, not an argument'. One might legitimately draw the inference that Socialism is an argument, and Conservatism is or should be a conversation. It is equally an illusion to believe that society can summon to its aid some ever-reliable independent guide. There is no such thing. All we have are 'the relics of [society's] own tradition of behaviour . . .'[5]

This scepticism about the value of general principles in politics is accompanied by a repudiation of one of the main strands in the European political tradition, that of Rationalism. The disease of Rationalism has spread wide and deep. And Rationalism has been more triumphant in politics than anywhere else except religion. Virtually every country and party in Europe suffers from it. Indeed 'almost all politics today have become Rationalist or near-Rationalist.' Many examples are given. 'The notion of founding a society, whether of individuals or of States, upon a Declaration of the Rights of Man is a creature of the Rationalist brain, so also are "national" or racial self-determination when elevated into universal principles. The project of the so-called Re-union of the Christian Churches, of open diplomacy, of a single tax, of a civil service whose members "have no qualifications other than their personal abilities", of a self-consciously planned society, the Beveridge Report, the Education Act of 1944, Federalism, Nationalism, Votes for Women, the Catering Wages Act, the destruction of the Austro-Hungarian Empire, the World State (of H. G. Wells or anyone else), and the revival of Gaelic as the official language of Eire, are alike the progeny of Rationalism.' In short, 'the ordinary practical politics of European nations have become fixed in a vice of Rationalism'.[6]

The Rationalist, Oakeshott observes, is preoccupied with certainty. He believes in the independence of his mind, and the only authority he recognizes is that of Reason. Custom and prejudice and any other authority are all his enemies. His unaided reason will infallibly tell him what is right. Nothing therefore is immune from his scrutiny, and the existence of something in no sense raises a presumption in its favour. The Rationalist's 'disposition makes both destruction and creation easier for him to understand and engage in, than acceptance or reform . . . he always prefers the invention of a new device to making use of a current and well-tried expedient'. The Rationalist sees himself as an engineer, and he must always be active. Abstraction not experience is his tool. Rationalist politics are 'the politics of perfection' and 'the politics of uniformity'. Only 'the best' will do, not 'the best in the circumstances'. Political activity is recognized by the Rationalist 'as the imposition of a uniform condition of perfection upon human conduct'.[7] In contrast, Conservative politics recognizes the diversity of human purposes and has no place for a belief in the evanescence of imperfection.

As a result of the Rationalist temper, 'traditions of behaviour have given place to ideologies', even in England, and the consciously planned is preferred to what has grown up over the years. This malign change from unfixed and adaptable habits of behaviour to comparatively rigid systems of abstract ideas was in the past baulked by 'the informality of English politics'. But now even the resistance to such change has become an ideology.[8]

Marxism is 'the most stupendous of our political rationalisms . . . this greatest of all political cribs . . . No other technique has so imposed itself upon the world as if it were concrete knowledge; none has created so vast an intellectual proletariat, with nothing but its technique to lose'. Marx and Engels were of course seeking to instruct a politically uneducated class. Indeed, 'the generation of rationalist politics is by political inexperience out of political opportunity'.[9]

In morals the rationalist damage was begun long ago. 'The urge to speculate, to abstract and to define, which overtook Christianity as a religion, infected also Christianity as a way of moral life.' By the middle of the third century Christian morality had largely become a self-conscious pursuit of moral ideals instead of being a way of life. And from then on 'a Christian habit of moral behaviour . . . was swamped by a Christian moral ideology . . .'[10] The morality of the Rationalist, like his politics, 'is the morality of the self-made man and of the self-made society: It is what other peoples have recognized as "idolatry"'. But to have significance moral ideals must belong to a religious or a social life. And Rationalists have abstracted moral ideals from a religious and social tradition, which they have done their best to destroy. In consequence Rationalist morality is fatally flawed. It leads us for example to try 'to destroy parental authority (because of its alleged abuse), then we sentimentally deplore the scarcity of "good homes", and we end by creating substitutes which complete the work of destruction'.[11]

The existence of liberty in England, Oakeshott wrote in 1949, depended not on parliamentary government or any constitutional contrivance, but on 'the absence from our society of overwhelming concentrations of power'. All our other freedoms depended on this one condition of freedom. Authority is diffused between past, present and future. Power also is dispersed 'among all the multitude of interests and organisations of interest which comprise our society', and it is shared between the Administration and the Opposition. Indeed our society is both integrated and made more free by the proliferation of voluntary bodies which is the direct result of freedom of association in this country.[12] It is free because by law no one is allowed unlimited power – 'no leader, faction, party or "class", no majority, no government, church, corporation, trade or professional association or trade union'.[13] Plainly that was much truer in 1949 than it is today.

Freedom of association necessarily implies the right not to join and the right to leave associations. And any association which deprives others of any of their rights is not an exercise in freedom of association, it is a denial of freedom of association. A 'compulsory-voluntary' association – the closed shop, for example – is plainly a contradiction in terms; it is an infringement of the right of association, as well as a concentration of power that endangers freedom. Oakeshott recognized that it is a constant struggle to preserve the diffusion of power. Arrangements which at one time promote the dispersion of power may at another promote its con-centration. We need to be alert enough to recognize any such change, and energetic enough to deal with it when it is still possible to do so.[14]

The office of government is to prevent coercion, and normally therefore the Government needs to be only more powerful than which-ever is the greatest concentration of non-governmental power at the time. The rule of law which binds the governors and the governed alike 'is itself the emblem of that diffusion of power which it exists to promote, and is therefore peculiarly appropriate to a free society'.[15] Prophetic words! In 1974 the rule of law broke down because a concentration of non-governmental power was stronger than the Government, and acted in a way inconsistent with a free society. The rule of law, Oakeshott continued, removes from us 'the fear of the power of our government'. Regrettably, that is not so today. The rule of law is now threatened by Government itself as well as by the arbitrary actions of extra-parliamentary bodies.

Ownership diffuses power, and so a right to private property as little qualified as maybe is the form of property most favourable to liberty. All monopolies or near-monopolies are infringements of liberty, and the greatest barrier to monopoly is private property. The libertarian knows 'that no individual, no group, association or

union can be entrusted with much power, and that it is mere foolish-
ness to complain when absolute power is abused. It exists to be
abused.' In consequence, the libertarian has faith only in arrangements, such as competition, which are hostile to monopoly and
absolute power.[16] To dole out power to the National Union of
Journalists, therefore, would have been an act of folly if those
concerned had been interested in the freedom of the press. But then
Mr Foot and Mr Booth were more interested in trade-union power
than free speech; so they cannot be accused of folly. They knew what
they were doing.

A free society has of course no preconceived purpose, but finds
'its guide in a principle of continuity . . . and in a principle of
consensus'. The two great enemies of freedom are collectivism and
syndicalism. 'Collectivism' means any form of managed society and
may be called 'National Socialism', 'Communism', 'Socialism' or
'Central Planning'. If we choose collectivism we cannot have freedom, and the converse is equally true. Collectivism is inimical to
freedom because it rejects the idea of the dispersion of power and of
'a society organized by means of a multitude of genuinely voluntary
associations'. Under collectivism the government requires great
power, is intolerant of opposition and becomes increasingly involved
in every conflict of interest in society.[17] But, dangerous as collectivism is, syndicalism, which seeks to transfer the control of the means
of production and distribution to trade unions for their benefit, is the
greater enemy of freedom. 'Syndicalism is a contrivance by means of
which society is disposed for a perpetual civil war in which the parties
are the organized self-interest of functional minorities and a weak
central government, and for which the community as a whole pays
the bill in monopoly prices and disorder.' Yet syndicalism is also the
enemy of collectivism. This is because the collectivist government
derives its strength from syndicalist monopolies yet cannot control
them.[18] Thus in 1949 Oakeshott accurately prefigured the situation
in Britain that followed the 1974 election.

The libertarian, he wrote at that time, does not favour unregulated
competition, which he knows to be 'a chimera'. But he will establish
effective competition wherever it is possible, and he will suppress all
monopolies, including labour monopolies. Wherever competition is
impossible, the monopoly should be publicly controlled. The third
objective of his economic policy is a stable currency, since 'inflation
is the mother of servitude'.[19]

D

Oakeshott expanded his ideas in his recent book, *On Human Conduct*, a work of considerable profundity and, at least to the layman, of some difficulty. What chiefly concerns us in it is his views on human association, for here we may expect a reflection of his opinions about current politics.

He distinguishes two modes of human association. First, there is what he calls '*enterprise association*'. This is human beings joined in pursuing some common purpose, in seeking the satisfaction of some common want or in promoting some common substantive interest. Since such purposes can be pursued only in the day-to-day doings of the members, association here is not merely in terms of the common purpose but of decisions about what shall be done, of the performance of cooperative actions and also of the acknowledgement of some instrumental rules of procedure. And since such associates are bound to the performance of actions, they may be free only when they have joined the enterprise voluntarily and when they are permitted to contract out if they no longer approve of the purpose or of the manner in which it is being pursued. This, he says, is the most common mode of human association and there may be as many associations in this mode as there are purposes which invoke joint pursuit.[20]

Secondly there is what he calls moral association. This is human beings joined, not in pursuing a purpose or in together performing substantive actions, but in the acknowledgement of an obligation to subscribe to a practice composed of non-instrumental conditions of conduct. This mode of association may, of course, be enjoyed by those who are also associated in pursuing a common purpose, but it is a distinct relationship; these conditions of conduct do not specify purposes or actions to be performed, but proprieties to be observed in seeking the satisfaction of any want.

When the conditions of 'moral' conduct are rules (laws) enacted and capable of being modified or repealed by a legislature, and there is a judicial procedure for determining the adequacy of subscription to them in particular cases, and there are known penalties assigned to inadequate subscription, the form of association they specify may be called '*civil association*'. Thus, persons associated in this manner (*cives*) are not joined in any undertaking to promote a common interest (they may have wholly different interests and be pursuing different and perhaps conflicting purposes), but in the recognition of non-instrumental rules indifferent to any interest. And their freedom lies not in being permitted to contract out of a joint enterprise but in not being bound to any joint enterprise.[21]

Having distinguished these two modes of association, Oakeshott turns to consider what has been believed and said about the character of a modern European state as an association of human beings. He finds that each of these two modes of association has been attributed to it, that modern European states have characteristics which give plausibility to both these attributions, and that each carries with it an appropriate view of the functions of government: a managerial function when a state is understood as an enterprise association and a custodial function when it is understood as a civil association. But while the first seems to correspond to Socialist belief and the second to Conservative belief, there is no exact fit; political alignments have rarely been in these terms, although there would have been less muddle if they had. And he comes to the conclusion that, from the time of its emergence upon the scene, a modern European state has been an ambivalent mixture of these two modes of association and is likely to remain so. But he finds reasons for believing that one of these analogies for the character of a state is superior to the other and for thinking that it would be better if this ambivalence were resolved in favour of civil association.[22]

For a writer so concerned with political activity and so convinced that political activity in England and in Europe is dreadfully muddled, Oakeshott has remarkably little to say about how the true path should be regained. Probably he thinks that such advice is outside the province of the political philosopher. Or maybe his pessimism leads him to think that there is no escape from a politics apt to be dominated by those who understand a state in the terms of enterprise association; all that can be done is to chart the route to disaster. At least he has no answer to the question, How would a politician or a party which agreed with him have set about getting elected in the 1960s or early 1970s by the British voter who is highly conservative with a small 'c'?

Admittedly some of Oakeshott's specific opinions are much more fashionable today than when he first expressed them; and in a superb essay, 'On being Conservative', he has defended and celebrated the conservative disposition in politics. But, as we have seen, the general tenor of his thought is more revolutionary than conservative. Whether or not he can in his writings be considered a Conservative with a big 'C', there is probably no living writer who is further from being a conservative with a small 'c'. After all, Oakeshott is so striking a philosopher largely because he is so lonely and original.

Yet the Conservative has to work in an environment which has been partly shaped by Collectivism and Rationalism. And the traditional manners of behaviour in British politics, while still retaining some of the informality, the empiricism, and the practicality, which Oakeshott with matchless eloquence rightly extols, have become tinged by those alien and undesirable forces. Only a sharp break with tradition and practice could drive them from Britain. And the British do not like revolutions; or at least they are reluctant to vote for them. To be conservative with a small 'c' today means being at least partly a Collectivist and a Rationalist. So the paradox remains that the great protagonist of traditional manners of behaviour comes near to requiring a theoretical and practical revolution.

9. Lord Hailsham of St Marylebone

Vehement passion does not always indicate an infirm judgement.
Edmund Burke[1]

Though he has never been beaten in a parliamentary election, Lord Hailsham has been in and out of the House of Commons twice, and has changed his name three times. Most of these changes were imposed upon him, and his political beliefs have not similarly fluctuated. One apparent fluctuation, however, was to the benefit of the country. He was the victorious Conservative and pro-Chamberlain candidate at the Oxford by-election which took place immediately after the Munich agreement in 1938 and at which his opponent was supported by, among others, Harold Macmillan and Edward Heath; then eighteen months later he voted against Chamberlain in the Norway debate and thus helped to make Churchill Prime Minister. He was himself a candidate for the Tory leadership in 1963, but the party decided in his own words 'to play safe'[2] and chose Sir Alec Douglas-Home. Had Hailsham won, the history of the Tory Party and of the country would probably have been very different.*

Hailsham is in the Conservative religious tradition of Burke, Coleridge and Lord Hugh Cecil, and in his autobiography he has given an impressive philosophic justification of his beliefs. But he despises politicians who try to sell their politics by preaching religion almost as much as he despises preachers who try to sell their sermons by talking politics. 'The introduction of religious passion into politics', he wrote in *The Conservative Case*,† 'is the end of honest

---

*In 1952 I was then Lord Hailsham's pupil at the bar, which was a liberal education, and in 1963–4 I was the newly disenobled Mr Hogg's parliamentary private secretary, which was a Conservative education. I am therefore not a detached observer.

†The more theoretical parts of *The Conservative Case* published in 1959 are almost identical to those parts in *The Case for Conservatism* published in 1947.

politics, and the introduction of politics into religion is the prostitution of true religion.'[3]

'There can be no genuine Conservatism', Hailsham believes, 'which is not founded upon a religious view of the basis of civil obligation, and there can be no true religion where the basis of civil obligation is treated as purely secular.'[4] This may seem a trifle sweeping, but it has not been disproved by the contemporary combination of a decline of religion and a loosening of the ties of civil and communal obligation. Religion is, to Hailsham, the sole justification for morality, it provides the moral basis of culture, which enables men to live at peace with each other, and it is the 'great governing wheel on the engine of human passion without which no passion, no love, no moral or political principle is valid or even legitimate'.[5] For him, therefore, the necessity of religion in secular society is self-evident.

But religion is in no way opposed to science. As the first and indeed only Minister for Science, Hailsham showed a greater understanding of science than many scientists. He rejected the idea of the two cultures. Pure science, he believes, is, like history, philosophy and poetry, a branch of culture. Science has its limitations, as does philosophy. But religion, philosophy and science share the same fundamental premise that the universe is rational and intelligible.[6]

Hailsham's politics, characteristically, are much less dogmatic and more compromising than his religion. According to one of Mr Gerald Brenan's characters, the great advantage of 'being born a gentleman is that one need never behave like one'.[7] Similarly a man who believes in God, it has been said, does not have to believe in anything else. In any case man's appetite for dogma should ideally be satiated by religion and not extended to economics or politics. The perversion of politics into a secular religion is one of the plagues of the twentieth century.

Hailsham is immune from that danger. His faith in Christianity is secure, but, like Lord Hugh Cecil, he sees the New Testament as 'very largely devoid of political or social doctrine'. Biblical texts cannot, in his view, be profitably used to support exact doctrines, since scriptural quotations can be used to shore up almost any kind of nonsense. And no one, he believes, whether Christian or not, is obliged under either a dictatorship or a democracy actively to embroil himself in any way in politics.[8] In a much quoted apophthegm, he has laid down that 'Conservatives do not believe that political struggle is the most important thing in life . . . The simplest among them prefer fox-hunting – the wisest, religion.' Indeed, 'The man who puts politics first is not fit to be called a civilised being, let alone a Christian.'[9]

In the thirties, he writes, he 'was resolutely a man of the centre',[10] and he has been that ever since.* He does not believe that Conservatives have a monopoly of truth or even of Conservatism. It follows that a monopoly of power by the Conservatives would be a denial of the parliamentary democracy in which Conservatives believe.[11] Presumably, however, this self-denial, even if it were not reinforced by the action of the voters, is dependent upon the Conservatives' opponents being adherents of parliamentary democracy and not its enemies. An interchange of power between a Conservative and, say, a Communist party would be neither desirable nor possible.

In any case, Conservatives should, and do, learn from the good parts of their opponents' case, which in time becomes common ground. 'Conservatism is not so much a philosophy as an attitude.' And since the Conservative Party has no fixed theory of the state, its task is 'to criticize and mould the latest heresy of the moment in the name of tradition . . .' There is no inconsistency therefore in the Conservative Party defending the state and authority against excessive Liberalism in the nineteenth century, and then defending liberty against socialism and excessive state control in the twentieth.[12] Thus, though in the nineteenth century Liberalism was nearly true, Conservatives rightly did not accept it. Believers then as now in original sin, they did not concede that 'the curse of Adam' could be 'so easily removed by Adam Smith'. The twentieth century 'has moved far from liberal economic orthodoxy and no one can seriously hope to restore it'.[13]

But Socialists have reacted far too far from Liberalism. While the motives of many Socialists and the objectives of the pioneers of the movement must be respected, the dangers to liberty of the state being the only employer, the manifest inefficiency of nationalization, the Socialist threat to private property, and all the paraphernalia of Socialism summon the Conservative to the defence of freedom and the individual. Democratic Socialists do not want to go all the way to Socialism. But however short or far the distance they are prepared to go – and if he had been writing the book today Hailsham would

---

*During the leadership struggle in 1963 he was often assumed by the press and politicians to be a right-winger. This was untrue, but so far as Tory MPs were concerned the delusion was not necessarily to his disadvantage.

have pointed out how greatly that distance has varied over the years – their policy will not work, since they throw away the carrot and are reluctant to use the stick. They prevent the free-enterprise system from working properly while not putting anything viable in its place.[14]

'We must always defend the middle ground', Hailsham said in 1974, 'against attacks whether from outside or inside our party and we must beware particularly of destructive attacks coming from two directions at once and masquerading for that reason as public opinion.'[15] Hailsham's centrism can be seen in his attitude to particular issues. In the thirties he believed in 'publicly-organized social service and privately-owned industry', and in the sixties and seventies he favoured 'neither a policy of refusing all help to lame ducks nor one of heaping largesse on hopelessly uneconomic concerns . . .' He has always stood for the unity of the British Isles and regrets the departure of Southern Ireland from the United Kingdom; but he favours diversity within the country and therefore as much devolution as is 'compatible with safety from foreign invasion and economic prosperity'. He is in general opposed to legislation on race relations, but believes it would be dishonourable to attempt to curtail the rights of immigrants or to discriminate against them. Nor does he think it right that dependents should be prevented from joining the heads of their family. He was outraged by Enoch Powell's 'Tiber foaming with blood' speech, and would have resigned from the Shadow Cabinet had not Edward Heath dismissed Powell. Finally, he has pointed out that the Conservative Party when it is in power has to be responsive to the pressure of events and to the economic and international facts of life. This leads to the legend that they have lost touch with the party faithful (who wrongly identify themselves with public opinion) and are putting expediency before party principle. As a result, after an electoral defeat the party tends to become 'more extreme and dogmatic', when usually the right course for it is to show 'greater moderation'.[16]

Hailsham would agree with Disraeli that there is a salutary legal flavour about our politics. For him, a fine lawyer and advocate,* the

---

*The Bar customarily treat the Bench with considerable deference. Once in the Court of Appeal Hailsham, who had not yet taken silk, replied to a question by one of the Lord Justices with the words: 'There is no evidence at all for that suggestion, my lord, and I think that even this court should pay *some* attention to the evidence.' A short silence followed.

law does not come far behind religion. He believes that 'there is a golden thread which alone gives meaning to the political history of the West, from Marathon to Alamein, from Solon to Winston Churchill and after'. This is 'the doctrine of liberty under law'.[17] The conflict between liberty and authority can only be reconciled by the rule of law, which is one of the cardinal tenets of Conservatism. In consequence, Conservatives stand for both authority and liberty. The principle of authority 'requires a man to override his private judgement or desire in favour of a particular rule with which he does not agree simply because it is the law . . . Authority is always something which requires respect in despite of the freedom of the individual.'[18] But just as liberty must be controlled by law, if physical or economic chaos is to be avoided, so must the power of the state and individual ministers be subject to the rule of law. Hence laws cannot be 'made or unmade at will according to the whim of a sovereign body'. In other words Parliament 'controlled by its temporary majority' does not have the right to do exactly what that temporary majority may happen to want.[19] And plainly that must be even more true, when the temporary majority is scarcely a majority and represents a relatively small proportion of the electorate.

Rather surprisingly for a Conservative, Hailsham thinks the limit to what Parliament and people may politically and morally do is fixed by 'natural law, which is the same for all sovereign bodies' and 'is the basis of all actual law'.[20] Burke believed that the rights of Englishmen were far more secure than the alleged natural rights of man, and events bore him out. In the *Reflections* he remarked that in the Petition of Right Parliament referred to '*inherited*' freedom and did not base their claims 'on abstract principles' but on 'a patrimony derived from their forefathers'.[21] Certainly natural law seems a frail and abstract defence against potentially tyrannical Parliaments.*

Yet patriotism, together with religion, law and moderation, is one of the foundations of Hailsham's Conservatism. It shines clearly through nearly all his speeches. 'Country,' he has written, 'though not entitled to the absolute devotion due to God, is perhaps the highest of all the natural relationships which command affection . . .'[22] In his view, free government cannot work without patriotism, since without it people will put some other interest or loyalty

*Indeed Hailsham has put forward detailed constitutional proposals, including a Bill of Rights, judicial review and fixed-term Parliaments, to curb the tyranny of the temporary majority.[23]

before their loyalty to the constitution. Hence Labour's emphasis on class, on trade-union solidarity, or on Socialist dogma is a threat to free government.[24] The validity of that warning was starkly confirmed in 1974.

A man of great intellectual gifts, whose oratory is even better than his writing, Hailsham has never shirked the party battle. Yet he once said on television that he had often questioned his party allegiance. He has been firmly anti-Socialist without ever being infected by the extremism or the doctrinaire posture of his opponents. He is a philosophic partisan. He has thus managed to be both a fiercely controversial party politician and the leading Tory thinker in politics since the war.

Part Three

There is not, there never was, a principle of government under heaven that does not, in the very pursuit of the good it proposes, naturally and inevitably lead into some inconvenience which makes it absolutely necessary to counterwork and weaken the application of that first principle itself, and to abandon something of the extent of the advantage you proposed by it, in order to prevent also the inconveniences which have arisen from the instrument of all the good you had in view.

Edmund Burke[1]

Parliaments are now grown to be quite other things than they were formerly.

Halifax[2]

... Conservatism has in this book only been considered in its nobler aspects. There are undoubtedly operating on the Conservative side in party politics, as on the side of other political parties, much baser elements. A critic of Conservatism might complain that selfishness, avarice, and an uncontrolled taste for alcoholic liquors were all elements that made for the success of Conservative politicians.

Lord Hugh Cecil[3]

1. Conservative Philosophy

Can it be forgotten how frequently, in the course of the French
Revolution, the world has seen sanguinary minorities riding in blood
over the necks of their prostrate countrymen? As little should we
lay to our souls the flattering hope that the bare absurdity – the
monstrousness of any doctrine is a sufficient security against the
attempt to reduce it into practice.

George Canning[1]

Ideas can not be too much prized in and for themselves, can not be
too much lived with; but to transport them abruptly into the world
of politics and practice, violently to revolutionize this world to their
bidding – that is quite another thing. There is the world of ideas
and there is the world of practice.

Matthew Arnold[2]

It is easier to write ten volumes of philosophy than to put a single
precept into practice.

Tolstoy[3]

So far, then, as philosophy or doctrine is concerned, the wise Conservative travels light. Conservative principles cannot be precisely
tabulated. To ask what is the nature of Conservatism is more to the
point than to seek to categorize it. Yet certain themes are apparent
from the writers we have considered. From Halifax we get the idea of
'trimming'. In the past, Conservatives 'trimmed' in favour of the
state and against *laissez-faire*. Today they 'trim' against the state and
in favour of the individual. And both today and in the past, the
purpose of their 'trimming' was the same as that of the 'Great
Trimmer' himself: to achieve balance.

From Bolingbroke, and from others, we get the idea of a national
party. All parties and all party systems have a tendency towards
factionalism. That tendency will be the better resisted, the more

comprehensive a party becomes, and the more mindful it is that party is only a means, not an end.

From Hume we get scepticism, the sense of the fallibility of human reason, and the instinct for enjoyment. There is no virtue in being miserable, even less in making others miserable. Tory abstinence should be from dogma and fanaticism not from enjoyment. The aim of statesmanship is the public benefit.

From Burke, we get prescription and a preference for things that have grown over things that have been made. We get reverence for the nation, the national institutions and national continuity, prudence, the need for parties, and the necessity of complexity if freedom is to be preserved. We get the love of the concrete and the hatred of abstraction. Experience and human nature are our surest guide.

From Coleridge, we get the reminder that no individual can be treated merely as a means, and that the worth and workability of a constitution depend upon the ideas of those who operate it. Misery and hardship cannot be shrugged off by the state or by the well-to-do as the inevitable results of quasi divine economic laws and forces.

From Disraeli, almost echoing Bolingbroke, we get the idea that it is the duty of the Tory Party to be national, and the reminder that the preservation of the national institutions and the improvement of the condition of the people are the overriding objectives of the party. These two objectives are inextricably joined together. If the country's institutions are defective, the condition of the people will deteriorate. And if too little is done to safeguard or improve the living conditions of the people, the national institutions will be endangered.

From Lord Hugh Cecil, we get the warning that there is no antithesis as such between Conservatism and Socialism or between Conservatism and Liberalism. Blind anti-Liberalism or blind anti-Socialism is not Conservatism. And law and morality are not at all the same things.

From Lord Hailsham, like Burke, Coleridge, Disraeli, and Cecil, we get the belief that religion is an integral part of Conservatism; but religion and politics are liable to prostitute each other. Conservatives hold no monopoly in truth. The rule of law is of overriding importance.

By Michael Oakeshott we are warned of the danger of political rationalisms and of the limitations of politics. We are reminded of the importance of 'traditional manners of behaviour'. Liberty in this country depends upon nothing so much as the absence of any over-whelming concentration of power.

All of our writers profoundly believed in the rule of law and in civil and political liberty; and they knew that law and liberty could only be preserved if they were buttressed by private property. For them balance, prudence and moderation were cardinal political virtues, and tranquillity and national unity primary political objectives. They were all acutely aware of the crucial importance of 'circumstance'.

Only British writers were considered, not because American or Continental Conservatives have not had much of interest to say, but because the British political tradition, and in particular the British Conservative tradition, is different from that of any other country. And we are not concerned with Conservatism in the abstract, whatever that may be, but with British Conservatism. Plainly many other writers could have been summarized. Hooker is a prime example. A recent anthology of Conservative thought contained extracts from Carlyle, Matthew Arnold, Bagehot, Maine and others.[4] But even if all possible candidates had been included here, there still would not have been a great phalanx of British Conservative writers. This is because of the nature of British Conservatism.

No British Conservative has produced a system of abstract political ideas or an ideology. Hume produced a philosophical system, but it was not political and it was not a system that could do anybody any harm – at least in this world. The others considered here produced nothing approaching a system. Apart from Hume, Oakeshott is the only thinker who has been primarily a philosopher, and his favourite medium has been the essay. Of the others, Halifax, Bolingbroke, Burke, Disraeli, Cecil and Hailsham were politicians; Coleridge was a poet.

The lack of Conservative systems is not due to those writers having been too busy or to their not thinking politics important. Some of them probably had some sympathy with the remark the Tory Dr Johnson made about George Lytleton: 'Politics did not, however, so much engage him as to withhold his thoughts from things of more importance.' And all of them would have agreed that politics are not the be-all and end-all of life. But obviously they thought politics important, or they would not have devoted so much of their life to politics or political thinking. The reason for the absence of British Conservative systems is the Tory dislike of abstract theorizing.

Salisbury even said that he would like 'to make political abstractions penal'.[5] Conservative thinking is seldom purely speculative. It is, or should be, always grounded in practice. Some attention, therefore, was earlier paid to whether or not the writers, who were considered there, more or less practised what they preached. Had we been considering 'pure' reasoning, that would have been pointless. But since Conservative thinking is based on facts and human nature, the degree to which that thought accorded with action is relevant to the assessment of it.

It is thus part of the essence of British Conservatism to be free from systems. Any right-wing system is merely reactionary or, simply, right wing; it is not Conservative. This hostility to systems is based on experience. A Conservative can well see the insincerity of the political systems-builders, and he is all too aware of the havoc they have caused. 'Most systematizers in relation to their systems', wrote Kierkegaard, 'are like a man who builds an enormous castle and himself lives alongside it in a shed; they themselves do not live in the enormous systematic building. But in the realm of mind and spirit this is and remains a decisive objection. Spiritually understood, a man's thoughts must be the building in which he lives – otherwise the whole thing is deranged.'[6] Systematizers are not of course the only people whose lives are divorced from their ideas and principles. Politicians are frequent offenders; all the same, 'Bollinger Bolsheviks' are probably less dangerous than their more ascetic comrades.*

Yet much more important than their insincerity is the violence and suffering caused by the systematizers. Any attempt to put a system into practice implies dictatorship and force. Free life is not tidy, and human beings if left to themselves do not fit into a system; therefore they have to be forced. And this is so, however much the system, or the regime which seeks to impose it, claims to be embodying or creating liberty. Indeed the more a regime claims to be the embodiment of liberty the more tyrannical it is likely to be. Both Marat, exulting in '*le despotisme de liberté*', and Mme Roland, lamenting on her way to the guillotine, 'O liberty! what crimes are committed in thy name', in their very different ways expressed that truth.

As Professor Talmon has pointed out, 'when a regime is by definition regarded as realizing rights and freedoms, the citizen

*Probably most people prefer a Bevan or a Foot to a Wigg or a Benn.

becomes deprived of any right to complain that he is being deprived of his rights and liberties'.[7] Indeed a system or a utopia is almost by definition tyrannical. If a state is run in the best possible way according to infallibly true and beautiful principles, then clearly nobody must be allowed to change them, for any change must by definition be for the worse. Therefore in utopia liberty will be denounced as licence or fascism or folly or counter-revolution or subversion or bourgeois selfishness; and it will be suppressed, so that the utopian bliss of the perfect system can prevail undisturbed. Conservatives are not perfectibilians, they accept 'original sin' as an obvious truth. And if human nature is flawed, both society and the state will also be flawed. Utopia is a myth and not even a helpful one.

Systems, if people attempt to put them into practice, produce tyranny. It was not the invasion of France by Austria which produced the Terror; it was Jacobinism. 'Maximilien Robespierre', said Heine, 'was merely the hand of Jean-Jacques Rousseau.'[8] The death of five million Kulaks, and Stalin's great purge in the thirties, were not the result of an imperialist–bourgeois conspiracy. They were the direct result of Marxist-Leninism. 'Men love abstract reasoning and neat systematization so much', Dostoyevsky wrote prophetically in *Notes from Underground*, 'that they think nothing of distorting the truth, closing their eyes and ears to contrary evidence to preserve their logical constructions . . . And through this development, man will yet learn how to enjoy bloodshed.'[9] Even Dostoyevsky, however, can scarcely have guessed just how much blood would be spilt by the systematizers, or how greatly they would enjoy it.

The mind, when it is allowed to indulge in speculative thought on political matters, is an ambitious, organizing and dictatorial instrument. It is drawn to absolutes and systems. It seeks to impose rational order upon natural disorder. Chekhov claimed that 'all the great sages are as despotic as generals . . .'[10] Certainly, many intellectuals have been fascinated by force and autocracy. 'In spite of my democratic convictions', the anarchist Bakunin wrote to Tsar Nicholas I, 'I have worshipped you profoundly in the last years, as it were against my will.'[11] In similar fashion, the Webbs made a deep obeisance to Stalin's Russia at a time when the Soviet regime was surpassing itself in evil, while Bernard Shaw managed at various times to admire not only Stalin but Hitler and Mussolini as well.[12] Writing in the thirties, Orwell saw the press lords and the bureaucrats as 'the *immediate* enemies . . . of freedom of thought', but on a longer view he thought the most serious symptom was 'the weakening of the desire for liberty among the intellectuals themselves'.[13]

So Conservative abhorrence of systems, of what Coleridge called 'metapolitical' arguments,[14] explains why there are relatively few Conservative philosophers. The Conservative belief that no general principle is universally applicable is a stumbling-block to many intellectuals. The distinguishing mark of British Conservative writers – and of Toryism – is the recognition of the overriding importance of 'circumstance'. Byron may have been justified in censuring 'Circumstance' as 'that unspiritual god and miscreator',[15] but politically circumstance is a far more beneficent god than more portentous deities which claim spirituality or infallibility; and its very lack of pretension is a protection against retribution. Yet because of its emphasis on 'circumstance', British Toryism is in a sense disorderly. Hence it does not appeal to those who wish to devise or impose a rational system; and this is the natural desire of political philosophers.

Bertrand Russell thought Byron was a link in one of the two schools of Liberalism that stemmed from Rousseau and Kant. The 'hard-headed' ran through Bentham, Ricardo and Marx to Stalin; the 'soft-hearted' through Fichte, Byron, Carlyle and Nietzsche to Hitler.[16] Russell admitted that this was too 'schematic' to be quite true, and certainly Professor Hayek's ideas would not lead to dictatorship except by revulsion. In his book *The Constitution of Liberty*, the most distinguished restatement of Liberalism to appear for many years, Dr Hayek has adopted some of the Conservative tradition, which is fair enough since Conservatism has adopted much of the Liberal tradition. He shares, for example, some of the Conservative distrust of reason, and he is very ready to be helped by by 'whatever non-rational institutions or habits' are of proved usefulness.[17] Hence, Hayek's great book contains much that is congenial to Conservatives; yet it clearly reveals the great gulf between Conservatism and Liberalism. Reading the book, one almost feels that Liberalism is Conservatism dogmatized, and therefore distorted.

On equality and progressive taxation, for example, Dr Hayek takes an extreme position that few Conservatives could accept. Conservatives do not favour the imposition of economic equality, but they can easily imagine a distribution of income that would be intolerable and would require adjustment. Hayek ignores such a possibility.[18] For him, apparently, whatever the existing conditions any egalitarian measure would be discriminatory and unacceptable. Similarly, Dr Hayek believes that progressive taxation is unjust. Conservatives agree that taxation is too high, and they concede that once progressive taxation is admitted there is no clear stopping point at which it can be said that to go beyond that point would be intolerable. Yet common sense and equity surely point to some degree of progression in taxation. Conservatives therefore agree with Adam Smith's remark that 'it is not unreasonable that the rich should contribute to the public expense, not only in proportion, but something more than in that proportion'.[19] To wheel up the rule of law against progressive taxation is more likely to discredit the rule of law than to bring down taxes.

Professor Oakeshott said of Dr Hayek's earlier book *The Road to Serfdom* that it was 'a doctrine'. 'A plan', he added, 'to resist all planning may be better than its opposite, but it belongs to the same style of politics.'[20] And that style is not of course a Conservative style of politics. Indeed Hayek himself believes that his position 'differs as much from true Conservatism as from Socialism'.[21] Presumably any doubts as to whether the rest of the book fully bears out that contention should be stilled by the realization that Hayek is a better judge than anybody else of his own position.

Dr Hayek's 'decisive' objection to Conservatism is that 'by its very nature it can not offer an alternative to the direction in which we are moving'. Moreover the Conservative is 'essentially opportunist and lacks principles'. Other deficiencies are that Conservatives 'lack the faith in the spontaneous forces of adjustment which makes the Liberal accept changes without apprehension'; Conservatism has been remarkably 'unproductive . . . in producing a general conception of how a social order is maintained'; a Conservative 'does not object to coercion or arbitrary power so long as it is used for what he regards as the right purposes'; and probably there can be no such thing as a Conservative philosophy, since 'the task of the political philosopher can only be to influence public opinion' which he will only be able to do effectively if he 'consistently defends "the general principles which are always the same" '.[22]

Most of these charges against Conservatism are merely pejorative descriptions of attributes in which Conservatives take pride. Thus what to Hayek is opportunism, is to Conservatives paying proper attention to circumstances. What Hayek calls the use of arbitrary power, the Conservative calls the legitimate use of the power of the state to promote the welfare of the people. What to Hayek is the Conservative inability to offer an alternative direction, is to Conservatives a concern to preserve the stability, unity and continuity of the country and the realization that violent upheavals or ideological strife threaten the fabric of society – and also, incidentally, weaken the hold of liberal ideas and values. Finally while Hayek complains of Conservative inability to produce a political philosophy, the Conservative points to the dangerous and unconservative nature of systems of political thought.

Perhaps free trade best illustrates the difference between Liberalism and Conservatism. The classical economists believed that trade should be as free between countries as within them. Governments should not interfere nationally or internationally. Speaking at Manchester in 1846, the Liberal politician, Cobden, said, 'I see in the Free Trade principle that which shall act on the moral world as the principle of gravitation in the universe, – drawing men together, thrusting aside the antagonism of race, and creed, and language, and uniting us in the bonds of eternal peace.'[23] In contrast, the American 'Tory' Alexander Hamilton, in his Report on Manufactures in 1791 and as Secretary of the Treasury, decided that free trade and *laissez-faire* were not suitable for a young economy. Government help, he believed, was necessary. Accordingly he recommended the use of both tariffs and bounties to encourage American industry.[24] Hamilton's ideas were in general followed by his successors, and the American economy is the most successful the world has known. As we saw earlier, the British Conservatives have not dogmatically stuck to free trade, but have moved in between free trade and protection according to the circumstances of the time.

Those who were not free-traders could be justly termed opportunists, only if the 'general principles', as Hayek and Adam Smith believed, really are 'always the same'. Hamilton thought they were not, and common sense supports him. The state of a country's economy relative to that of other countries and the extent to which other countries are practising free trade are anyway two factors which may be considered to affect the rules. In any case Hamilton's judgement has been vindicated by the history of America, while Cobden's belief that free trade was akin to gravitation has proved a delusion. Not only over free trade but throughout the economic and political field, Conservatives see that the facts change, and they believe that theories and policies should change with them. They are therefore opposed to the rigid rules of economic Liberalism. In the eternal dispute that Albert Sorel saw 'between those who imagine the world to suit their policy, and those who correct their policy to suit the realities of the world',[25] Conservatism is always on the side of the latter. Not so Liberalism. And not so, Dr Hayek.

In *The Constitution of Liberty* Dr Hayek calls the objection 'we can not turn the clock back' the 'most fatuous of all fashionable arguments', and wonders if those using the cliché realize that 'it expresses the fatalistic belief that we cannot learn from our mistakes, the most abject admission that we are incapable of using our intelligence'.[26] The chief Tory objection to Liberalism is indeed that it has not learned from its mistakes or from the past. And Tories would add that trying to put the clock back or at least not noticing that it had moved on was one of the Liberals' worst mistakes.

For Dr Hayek, the free market is the magic cure of nearly all ills, and almost any governmental interference with it will do political and economic damage. Conservatives are wholly committed to fighting for a free society, but they do not believe that undiluted Liberalism will achieve it. They do not see Liberalism as a seamless garment; or if it is a seamless garment, it is not suitable dress for the present day. Experience does not suggest that political freedom will be secure if the state confines itself to a few general laws and otherwise scarcely intervenes.

Dr Hayek has written elsewhere about the damage done to the Liberal cause by the 'wooden insistence' of some Liberals on *laissez-faire*.[27] But even within the civilized framework provided by Dr Hayek his insistence upon competition seems more than a little wooden. Conservatives agree that competition is indispensable to a free society. But they do not make a god of it, and even if they did they would not agree that it was the one and only god. In economics, Conservatives are not monotheists. They agree with Professor Hirschman that 'non-market forces are not necessarily less automatic than market forces'.[28] Above all a Tory knows that whatever his own views most people have a strictly limited faith in competition. They may accept it as a general rule, but if its effects are apparently disastrous they expect the government to act to rectify the situation. A state or a government which maintained that any governmental interference would in all cases be disastrous and that competition must be allowed to rectify itself would not retain their allegiance for long.

One of the lessons of the Fascist counter-revolution, Sir Denis Brogan pointed out, was that 'political liberty is not the only, perhaps not the main demand made by the average man on society', and he warned of the ease with which he could be persuaded to sacrifice it 'for other real or mythical goods'.[29] The history of modern trade-unionism raises similar doubts about the importance many people attach to liberty.

The preservation of freedom is a complex business. But if people are not to be seduced by other attractions, they must at least feel loyalty to the state. Their loyalty will not be deep unless they gain from the state protection and other benefits. Homilies to cherish competition and warnings against interference with market forces will not engender loyalty. People will not tolerantly sit back and wait for impersonal forces to overcome disaster. They expect and demand action, and if they do not get it they are likely to look elsewhere or take action themselves. If the state is not interested in them, why should they be interested in the state? Complete economic freedom is not therefore an insurance of political freedom; indeed it can undermine political freedom. Economic Liberalism, because of its starkness and its failure to create a sense of community, is liable to repel people from the rest of Liberalism. That is perhaps the fundamental point of difference between Liberalism and Conservatism. Liberalism does not produce a liberal society because it does not appeal to Professor Brogan's 'average man', and not surprisingly modern Liberal parties have not prospered.

British Liberalism, Lloyd George said in 1908, was not going 'to repeat the fate of continental Liberalism'. Continental Liberalism had 'been swept on one side before it had well begun its work, because it refused to adapt itself to new conditions'. It had concentrated exclusively on 'perfecting the machinery which was to grind corn for the people' but it had forgotten that 'people had to live whilst the process was going on'. British Liberalism, he believed, had not made that mistake since it promoted 'measures for ameliorating the conditions of life for the multitude'.[30] But despite Lloyd George's brave words, the British Liberal Party fared no better than its Continental counterparts. Both here and in Europe Conservative parties have proved better survivors than Liberal parties. This may be due to opportunism, but unless Dr Hayek would have preferred only Socialist parties to be in existence, he should find that opportunism welcome.

Conservatives may be unable in Dr Hayek's words 'to offer an alternative to the direction in which we are moving'. Unlike Canute's courtiers, they know that the waves cannot be commanded. As a result they have not been drowned. If the Conservative Party had followed Hayekian policies after the war, it would have become like the old European Liberal parties. It would have been a dwindling rump and never in power. But as it followed Tory policies, Conservatism is still politically significant and powerful. And in so far as Liberalism survives or is restored, it will be largely due to the Conservatives who have seen that Liberalism needs to be substantially strengthened by a large injection of the Conservatism that Dr Hayek despises.

Dr Hayek's system is different from other systems. It would not lead to a tyrant trying to impose it. But if it ever came into being, it would almost certainly lead to a tyrant overthrowing it. Hence even the Hayekian system is unacceptable to Conservatives. Dr Hayek himself emphasizes that he is far away from Conservatism, and Conservatives, while accepting much of Liberalism in general and of Hayek in particular, are firmly opposed to dogmatic Liberalism. That utopia is as unreal as all the other ones. Philosophers, said Hume, a writer whom Dr Hayek respects, 'confine too much their principles, and make no account of that vast variety which nature has so much affected in all her operations. When a philosopher has once laid hold of a favourite principle, which perhaps accounts for many natural effects, he extends the same principle over the whole creation, and reduces to it every phenomenon, though by the most violent and absurd reasoning. Our own mind being narrow and contracted, we cannot extend our conception to the variety and extent of nature, but imagine that she is as much bounded in her operations as we are in our speculation.'[31] That is a fair criticism of modern economic Liberalism.

Conservatives on the other hand try to take account of nature's 'vast variety'. Coleridge thought only fiends or angels could live in accordance with the principles of abstract reason.[32] In fact such people tend to be fiends, and they tend to impose their abstract principles on others rather than on themselves. In any case Conservatives avoid abstract reasoning. They do not believe that men's actions are determined by their reason. 'I will admit that reason is a good thing,' said Dostoyevsky's Underground Man. 'No argument about that. But reason is only reason, and it only satisfies man's rational requirements. Desire, on the other hand, is the manifestation of life itself – of all life – and it encompasses everything from reason down to scratching oneself . . .'[33] Tories accept that 'reason is only reason'. They do not believe that Conservatism is the whole truth. No Tory could ever say with the Abbé Sieyès, 'the science of government is one that I think I have mastered'.[34] Equally Tories do not believe that any other '-ism', or indeed anything else, is or can be the whole truth. They do not believe in total solutions. 'The people who bind themselves to systems', Turgenev somewhat tactlessly wrote to Tolstoy, 'are those who are unable to encompass the whole truth and try to catch it by the tail . . .'[35] Not surprisingly, Tolstoy paid no attention. But Conservatives do not try to catch truth by the tail. They accept that they will never possess more than a part of it.

All this perhaps makes Conservatives, as John Stuart Mill suggested, the stupid party. Yet Conservatism in some ways involves greater intellectual effort and sophistication than do Socialism or Liberalism with their simplifications, their abridgements of the truth, their slogans, their abstractions, and their claims to certainty. A distrust of reason and an awareness of its limitations may be more demanding than an easy acceptance of the latest intellectual trend or fad. Conservatism does not claim to possess the keys *or* the Kingdom. There is no certainty about the route and no certainty about the destination. As Burke said of himself, the lead has to be heaved every inch of the way.

2. What Conservatism is Not

The frightened, the defeated, the coward, and the knave run to the flanks, straggling out of the battle under the cover of slogans, false formulas, and appeals to passion – a welcome sight to an alert enemy. When the centre weakens piecemeal, disintegration and annihilation are only steps away, in a battle of arms or of political philosophies. The clear-sighted and the courageous, fortunately, keep fighting in the middle of the war.

Dwight D. Eisenhower in 1949[1]

In place of a preconceived purpose, then, such a society will find its guide in a principle of *continuity* (which is a diffusion of power between past, present and future) and in a principle of *consensus* (which is a diffusion of power between the different legitimate interests of the present).

Michael Oakeshott[2]

My views are a harmonious process which keeps them in relation to the current movement of events.

Winston Churchill[3]

British Conservatism then is not an '-ism'. It is not an idea. Still less is it a system of ideas. It cannot be formulated in a series of propositions, which can be aggregated into a creed. It is not an ideology or a doctrine. It is too much bound up with British history and with the Conservative Party. Yet equally it is not merely a practice, the practice of the Conservative Party.

Cromwell, talking of religion, once said, 'I can tell you, Sirs, what I would not have; though I cannot, what I would.'[4] And having looked at the ideas of the leading Conservative thinkers, it may be convenient to start seeing what Conservatism is by first seeing what it is not.

Conservatism is not opposed to change as such. 'Any change', said the Duke of Cambridge, 'in whatever direction for whatever reason is strongly to be deprecated.' In a similar spirit, the Pope on his return to Rome in 1814 abolished all street lighting because it was 'a revolutionary innovation'.[5] Neither the Duke nor the Pope was a Conservative, merely a reactionary. The Conservative attitude was well expressed by Salisbury, one of the most conservative with a small 'c' of Conservative leaders, when he said in 1883 that the object of the party was not, and should not be, simply to keep things as they are. 'In the first place,' he said, 'the enterprise is impossible. In the next place, there is much in our present mode of thought and action which it is highly undesirable to conserve.'[6]

Conservatives are conservationists. A conservationist finds much modern architecture shoddy if not barbarous. He may ask, with Wordsworth,

> 'Is there no nook of English ground secure
> From rash assault? . . .
> How can they this blight endure?'[7]

Surveying the London skyline he may regret the absence of an architectural police force to root out and punish architectural crimes. But while the conservationist regrets the knocking down over the years of much good architecture and its replacement by something that is usually a good deal worse, he does not believe that all old buildings of whatever date or quality should be preserved or that all new building can or should be prevented. While conservation is his primary concern, he is aware that there are other considerations such as health, economics or employment which cannot be ignored.

The Conservative has a similar attitude to the political landscape and to the architecture of the political world. In deciding how much change to accept or promote the political conservationist, like the architectural, has to take many conflicting factors into account. He cannot devote his entire attention to reconstructing and preserving a Williamsburg or a Bath. That would be abdication. It would also be self-defeating. Once he abandoned concern for, say, Liverpool and Wolverhampton, not even Williamsburg or Bath would be safe. The political conservationist is not an antiquarian. He is the guardian of the present and the future as much as of the past.

In much of the nineteenth century, progress, in the sense of change for the better, was commonly thought to be inevitable. Browning, for instance, confidently proclaimed in *Paracelsus*:

> '. . . Things tend still upward, progress is
> The law of life, man is not Man as yet.'

And the Whigs or Liberals were believed to be in the van of progress with the Conservatives reluctantly following a short distance behind. Thus Macaulay compared the two parties to the front and rear legs of a horse – one always a little ahead of the other. Meredith and Trollope expressed much the same thought. In *Beauchamp's Career*, Meredith says of the Radical Dr Shrapnel that 'he fortified his outlook by saying to Mr Lydiard that the Tories of our time walked, or rather stuck, in the track of the Radicals of a generation back. Note, then, that Radicals always marching to the triumph, never taste it; and for Tories it is Dead Sea fruit, ashes in their mouths.'[8] And in *Phineas Finn* Trollope has the Radical MP, Mr Monk, saying that it is the use of the Tories 'in creation, that when we split among ourselves, as we always do, they come in and finish our job for us. It must be unpleasant for them to be always doing that which they always say should never be done at all.'[9]

Quite aside from the Victorian complacency about progress, this greatly oversimplifies nineteenth-century history by making the party struggle seem much more uniform than it was. Of the leading politicians between 1827 and 1859, Russell, Wellington and Grey were almost alone in staying in the same party throughout their career. Tories often did oppose Whig and Liberal measures, but that was at least partly because in the years before Trollope and Meredith wrote their political novels they were normally in opposition. Yet they were more prominent than their opponents in seeking to improve working conditions in the factories; the most 'conservative' government England has had since the early days of Liverpool's administration was Palmerston's Whig–Liberal Government of 1859–66; and of the three great reforming administrations of the nineteenth century, two were Tory, Peel's from 1841 to 1846, and Disraeli's from 1874 to 1880.

More important, Trollope and Meredith ignored the Tory concern for the continuity and the unity of the nation. 'The central doctrine of Conservatism', wrote Salisbury, is 'that it is better to endure almost any political evil than to risk a breach of the historic continuity of government.'[10] To accept what was formerly opposed, perhaps to improve it a little here and there, is not a disagreeable process to those who know that in so doing they are aiding the tranquillity of the nation and fostering its political and social unity. Conservatives believe in stability, and acceptance of some unpalatable measures is more likely to lead to stability than is continued and relentless struggle. Tories, above all people, believe in the necessity and beneficence of traditions. Without them social and political life would be impossible. The acceptance of some undesirable measures and developments is a price worth paying for the preservation of the national tradition of peaceful change.

Of course if it is believed that mankind in general, and Great Britain in particular, are permanently fixed upon a course of progress and improvement, then those who seek to obstruct this felicitous process will to the enlightened seem stupid, selfish and obscurantist. Even a Conservative leader was tainted by this belief. 'There are, so far, no symptoms', Balfour reassured the women of Newnham in 1908, 'either of pause or regression in the onward movement which for more than a thousand years has been a characteristic of western civilization.'* But few people today believe in inevitable progress, except Marxists, and the tyranny of Marxist states is not most people's idea of progress.

Even in an age of 'progress', a party of scepticism and resistance has an important role to play, though the Tory Party was almost always more than that. 'You cannot', Disraeli said in 1867, 'form a party of resistance pure and simple.'[11] Or if you do, that party will be purely reactionary and will soon be an impotent rump. But once the idea of inevitable progress is given up, 'change' is no longer progress. It is merely change; and it may be change for the better, for the worse, or more or less neutral. Hence resistance to change becomes more respectable. Change cannot be prevented, for, as Machiavelli said, 'time drives all things before it . . .' But change can be guided and its pace can be adjusted. Obviously orderly change is a vital national interest, and the faster the general pace of change, the more important it is that some familiar landmarks should remain. That is as true of buildings, as the experience of tearing down whole districts and

---

*As a look into the future this was quite up to the standard of the Younger Pitt prophesying in February 1792, within a year of England embarking upon a war which lasted practically without a break for more than twenty years, that the country could count on fifteen years of peace;[12] or of the President of the New York Stock Exchange announcing in September 1929 on the eve of the great slump, 'we are apparently finished and done with economic cycles as we have known them';[13] or of Lloyd George, the Chancellor of the Exchequer, telling bankers on 9 July 1914, eleven days after Sarajevo, 'in the matter of external affairs the sky has never been more perfectly blue',[14] and then telling the House of Commons on 23 July 1914, the day of the Austrian ultimatum to Serbia, that he saw 'distinct signs of a reaction against armaments throughout the world'.[15]

replacing them with vandal-prone tower-blocks has disastrously shown, as it is of political institutions and traditional habits.

The Tory Party should therefore, in Newman's phrase about Coleridge, make trial of the age.[16] It should be a benevolent inquisition, checking and questioning what is in appearance the dominant orthodoxy of the day but is in reality the dominant heresy of the day. The heresy is the part of the truth* proclaimed by the new doctrinaires, and it has to be assessed against and, as best as may be, fitted into, the orthodoxy, which is the past and present of the country safeguarded by the Tory Party. This is all the more necessary since, as Sir Karl Popper has pointed out, 'nothing ever comes off exactly as intended'.[17] There are always unintended and unwanted consequences. Anybody who believes that his blueprint for social action will survive translation into reality without being altered deludes himself.

Naturally this inquisition occasionally becomes less than benevolent, and some Tory Torquemadas become violently hostile to all change. As was seen earlier, the marching song of the old guard down the ages has been that the Tory leadership has betrayed the Conservative cause and can no longer be considered truly Conservative. Because of their acceptance and promotion of change, Tory leaders are accused of putting expediency before principle, of being more interested in office than in party doctrine, of becoming a pale imitation of their opponents, and of drifting along with public opinion instead of moulding or overthrowing that opinion. Conservatives like other people are not rational, and some resemble Pope Pius VII or the Duke of Cambridge.

Salisbury was no Torquemada, but Rosebery once effectively satirized his fears that his opponents were trying to turn the House of Lords into an American Senate, and that even a small step in that direction was dangerous. 'It is, as if when one wanted to go to America', said Rosebery, 'the Noble Marquess offered you a hansom cab; it would take you to Euston Station, but there would still be very many miles to go before reaching his destination.' Excessive conservatism with a small 'c' is not, however, a monopoly of the Tory Party. Dalton complained of being obstructed in the Attlee Cabinet by 'the better-notters'. There are always those in every party

---

*It can claim this status if it is within the British political empirical tradition. If it is outside that tradition, as is Marxism or other totalitarian creeds, then it is no part of the truth.

who are fearful of setting precedents. 'The principle of the Dangerous Precedent', wrote Cornford, 'is that you should not now do an admittedly right action for fear you . . . should not have the courage to do right in some future case . . . Every public action which is not customary, either is wrong, or, if it is right, is a dangerous precedent. It follows that nothing should ever be done for the first time.'[18]

Something of such an attitude is to be found in all parties and in all walks of life. And during a period of rapid change, it is a useful corrective to those who automatically espouse every new idea and follow every trend of the day. For such people the time is always right, and the Government steamroller must be brought out on every occasion to impose the latest fashion. Yet to believe 'that what is new is true' is, as de Montherlant once observed, 'a sure sign of barbarism'.[19]

Being, as a rule, benevolent inquisitors does not prevent Conservatives from themselves taking the lead. They are not always on the defensive. Plainly over British entry into Europe the Conservatives led, and Labour followed at varying speeds and with varying degrees of honour. But when the Tories are the initiators they must beware that they themselves are not the carriers of heresy. In a well known passage, Disraeli distinguished between change 'carried out in deference to the manners, the customs, the laws, and the traditions of a people', which he favoured, and change carried out 'in deference to abstract principles, and arbitrary and general doctrines', which he deplored.[20] This distinction has been derided.[21] But while it cannot be reduced to exact definition, it seems valid. After all, who left to themselves would ever have thought it right that women and children should be made to work more than ten hours a day in factories? Those who were against the Ten Hours Bill had been deluded by the general doctrines of the economists. Again, who having seen the results of the Attlee Government's nationalization measures could, if left to himself, favour further large-scale nationalization? However much he was repelled by private enterprise, he surely could not evade experience unless he was hopelessly enmeshed in 'abstract principles and arbitrary and general doctrines'. Similarly, the educational system in Britain is obviously open to criticism, and has been criticized by many Conservatives including Baldwin and Harold Macmillan. There was and is a case for comprehensive schools. But to attempt to impose them on the whole country in the absence of evidence, to put it mildly, that this would improve the educational standards of the country is a clear example of the sort of change which Disraeli found objectionable.

A reactionary refuses, for ideological and temperamental reasons, to accept change or tries to reverse it. He is not a Conservative. Broadly there are two Conservative attitudes to change, and they may be termed Peelite and Disraelian. Peel was far from being a reactionary. Both as Home Secretary in the 1820s and Prime Minister in the 1840s, he carried through many far-reaching social and economic reforms. But on the greatest political issues of the day – parliamentary reform, Catholic emancipation, the Corn Laws, factory legislation – he lacked foresight. His attitude to change was almost wholly responsive. He accepted the inevitable at the very last moment, and occasionally even later. The contrast with Disraeli is marked. Disraeli's attitude to change was often anticipatory. Where Peel usually accepted the inevitable, Disraeli tried to forestall it. Both over parliamentary reform and over social reform, Disraeli saw what was needed and then tried to enact it. As a result he and his party gained credit, and the party was not split. This is surely a more dignified as well as a more politically effective approach than that of Peel.

The Conservative attitude to change must clearly often be purely responsive. Necessary change is often unpredictable, and Conservatives are the last people to favour change which is unnecessary. Yet the Disraelian attitude may in the end lead to less change than the Peelite attitude. For instance, if the Balfour Government, as Baldwin always believed it was their duty to do,[22] had legislated to undo the Taff Vale and other judgments of the House of Lords on trade-union cases, the country would have been spared the Trade Disputes Act of 1906 and the great damage that has flowed from it. Trade-union radicalism would have been diminished, industrial anarchy would have been avoided and the Tory Party would incidentally have benefited. Much the same thing is true of the failure of the Salisbury and Balfour Governments to bring in old-age pensions. For the Tories to have brought in a tax on the sales of land for development in the early sixties would have been an example of anticipatory change; for them to fail to do so until December 1973 was scarcely even responsive change. Again, if either party had been more sympathetic earlier to Scottish aspirations for greater control over their own affairs, probably less change would have been necessary than now seems probable.

How much the Tories should attempt to initiate is a matter of judgement at the time. That judgement should be formed by the needs of the country, the temper of the people, and the behaviour of the party's opponents. It cannot merely be formed by a judgement of what the party would like to do. 'However absorbed a commander may be in the elaboration of his own thoughts', Churchill wrote of General Nivelle's preparations for an offensive in 1917, 'it is necessary sometimes to take the enemy into consideration'.[23] The Conservatives' 1966 election programme was far too radical to make victory probable, but then they were unlikely to have won that election whatever they had said. Similarly the Heath Government, like the other great reforming Government of the post-war years, the Attlee Administration of 1945–50, tried to do too much.

Following an ineffective and damaging Socialist Government, an incoming Tory Government is naturally tempted to undo the damage, and repair omissions. Otherwise Britain will fall yet further behind its neighbours. Yet it is easily possible to have too much even of good legislation, and in the nature of things not all Tory legislation will be good. In Lecky's words, 'wise, frugal, moderate and skilful administration of affairs' is when possible preferable to legislating.[24] Yet it is not always possible. The reform of local government and of the administration of the Health Service point the Tory dilemma. The first was and is highly unpopular, but some reform was certainly necessary.* The second made the Health Service even more bureaucratic than before, but once again some reform was required.

There will be no easy solution for the Conservative Party until Labour Governments stop spending their time nationalizing industries and, at least for the first part of their term of office, spreading general havoc. A Tory Government will always find it difficult to function as it should until the Labour performance improves. In a two-party system, the parties are opponents, but they are also partners; and it is hard for one of them to succeed in government when the other has badly failed.

To build upon experience, rather than to attempt to overturn it, to pay attention to the available evidence, is the way to effect change in accordance with 'the manners, the customs, the laws, and the traditions of a people'; in contrast, to treat institutions and individuals as raw material to be moulded into some allegedly ideal pattern

---

*I would have preferred reform on the lines of the Redcliffe-Maud Report, which would probably have been even more unpopular.

is to carry out change 'in deference to abstract principles and arbitrary and general doctrines'. Just as modern medicine favours surgery only when it is palpably necessary and prefers to give the healing powers of nature full rein, so Conservatives favour the development of old institutions and customs and the grafting of the new on to the old rather than outright abolition and brand-new creation. Obviously this is not always possible, especially in international affairs. Change may be almost forced upon this country by events abroad. Entry into the E E C is a prime example. But in general to cut with the grain rather than across it is surely sensible. Britain is not an organism. But it is much more like an organism than a piece of machinery or a random memoryless collection of atomized individuals. Hence the path of wisdom is to treat it as though it were an organism, and to avoid causing it pain or giving shocks to its system.

Anticipatory change is not only likely to help the Tory Party to stay in power and therefore to lead to less change of the sort that Conservatives think is undesirable. By removing grievances before they fester, it is also likely to lead to greater moderation by Labour Governments. If Labour has now become a dogmatic or Marxist Socialist Party, there is little or nothing that a Tory Government or Opposition can do to make it more moderate. But if there is a possibility of the Labour Party returning to its former empirical or revisionist past, then there is much the Conservative Party can do. After all it was the success of the Churchill Government in operating a mixed economy, in running the welfare state, and in getting on with the trade unions, as well as the Labour right wing's fear of Communism within their ranks, that produced Labour's great move to revisionism and moderation in the late fifties.* Had the Churchill Government (assuming it could ever have been elected on such a policy) attempted wholesale denationalization, partial dismantling of the welfare state, high unemployment, or a disregard of the T U C, Labour would surely have moved in the opposite direction and claimed that the only fault of the Attlee Government was that it had been insufficiently Socialist. The apparent shift to the Right of the new Conservative Government in 1970 was largely rhetorical. But the rhetoric may have played some very small part in furthering the disastrous Leftward lurch of the Labour Opposition from 1970 to

*I remember a conversation with the formerly very left-wing John Strachey in 1956 or 1957, in which he explained to me that now that capitalism was working so well it was obviously pointless to try to get rid of it.

E

1974. The overriding causes of that lurch, however, were the push from the Left and the time-serving timidity of the Labour leadership.

Baldwin's ambition to make the Conservative Party face Left in its anti-Socialism was not only good for the Conservative Party; it was good also for the Labour Party, and above all for the country. In the British two-party system, moderation in one party is likely to engender moderation in the other, and extremism is likely to breed extremism. The true Conservative course therefore is to stick as closely as possible to the centre with a slight Right incline. This may well produce acceptance and consensus, and at most only a Left incline in response. A sharp Right turn on the other hand is likely to be followed by an even sharper Left turn. Hence Conservative moderation brings its own reward.* The best way of safeguarding the future is by not trying to return to the past.

The second thing British Conservatism is not, is a pressure group. The party is of course usually supported by a number of pressure groups, but it is not itself a pressure group. The importance of the distinction is that under our political system a political party is an organization whose purpose is the winning and wielding of power. It is an organized instrument for gaining consent. A pressure group, on the other hand, seeks to further the interests of its members or to multiply its adherents and the number of true believers without seeking itself to take over the machinery of state or to instal its leader in 10 Downing Street.

The distinction between party and pressure group is not absolute. The constitution of the Labour Party makes the trade unions part of a political party as well as being the most powerful pressure group in the land. But so far as the Conservative Party is concerned, the distinction is clear. The Tory Party seeks, for example, to uphold the interests of agriculture in England; it is not a pressure group for farmers. No doubt it seeks to conciliate the NFU and to secure the support of the great majority of farmers. But having listened to the NFU and other agricultural interests, the Tory Party produces its own agricultural policy, and that policy is only part of its whole national policy.

Similarly, the Tory Party upholds private property, and for both political and economic reasons it supports private enterprise. But it is not a pressure group for capitalism. The Labour Party achieves

---

*This will not be true if the Labour Party remains in the grip of extremists. But, as will be argued below, that raises a constitutional issue.

electoral success by playing down its commitment to Socialism. Even in 1929 the word 'Socialism' did not appear in Labour's election programme. And that great electoral conjuror, Sir Harold Wilson, in his election broadcasts used words like 'government' and 'Britain' with great frequency, but during election campaigns the word 'Socialism' largely disappeared from his vocabulary. Similarly, nationalization is always heavily played down at election times by Labour politicians. Only by such subterfuge does a Socialist Party manage to win elections.

Now capitalism as such, whatever exactly it may be, and in so far as people know what it is, is not very much more popular in this country than Socialism as such.* Of course we have to make private enterprise work, and we have to persuade people of the need for it. Tories must put forward their ideas as was very effectively and judiciously done in the party document 'The Right Approach' in 1976. But the formation of opinion is not the main purpose of political parties. They are at least as much the conveyors of opinion as its formers. Their aim is less to convert people than to gain their vote. And votes will not be fully harvested if the case is put in too extreme a form. 'It is not at all easy', Cardinal Newman pointed out, 'to wind up an Englishman to a dogmatic level.'[25] That is probably even truer today of politics than it was in Newman's day of religion, and Conservatives have no cause to regret it. Hence the notion that the Conservative Party against which the psephological terms of trade have moved since before the war could better its electoral prospects by becoming explicitly and primarily a capitalist party and talking about what Harold Macmillan calls 'the old *laissez-faire* doctrine of classic Liberalism',[26] in the way, say, that Mr Wedgwood Benn or Mr Foot talk about Socialism, is almost as bizarre as the idea that the Labour Party could win an election by threatening to carry Clause 4 of its constitution into full legislative effect in the next Parliament. Indeed it is in one respect even more bizarre. Many industrialists do not have the simplistic feelings about the joys of the free market that are promulgated by some evangelists for capitalism. In the past, many members of the T U C had far greater secret reservations about Socialism than the C B I, say, had about capitalism. Now the ideologists are running amok at Congress House, and

---

*Public-opinion surveys show that 'private enterprise' or 'free enterprise' are much more popular than 'capitalism'. Similarly 'nationalization' or 'Socialism' are much more unpopular than 'public ownership'.

it is the CBI and industrialists who are seeking a middle way and who do not believe that a free market works in the way that the classical economists said it did. So if the Conservative Party began to look upon itself as a pressure group for capitalism, it would be being more capitalist and more extreme than the existing pressure group for industry. More important, by crippling the Tory Party as an electoral force, such a development would ensure a steady succession of Labour Governments and the accelerating imposition of full Socialism upon this country. There could hardly be a clearer instance of a move having the precisely opposite effect of what was intended. The Tory Party is a party of power not a party of protest. Any Conservative who wants to belong to a party of protest should join the Liberals.

The third thing British Conservatism is not, is ideological. Conservatives avoid ideology because they have seen that all ideologies are wrong. They strongly suspect, too, that the adoption of an ideology would make them a party based on class. Ideology seems inseparable from class; hence the Tories can only remain a national party if they remain free from ideological infection.

Some Conservatives would say, however, that to embrace capitalism with both arms and preach its virtues in the highways and byways, or at least in the columns of newspapers, is not to foist a new ideology on Conservatism and the Conservative Party; it is merely to persuade the party to recover its lost virtue and by its example to lead the country on the only route to salvation. But as we have seen, such a belief stems from an erroneous view of Tory history and a faulty reading of Conservative philosophy. A foundation of Toryism is the belief in national unity, and, which is largely the same thing, in the continuity of the nation. Nothing is more divisive than ideology. The consequences of ideological battle are at least as disastrous as those Hume discerned in religious conflict. Conflicts of interest can be composed by compromise. Conflicts of ideology, as Baldwin told G. M. Young,[27] are far less tractable. Ideology is therefore a threat to national unity, and as such is abhorrent to Conservatives. Besides, in a two-party system, the alternation of the two parties in power and opposition makes a basic ideological difference between them deeply damaging, since it implies large fluctuations in policy. As well as harming the economic and other national interests of the country, such swings would inevitably bring the political institutions of the country into great disrepute. If the parties could not prevent such fluctuations, and *a fortiori* if they seemed to exacerbate them, then the feeling would strongly grow that they had outlived their usefulness and were a luxury the nation could no longer afford. National continuity would thus be threatened on two levels: fluctuations of policy every few years; and, in consequence, an erosion of the ability of our national institutions, because of lack of public confidence in them, to safeguard such continuity as still existed. In other words, our already fairly fragile national unity would be unlikely to survive.

The nearest thing the Tory Party has, or rather had, to an ideologue is Mr Enoch Powell. And since Mr Powell's intellectual gifts are beyond question, a study of his opinions and career may tell us whether a more ideological approach would benefit the Conservative Party.

Mr Powell has not had much chance to demonstrate administrative skill in office. He was made Under-Secretary at the Ministry of Housing in December 1955, and then Financial Secretary to the Treasury, from which he resigned in January 1958 in company with Lord Thorneycroft and Lord Rhyll, an incident which Mr Macmillan described as 'a little local difficulty' before setting off on his tour of the Commonwealth. Mr Powell was brought back into the Government as Minister of Health in 1960 and in 1962 he was made a member of the Cabinet. When Sir Alec Douglas-Home became Prime Minister in 1963, Mr Powell refused to join the Government.

His political reputation does not therefore rest on any body of legislative or administrative achievement. It rests entirely on his oratory, and overwhelmingly indeed on his pronouncements upon race and immigration. British politicians of all parties in the fifties and early sixties showed themselves to be lamentably short-sighted on these questions. Although the immigrants have brought many benefits to Britain, they have brought dangerous problems as well. But leaving aside the balance sheet, the great immigration took place without the British people feeling they had been consulted, an omission which has produced much natural resentment. Most British politicians acted from admirably pure motives. They thought that to allow immigration was part of the obligations of Empire, and they shuddered at the idea of imposing a colour bar. When the Conservatives did finally bring in a mild law in 1962 to restrict immigration, it was vehemently opposed by the Labour Party, by most of the media and by some members of the Conservative Party.

In any case Britain was by then well on the way to becoming a multi-racial society; and the failure of politicians of all parties to respond earlier to the fears and discontents that were being expressed in the country did much to diminish public faith in British institutions.

Not all politicians lacked foresight. In Downing Street shortly before he gave up the premiership, Sir Winston Churchill questioned me about the attitude of *The Spectator* to the arrival of immigrants from the West Indies. After expressing some measure of approval, Churchill said: 'I think it is the most important subject facing this country, but I cannot get any of my Ministers to take any notice.'

Millions of people in this country believe that Mr Powell was similarly far-sighted. Indeed Enoch Powell has hinted so himself. 'For over ten years', he wrote in February 1967, 'from about 1954 to 1966, Commonwealth immigration was the principal, and at times the only political issue in my constituency of Wolverhampton.'[28] If that is true, Mr Powell's silence on the issue is indeed remarkable. So far from making a volley of speeches alerting the country to the danger and expressing the worries of his constituents, he seems not to have made a single reported utterance on the subject during the fifties or early sixties. His first signed published reference to immigration was in June 1964, when he declared his faith in a multi-racial society. 'Money is colour-blind', he wrote, 'and economic forces will help the work of integration which must be done if a homogeneous community, local and national, is to be restored.'[29] It was only after the 1964 election that Mr Powell in common with many other people publicly called for greater control of immigration. And, as late as the general election of March 1966, immigration was of such little importance to Mr Powell that in his election address he mentioned it only in passing.

Mr Powell was therefore no more far-sighted than his ministerial colleagues on the issue, and indeed he was rather more culpable than them. His constituency, unlike theirs, was in a town to which immigrants had flocked in large numbers, and unlike them he was out of the Government for two periods between 1955 and 1964. From 1958 to 1960 and from 1963 to 1964 Mr Powell was not constrained by the silences of office. He had full opportunity to warn the country, and he did not take it. He was not a Cassandra.* Only when the problem

---

*Lord Hailsham has pointed out that, as Minister of Health, Mr Powell 'certainly did not resign or, so far as I know, discourage the importation of Jamaican or Indian nurses'.[30]

was widely recognized and had grown full-sized, did he draw attention to it. Since then he has done nothing to help those seeking to
improve relations between the races. A 'race' speech by him nearly
always produces headlines. It is race on which Mr Powell's political
strength is almost exclusively founded; and by his prophecies of
doom accompanied by his obviously impossible 'solution' of repatria-
tion, he has not shrunk from the risk of making race relations worse
or from lending some credibility to his prophecies of violent racial
conflict.

Enoch Powell now thinks that Britain's accession to the EEC
irretrievably impaired the country's sovereignty and unacceptably
downgraded the House of Commons. This was not always so. Mr
Powell voted for entry into the EEC in 1961 and 1967. He was in the
sixties a member of the very pro-European 'One Nation' group in
the House of Commons, and he supported, though because of his
membership of the Shadow Cabinet he did not sign, a strongly pro-
EEC pamphlet written by Mr Nicholas Ridley and other members
of 'One Nation'. Moreover he ended his election address in 1966
with a strong plea for the removal of the barriers between Britain
and Europe. Admittedly he did not mention the Common Market.
But the only possible method of getting rid of those barriers was to
join the EEC, and it was the aim of the Conservative Party to do so.
Moreover Mr Powell was then in the Shadow Cabinet, and his
constituents must have thought he was referring to Britain joining
the Common Market. Since he would not have tried to deceive his
constituents, he was plainly advocating British entry into the
EEC.

Judgement on the economic effects of joining the EEC might vary
from time to time. But Mr Powell bases his case on the sovereignty
issue, and that has not varied over the years. The inference is therefore irresistible. The issue and Tory policy have remained the same.
It is Mr Powell who changed. Up to 1967 he was a strong supporter
of British entry; after his break with the leadership he became an
implacable opponent.

In the fifties Mr Powell was one of the original members of the
Suez Group and voted against the Anglo-Egyptian Agreement of
1954. In the sixties he favoured the opposite policy. He was opposed
to the maintenance of large military commitments east of Suez and
favoured concentration on the defence of Europe.[31] He was also an
early and courageous critic of American policy in Vietnam. But a

defence policy which principally involved a big contribution to the defence of Western Europe sat uneasily with a political policy of extreme opposition to the European Economic Community. Mr Powell's U-turn on the Common Market evidently entailed a new defence policy. Accordingly, he came to the conclusion that Britain could not after all contribute more than 'marginally to the outcome of the Continental battle'. Instead we should concentrate on defending 'our sea and air space'.[32] Clearly Britain should secure her own base, but the idea that she could remain free and independent if the rest of Europe were overrun by the Russians is fantasy. It has little to do with the realities of British interests, and much to do with Mr Powell's latter-day obsession about Europe.

On Ulster, where Mr Powell is now a member,* he originally supported 'everything done under the reform programme' of 1969–71.[33] That of course included the Hunt Report, the disbandment of the 'B' Specials and the disarmament of the RUC. But he soon altered course and became a fierce critic of the measures taken by the Heath Government. Originally, too, he was opposed to the Stormont system, talking disparagingly of 'the quaint anomaly of a narrow-gauge Parliament and government', and urging Ulster to demand 'full, proper and exclusive [sic] representation at Westminster'.[34] When he became Member for South Down, his position became less clear-cut. But Mr Powell has been fully consistent throughout in not supporting reconciliation between the communities in Ulster by compromise, and he seems to have played an important part in wrecking Mr Craig's initiative in 1975.

It is on economics that Mr Powell has recently, at least, been most consistent. But 'what has to be explained', writes his biographer, Mr T. E. Utley, 'is the almost incredible contrast between Powell in the early 1950s and Powell today [1968] . . . The moderate Butlerite, the defender of a tempered form of capitalism, has become the apparently fanatical advocate of a *laissez-faire* economy in which the state is limited to the function of an overall monetary regulator and a

---

*'It is an excellent thing that Mr Powell has joined the Ulster Unionists,' Lord Hailsham said during the October 1974 election. 'They have found a new leader to desert, and he a fresh cause to betray.' The comment of a former Ulster Minister of Education, Captain Long, after Mr Powell had been selected to contest South Down, was more charitable. 'If,' he said, 'the two anonymous candidates who withdrew in South Down were General Amin and Cassius Clay, I think that, on balance, the constituency made the right decision.'[35]

keeper of the general rules.'[36] Mr Powell was prudent enough to remain a member of the Macmillan Government, when Mr Macmillan, Mr Selwyn Lloyd and Mr Maudling produced incomes policies and pursued an interventionist course. But that did not prevent him denouncing those policies as 'nonsense' after he had refused to be a member of the Douglas-Home Cabinet. And for the present-day Mr Powell there can be no compromise between capitalism and Socialism – except electorally. Either all economic decisions must be made by the market or they must be made by the men in Whitehall. If they are all made in Whitehall we shall have a Socialist dictatorship. Therefore none of them must be made there. But why some should not be made by the market and some by Whitehall is not clear.*

It is in economics and finance that the caste of Mr Powell's mind is most clearly revealed, and his habitual manner of argument most characteristically displayed. His apparent logic often seems to amount to the rejection of one extreme premise, the adoption of another, and then the ruthless exclusion of all dilutions, shadings and qualifications. But, as Montesquieu put it, '*Le bon sens consiste beaucoup à connaître les nuances des choses,*'[37] and Mr Powell's disregard of this truth presumably explains the often bizarre results of his 'logic'.

His style of argument may be caricatured as follows: 'Britain is under attack. We could in theory defeat the enemy within by going to the North Pole. But in practice we cannot go there, because the North Pole is too far away and it is too cold. It would be a denial of our essence as a nation to go to the Equator or to the Tropics because they are too near to the North Pole and anyway do not exist. Some people have been hypnotized into the belief that the temperate zones are compatible with Britain's history and national genius. But that is the work of the enemy within. All these expedients are tainted with inconsistency. It is manifest therefore, indeed it is true by definition, that the only solution, the only place to which we can and must go is the South Pole.'

Mr Powell is reported by his biographer to have told a small collection of journalists without a hint of irony or levity: 'Often when I am kneeling down in Church, I think to myself how much

---

*In about 1965, Iain Macleod remarked of Powell's economics that he was 'a fellow-traveller, but I prefer to get out one or two stops before the train crashes into the buffers at the terminus'.[38]

we should thank God, the Holy Ghost for the gift of capitalism.'[39]
Mr Powell sometimes seems to forget that capitalism depends at
least as much on businessmen as it does on the Holy Ghost. And
people who are actually engaged in industry as opposed to merely
talking about it do not usually see relations between industry and
government in the black-and-white terms of Mr Powell. They are
often impatient of Government policies and interference, but they
are aware of the complex relations between government and industry. The man in Whitehall and the businessman in Wolverhampton may often have a good deal more in common than either
of them has with Mr Powell.

Mr Powell's views on capitalism make his behaviour in 1974 hard
to understand. In February of that year he gave up his seat without
a word of notice to his constituency which had faithfully supported
him for nearly a quarter of a century. Not content with that, he
advised the electors to vote Socialist because of the Common
Market issue. It may, of course, be fully permissible to put Conservatism or high Conservative principle above the interest of the
Conservative Party. But that is not what Mr Powell did. After all, he
can scarcely have concealed from himself that despite all the con-
temptible waverings of the Labour leadership in opposition, a
Labour Government after putting down a smokescreen was likely to
find it impossible to leave Europe. Yet the High Priest of Capitalism
helped to put in a Socialist Government, which in his view is likely
to lead to the destruction of capitalism. And his *casus belli* was an
issue about which the Labour Party was equivocal and on which he
himself had only reached his current view after quarrelling with
Mr Heath. This was not a coat-turning which could be explained, let
alone defended, on political grounds.

The impression that it is not logic or high Conservative or Liberal
or indeed any other principles which are at the root of Mr Powell's
conduct was powerfully reinforced by his treatment of Sir Keith
Joseph and Mrs Thatcher. In September 1974 Sir Keith made a well-
publicized speech at Preston which extolled the virtues of the free-
market economy. Mr Powell might have been expected to praise the
speech, or even thank the Holy Ghost for it. Instead he rather sourly
commented that it read like an anthology of his own speeches. And
when Mrs Thatcher became Leader of the Party, his graceless
reaction was to say that it was a matter of chance: had the election
for leader been held a little earlier, a different choice would have been

made: had it been held a little later, yet another candidate would have been chosen.

In other words he went out of his way to avoid a reconciliation with a new Tory leader, whose economic views were widely thought to be much nearer his than Mr Heath's had been, and to rebuff a leading Conservative thinker whose economic enthusiasms were similar to his own. Of course if Mr Powell had not treated his constituency so badly, and if he had not worked for a Socialist victory in 1974 he might now have been leader of the Conservative Party. And it is perhaps chagrin at opportunities wantonly cast away, which has hardened Mr Powell in his apostasy from the Conservative Party. The referendum decided the issue, which was the ostensible cause of his breach with his former colleagues. Yet Mr Powell's hostility to the Tory Party remains unabated. In any case, whatever his motives, for a free-market ideologue to prefer Socialism to the Tories is not politically rational. In 1966 Mr Powell warned his constituents that another five years of Labour Government would 'turn Britain into a nation where all the decisions that govern our lives would be taken and forced upon us by a little group of men in Whitehall'.[40] The Labour Party was much more Socialist and left-wing in 1974 than in 1966. Yet Mr Powell in 1974 twice advised the British people to hand over the decisions which govern their lives to a little group of men in Whitehall. Certainly it does not lie in Mr Powell's mouth to complain of the inconsistencies of former colleagues, when he himself has not only reversed himself on many issues but has betrayed his party as well.

All in all, then, on the evidence of Mr Powell's career, an ideological approach does not produce loyalty, consistency, Conservatism or chivalry; and the Tory Party should persist in avoiding it.

From Powell to Balfour is a far cry. Balfour thought that for a politician anything which looked 'like a sudden conversion must be a source of at least temporary embarrassment'.[41] Party leaders are naturally averse to too sudden changes of policy because of the need to preserve the confidence and sustain the morale of their followers. As Gladstone put it, 'change of opinion in those to whose judgement the public looks more or less to assist its own, is an evil to the country, although a much smaller evil than their persistence in a course which they know to be wrong'.[42] Yet the weakness of the British economy and the general weakness of modern governments in the face of social forces in their own country as well as in face of developments in the rest of the world make some changes of policy by a government both necessary and desirable in the course of a five-year Parliament. The consequent dilemma is best resolved not by the avoidance of such changes, but by the avoidance of specific pledges and grandiose promises. Flags should only be run up when the mast will be capable of withstanding the buffeting of even the dirtiest weather.

In other words consistency will paradoxically be best preserved by the absence of ideology not by its presence. Dogma will be broken by events, and will have to be discarded chunk by chunk to the disappointment and consternation of the party. But if error is not espoused in the first place, if the party remains true to its traditions and eschews doctrine like the plague, party policy can be kept in harmony with events. There will then be a few alarming changes, and nothing to dismay the faithful. By such moderation, the party will also incidentally find it much easier to gain the nation's consent in the first place.

Sir Keith Joseph is right to prefer the expression 'common ground' to 'the middle ground'. And the common ground, which is occupied by moderate voters and which is largely staked out by events, is where the Tories should always be camped. But in fact much of the argument is based on what Palmerston called 'the abuse of metaphors, and . . . mistaking general resemblance or imaginary similarity for real identity'.[43] Plainly, if the middle ground is taken to be some exact spot equidistant from the extremes of Left and Right, and the Left extreme is then moved further to the Left, the middle point will also be shifted to the Left. (The same would of course be true if the Right extreme was moved to the Right, but that is scarcely in issue.) But 'ground' is only a metaphor; and that is why 'middle ground' and 'common ground' mean much the same thing. Politicians do not fight battles for ground; they compete for the support of people. When they talk about occupying, or appealing to, the middle ground, they mean they are appealing for the support of voters who are not irremediably committed to either party. This has nothing whatever to do with literal ground. Uncommitted voters, unlike the metaphorical middle ground, do not shift to the Left, when the extreme wing of the Labour Party moves to the Left, or to the Right when the right wing of the Conservative Party moves to the Right. They stay where they are, or they move away from the extremists.

A party cannot win an election unless it wins the support of a high proportion of the uncommitted voters. And, as the common middle ground means the uncommitted voters, anybody who says he is not concerned with that ground is in effect saying that he does not ever want to win an election. There are possible ideological grounds for such a wish, but they have nothing to do with serious politics. As Disraeli said in *Endymion*, 'real politics are the possession and distribution of power'. Furthermore with the increased volatility of the electorate, the number of uncommitted voters at any one time is continually increasing. And it is not only the uncommitted who are moderates. Although most people are extremists on some matters, they are moderate on most issues. What Coleridge called 'the magic rod of fanaticism' has struck only a few of them.[44] The great majority of voters, indeed, are not much interested in politics of any sort, and only a very small porportion see things in ideological terms. Hence, for the Conservatives, there is no alternative to moderation.

What has been said here would probably have been fairly generally accepted by most Conservatives up to a few years ago. But many would now argue that it has a distinctly old-fashioned look, since it appears to ignore the fundamentally different situation in which the party now finds itself. Up to 1970, the Tories faced a Left-of-Centre party, which was theoretically committed by Clause 4 of its constitution to the nationalization of the means of production, distribution and exchange, but which was in practice reluctant to increase the size of its sacred herd of state-owned industries. It was avowedly pragmatic in its approach to politics under a leader whose pragmatism excluded even a glimpse of political principle. After 1970 the Tory Party suddenly found itself facing a party in practice controlled by extreme left-wing trade-union leaders, which was even prepared to support political strikes, and which committed itself to a vast extension of nationalization, heedless of the consequences to the economy or to the constitution.

Faced then by an animal which had become much more like a Continental Socialist Party of many years ago or like a Continental Communist Party of the present day than like the traditional British Labour Party, many Conservatives decided that the old 'middle of the road' Conservatism of the past had failed (or at least was seriously out of date) and that something quite different was required. If the Conservative Party continued to act as it had acted in the past, they argued, the triumph of Socialism was certain.

If the Labour Party has changed in this way, then the two-party system has broken down. And even though the International Monetary Fund has forced the Callaghan Government back towards the middle of the road, there is no sign that the Labour Party in the country has similarly changed direction. The fundamental condition for a successful two-party system is that the parties should never be far apart. This 'centrism' used to be achieved in this country. Both parties were competing for the votes of much the same people, and both accepted certain conventions. Under a system which is working properly, when one party sees disaster ahead and wishes to put on the brakes or go into reverse, the other will also see the danger and take similar action. But if the parties want to go in opposite directions for any length of time, the two-party system cannot survive. The constitutional significance of this will be discussed in Chapter 6.

For the moment, however, we are concerned only with the Tory Party's political response to Labour's reversion to Socialism. Certainly Conservatives must, as Burke adjured, 'model our principles to our duties and our situation'.[45] But *politically* how much has the Tory situation altered? The more the Labour Party has keeled over to the Left and become committed to the imposition of full-blooded Socialism upon Great Britain, the more vital it is for the Tories to win elections and to be in power. And they are far more likely to win elections if they remain the moderate non-ideological party they have always been, than if they pay their opponents the compliment of imitating their ideological extremism. In other words the more Labour moves to the Left, the more relentlessly should the Conservative Party cling to moderation and the Centre.

That after all is its historic ground. Whether or not Carlyle was right in calling Herbert Spencer 'the most unending ass in Christendom',[46] the Tory Party has always rejected Spencer's extreme doctrines of *laissez-faire*. John D. Rockefeller may have been premature in saying in the 1880s, 'individualism has gone, never to return'.* But his fears are more likely to be proved unfounded by a steady enlargement of the rights of the individual and by a steady control over the activities of the state than by an all out doctrinaire war against collectivism in favour of individualism.

If England is to remain free, private property and free enterprise must survive, and the Conservative Party must regain the position in

*Rockefeller was of course talking about business individualism. His previous sentence was: 'The combination is here to stay.'[47] But this merely reinforces the point.

the country that it once held. But none of these objectives will be achieved by the Conservative Party waging a holy war. For one thing holy warriors are rightly suspect to Conservatives and, probably, to most people in this country. For another, as we have seen, such a development would be self-defeating.

The Conservative Party can and should try to give a lead to public opinion. But the party cannot usefully skirmish very far ahead of it. Political parties are only one influence upon the public mind. They do better, in Burke's words, 'to follow, not to force, the public inclination'.[48] Not only will they in so doing reap electoral benefits, they will also be suitably recognizing the proper sphere of politics and politicians. What de Tocqueville called 'the slow and quiet action of society upon itself'[49] is surely much to be preferred by Conservatives to noisy political action injected with ideology.

But, it may be objected, even if moderation wins the Tories the next election, this will not stop Labour winning the one after or the one after that. Therefore the march to Socialism will have only been slowed, and the holding of the middle ground will have done no lasting good. That remains to be seen. 'Guidance in these mundane matters', as Churchill once wrote to Eden, 'is granted to us only step by step.'[50] Elections can only be won one at a time, and to gain power even only occasionally is surely better than never to gain it at all. Certainly Conservatives should try to win the future, but not at the cost of losing the present. In any case, the constitutional problem should be distinguished from the political. Under a two-party system and under a constitution which gives almost unlimited power to the existing parliamentary majority if it has no scruples about exercising it, one of those parties cannot be prevented from coming to power sooner or later and carrying out its programme. If the consequences of its doing so are unacceptable, the constitution should be changed. That is a constitutional problem and no amount of ideological fervour will solve it.

Meanwhile the fundamental concern of Toryism is the preservation of the nation's unity, of the national institutions, of political and civil liberty, and not the achievement of some ideological victory. Hence the Tory objective is limited, and, like wars in the eighteenth century, relatively civilized. And it can only be accomplished by a Conservative Government.

3. Tory Themes

For my part I love life and cultivate it as it has pleased God to grant
it to me . . . I accept cheerfully and gratefully what nature has done
for me, and am pleased with it and proud of it . . . Of philosophical
opinions I more willingly embrace those which are the more solid,
that is to say, the most human and the most of our own . . . Nature
is a gentle guide, yet not more gentle than she is prudent and just.
I hunt everywhere for her trail . . . The fairest lives, to my mind, are
those which are regulated after the ordinary human pattern. without
miracle, without extravagance.
Montaigne[1]

Toryism is as much a matter of taste as a body of doctrine.
W. E. Henley[2]

But he [Justice McKenna] not infrequently recurs to the tyro's
question: Where are you going to draw the line — as if all life were
not the marking of grades between black and white.
Justice Holmes in a letter to Harold Laski[3]

The Conservative Party is an historical party; not in the sense that
Christianity is an historical religion looking back to definite events in
time, but in the sense that it is never complete, never unalterable and
always closely linked with both the past and the future in an un-
broken continuum. Freud compared the human mind with the city
of Rome, as Rome would be if each age of the city remained intact.
The Tory Party is more like an archaeological site, on which successive
civilizations have left layer upon layer of structure and remains:
each layer being different from the others but having certain common characteristics imposed upon it by the geography and topo-
graphy of the site. And just as the existing buildings upon an archaeological site do not provide a key to what lies beneath, so the Tory Party
at any given moment in the present provides only a very indifferent
representation of its whole.

Conservatism is indissolubly joined to the Conservative Party. Yet Conservatives do not believe that Conservative Governments or Oppositions are always right. It is not in the nature of Governments, even Conservative Governments, to be always right; still less is it in the nature of Oppositions. Nor do Conservatives believe that they alone should always be in power. Many Socialists, convinced they are the possessors of absolute truth, would like to be able to get on with the business of creating the millennium undisturbed by people who do not like Socialism, or who are mindful of the dangers both of millennium-builders and of absolute power. 'We want', Aneurin Bevan said in 1945, 'the complete political extinction of the Tory Party, and twenty-five years of Labour Government.'[4] The Tory Party never wants the political extinction of its opponents, though it would welcome their conversion. It does not believe that it possesses absolute truth, and it does not believe in one-party rule even by itself. To some degree, therefore, Conservative policy is determined by its opponents. If there were no Socialists, say, and if Tories did not have to deal with the consequences of Socialist Governments, Conservative policy would be different from what it is. According to his daughter, Salisbury 'did not shrink from facing the fact that according to his views the success of his own party was dependent on the existence of the other; "I rank myself no higher in the scheme of things than a policeman – whose utility would disappear if there were no criminals".'[5]

This relatively modest role and the necessary flexibility of Conservatism are sources of pride to Conservatives. After all, even those parties which suffer from ideologies frequently have to adapt their objectives and policies. Indeed, as Dr Chadwick remarked of the nineteenth-century controversy over the Thirty-Nine Articles, 'static doctrinal formulas do not always, whatever the appearances, maintain doctrine in a static condition'.[6] And political formulations of doctrine are naturally much more subject than religious formulations to changes in meaning. Conservatism has no such pretensions. It cannot remain the same because it takes account of its opponents, the political system, the general conditions prevailing, and the state of public opinion. All these things change, and the Conservative Party, which is embedded in national life, changes with them. That pre-Tory, Hooker, thought in the sixteenth century that even the laws of God were not immutable.[7] Conservatism does not presume to be either immutable or infallible.

Yet there are perennial themes, though they have been variously treated. Some have grown fainter over the years. 'Church and King' was the foundation of the old Tory Party; the Empire was a corner-stone. The monarchy is one of the few British institutions that is working well, and Conservatives revere it as the symbol of national unity and continuity. But except for a few well publicized dissidents the monarchy is now almost as popular among Labour supporters as it is with Conservatives. In any case it has no political power, and its constitutional power is held in reserve. If the throne is now almost equally regarded by all, the altar is almost equally disregarded. However religious many Conservatives still are, religious observance in this country has substantially declined. The Church of England, because of its history and because of its liking for the middle way has immense appeal to many Conservatives, but neither the Church of England nor any other Church now enjoys much political power. Clearly, too, imperialism as a theme has vanished with the Empire.

Nevertheless the themes of freedom, patriotism, a national party, one nation, national unity, authority, continuity, the rule of law, the improvement of social and economic conditions, balance and moderation, as well of course as the importance of 'circumstances', have not faded. These themes are not single or separate. Each by itself would be discordant. They intermingle, and they have to be worked out together.

'The world', Lincoln said during the Civil War, 'has never had a good definition of the word liberty, and the American people, just now, are much in want of one . . . in using the same word we do not all mean the same thing.'[8] Both the threat to liberty and the confusion about its meaning have grown in the last hundred years. Yet the absence of an agreed definition does not greatly trouble Conservatives. To them, liberty in the abstract is meaningless at best and dangerous at worst, since it is all too likely to turn into the suppression of liberty.

Freedom, said Cobbett, 'is not an empty sound; it is not an abstract idea; it is not a thing that nobody can feel.'[9] Liberty, for Conservatives, is a concrete thing in the sense that its existence or absence can be established by tests. By it they mean, for instance, freedom to say what they think and meet where they like, freedom to worship as they choose, freedom to bring up their children and to own property, freedom to change the Government without armed

Tory Themes **147**

force, freedom from coercion by any entity other than the state, freedom from foreign intervention and freedom from invasion. They are concerned with certain definite liberties not with any abstract condition of liberty.

If the existence of liberty can be established by simple tests, there is nothing simple about its preservation. The survival of freedom depends not on a simple declaration of rights, on incantations to the primacy of the individual, on proclamations of the freedom and supremacy of Parliament, or on any simple formulation, doctrine or institution of any sort whatever. British liberties are the outcome of a highly complex combination of traditions, ideas, laws and historic rights and institutions. And they will only be preserved by the continuance of that intricate structure, modified and varied though it is by the necessities of time and circumstance.

Burke saw that the insistence of the ideologues of the French Revolution upon simplicity of institutions would be fatal to freedom and would infallibly produce tyranny. He denounced Jacobinism for 'taking the people as equal individuals, without any corporate name or description, without attention to property, without division of powers, and forming the government of delegates from a number of men, so constituted; in destroying or confiscating property, and bribing the public creditors or the poor with the spoils . . .'[10] That is an accurate description not only of Jacobinism, but of revolutionary movements in the last two centuries. The stripping down of the national institutions to bare essentials leaves the individual naked and defenceless. The ruler can then impose his own will in the guise of the so-called general will in the knowledge that nothing remains powerful enough to frustrate him.

All ideologues believe in simplicity, in the simplicity of their system; and they believe rightly that complexity would thwart them. Bentham denounced complication as 'the nursery of fraud', and extolled simplicity. 'O rare simplicity! handmaid of beauty, wisdom, virtue – of everything that is excellent.'[11] Of course complication can be the cover of fraud and abuse. Bentham was right in thinking that much of the exceedingly complicated legal system of his day benefited only the lawyers. The same is often true of a bureaucracy. But simplicity is the enemy of freedom, and complexity is its friend. Thus, for example, a single chamber does not infallibly lead to dictatorship, but it is more likely to do so than two chambers. Any single dominating principle or institution is a threat to freedom. Burke contrasted a tyrannical assembly in France with historic rights, liberties and corporations in England. Parliamentary sovereignty, if overstressed, is Jacobin not Conservative. Hence Conservatives from Burke and Disraeli onwards have been pluralists. They do not believe in what Carlyle called the liberty of 'social isolation'.[12] That sort of liberty, as Carlyle saw, could never last for long. They believe in the liberty which is fashioned and safeguarded by a multitude of associations, interests, laws and institutions. They heed Johnson's warning that 'a man is to guard himself against taking a thing in general'.[13] Instead they look to many particulars. 'We compensate, we reconcile, we balance,' said Burke. 'We are enabled to unite into a consistent whole the various anomalies and contending principles that are found in the mind and affairs of men.'[14] That is far better and far safer than any systematic simplicity. And in consequence one of the foundations of Conservatism is complexity.

In defending British liberties, Conservatives are helped by being free from dogma about the state and the individual. Even before Burke, they had not seen these as mutually antagonistic entities. They regard them as mutually dependent and mutually sustaining. Conservatives believe in both authority and liberty. In defending in the nineteenth century the state and authority against excessive individualism, and in defending in the twentieth century the individual against excessive state authority and Socialism, the Conservative Party has not changed its ground. In Morley's phrase about Burke, it has merely changed its front. The old 28th Regiment of the Line, The Gloucesters, won the right to wear a badge on the back as well as on the front of their cap because when, at the battle of Aboukir they were attacked from the front and then in the rear, half the regiment turned about and fought off its assailants. The Conservatives Party, like the 28th, is always fighting on two fronts, but at present it is the attack by the Socialists which is infinitely the more dangerous.

In their defence of the individual against Socialism and excessive state power, Conservatives rely chiefly upon the family and private property. 'Men are necessarily born', wrote Hume, 'in a family society, at least; and are trained up by their parents to some rule of conduct and behaviour.'[15] The family is the natural social unit, and is the primary support of the individual. Man is a member of a family before he is a member of anything else. The family is the centre of affections and the transmitter of traditions. Because the bonds of the family are so strong, many tyrants have correctly seen it as their enemy and have aimed to disrupt it. Modern dictatorships have tried to make children inform against their parents.

The family is the citadel of individual freedom, but that citadel needs its moat of private property. According to Cobbett, freedom meant, 'and it means nothing else, the full and quiet enjoyment of your own property'.[16] That is too restrictive. But if Conservatives do not go all the way with Cobbett, they agree that liberty and property are indissolubly joined together. If there is no private property, there will be no freedom: the state will be unchallengeable and supreme. On similar grounds, Conservatives support the system of private enterprise. State monopoly spells tyranny. There are, of course, other strong reasons for private property and private enterprise. People have a natural instinct for ownership and possession, and private enterprise provides an incentive, other than force, for work. But Conservatives value private property and private enterprise primarily as the protectors of the family and of freedom.

They therefore want the maximum possible number of people to own as much property as possible. They believe with Bacon that 'money is like muck, not good except it be spread'.[17] They further the creation of a property-owning democracy as a good in itself, but also because no other form of democracy will long survive. Accordingly a high Conservative priority must be to lower taxes on income and capital to enable people to keep more of what they earn. The Conservatives as they always do will cut high Socialist taxes. More specifically, one way of spreading wealth is to give tax incentives to firms wishing to develop share ownership among their employees.[18]

Another way of spreading property in Britain today and reversing the concentration of economic power in the state is to allow council tenants to buy their houses. It is no accident that Socialists have up till now strongly opposed the sale of council houses. To break up the local-authority fiefdoms of council houses by turning the erstwhile tenants into home owners is a blow against Socialism and an extension of freedom. If the conversion of virtually the whole stock of council houses into individual ownership is unfortunately impracticable, the Conservative aim must be to ensure that very large numbers are sold on the easiest possible terms. The so-called 'ratchet effect' of Socialism can thereby be given a decisive downward twist.

Conservatives also favour inherited wealth, though they appreciate that such wealth must be taxed. But as more and more people, as a result of Conservative policies, come to own their own houses, Conservatives take it as axiomatic that the owners of these houses should be allowed to leave them to their children. They cannot see that it is right for a man to earn money for himself, but wrong to earn it for his children. Indeed anybody who believes in the importance of the family and anybody who does not believe that the nation is merely a conglomerate of atomized individuals is bound to favour some transmission of wealth and possessions from one generation to another. Conservatives, as Margaret Thatcher has emphasized, do not believe in 'the one-generation society'.

Nor, for similar reasons, are the Conservatives against the accumulation of large fortunes or the much diminished inheritance of them. They do not understand why the only people able to make a lot of money should be the winners of football pools or pop singers domiciled for tax purposes in Switzerland. Widely spread private property is an important element of stability and continuity in the country. It provides a defence against the prevalent ideology of the time. Sensible people are less likely to become enthusiasts of the latest quack remedy, if they are well aware that its adoption may entail the loss of their possessions and the uprooting of their stake in the country. Similarly, but to a lesser extent, the existence of large private fortunes provide a few earthworks against the encroachment of the state. They may also help the Left: in the early fifties *Tribune* was financed by very rich Socialists, as was Sir Harold Wilson's private office in the seventies. In any case Conservatives want to see more people with more wealth, not fewer people with less.

The Conservative insistence upon private property as a bulwark of freedom implies not only a rejection of equality (which is discussed in the next chapter) but also of a classless society. Class is a declining factor in Britain and other Western countries, but some distinctions and stratification will presumably continue. Yet these stratifications are certainly no greater in the West than they are in Russia. At present the so-called classless societies are neither classless nor free.* When Conservatives see anywhere in the world a classless society which is free, they may begin to favour such a society. Until then, they will forgo unattainable ambitions, and stick to freedom.

*In the Soviet Union, Daniel Bell writes, 'the political and scientific elites live in special sections, have special shops for foods, and even have special hospitals reserved for them'. They are 'now passing on their privileges directly to their children'.[19]

The institution of private property also prevents exact equality of opportunity. So of course does the family, since parents can and do help their children in other ways than money. Complete equality of opportunity could only be achieved by taking children away from their parents, and bringing them up in baby farms, which is, or should be, unthinkable. The Conservative ideal, therefore, is best expressed not as equality of opportunity but as *la carrière ouverte aux talents*. Everybody should have a chance to get on in the world and rise as high as his abilities permit, unhindered by antique privilege. In this country that aim is near achievement,* though the doctrinaire Socialist abolition of the direct-grant schools and the consequent penalization of the clever child from a poor home has set it back. The Socialist ideal is equal opportunity for all who live in good residential areas such as Hampstead or Oxfordshire. Conservatives have nothing to do with such hypocrisy.

The family and private property are, then, the principal safeguards against the over-mighty state. But a state kept within bounds is not an enemy. Conservatives following Burke, see the nation as a partnership, and in that partnership the state cannot sleep. The Tory reconciliation between the state and the individual is dependent upon the presence of many non-government institutions to which people owe loyalty. But loyalty to the state is even more important. Rational self-interest might be enough to ensure that loyalty, if man was guided by rational self-interest. But he is not. Dostoyevsky was nearer the mark when he said that 'human nature unfailingly demands [something] to worship'.[20] Conservatives do not want people to worship the state. In any case there has been little danger of that in post-war Britain. But they believe that respect for authority and loyalty to the state are indispensable to freedom and the maintenance of order. Without them the social bonds will be so weakened that anarchy and then tyranny will be the outcome. The monarchy is a useful focus for loyalties, but symbols are not enough.

The Tory emphasis on authority and loyalty has always ruled out the night-watchman state. Loyalties have to be won, and authority has to earn respect. No partnership can be real, if no benefits flow from it. The family is the primary social unit. But if it cannot provide for its members, the state must supply the deficiencies. The family has

---

*That is not true, of course, of the West Indian or Asian communities, which is why the Race Relations Acts are necessary.

to be supplemented by the state. In the *Reflections* Burke wrote that government was 'a contrivance of human wisdom to provide for human wants. Men have a right that these wants be provided for by their wisdom.' Only Liberal ideologues, not Conservatives, see something fundamentally wrong with the welfare state as such. State provision for welfare is fully in accordance with Conservative principles. The welfare state is a thoroughly Conservative institution, which is why Conservatives did so much to bring it into existence; and its roots go deep in English history. Beyond doubt, the balance now needs to be redressed. More and more money has been poured into the social services and increasing numbers of people have been employed in them without much discernible improvement at least recently in the quality of the service provided. Moreover the object of state benefit and state welfare is to do for the individual what he cannot do for himself. Increasingly, however, under Labour Governments state welfare has become an end in itself, and a means of preventing the individual from satisfying his own wants. That is prohibitively expensive, damaging to the economy, socially harmful, and a threat to freedom. The social wage must not be allowed to turn our people into wage slaves. The welfare state must be pruned in places, and pruning will strengthen it like roses. More private provision must be encouraged, and private competition with public services has economic as well as social advantages. Yet in the present state of industrial society, public welfare on a large scale is inescapable.

At the back of all utopian projects, Sir Karl Popper has said, 'is the hope of casting out the devil from our world'.[21] The welfare state is not utopia, and Conservatives have no hope of casting out the devil from our world. They believe he is a permanent part of it. But the absence of any grand Conservative goal, caused by the Conservative disbelief in utopia, does not imply the absence of a large number of lesser objectives, which can be furthered by the sensible use of the power of the state. The elimination of poverty, the redress of grievances, and the purging of abuses are perpetual Conservative aims. The politics of indifference are no more part of the Tory credo than are the politics of envy.* 'It is true,' wrote Carlyle, 'evil must continue; yet not this evil and that evil.'[22] Neither the world nor man

---

*Tories are as strongly opposed to Poujadism, which is the right-wing politics of envy, as they are to Socialism which is the left-wing variety.

will ever be perfect. But Tories are involved in a ceaseless struggle to improve the world, while not embarking on the impossible and dangerous project of trying to change human nature. The distinction is an important one.

Popper has suggested 'the principle that the fight against avoidable misery should be a recognised aim of public policy, while the increase of happiness should be left, in the main, to private initiative'. 'Work', he advises, 'for the elimination of concrete evils rather than for the realisation of abstract goods. Do not aim at establishing happiness by political means. Rather aim at the elimination of concrete miseries.'[23] This principle is wholly congenial to Conservatives. Firstly it emphasizes that there is always work to be done to help the needy; in a free society not everyone can succeed. Secondly it leaves no scope for the system builders to impose upon us their version of earthly bliss. Thirdly it shuts out the busybodies anxious to interfere with and 'improve' other people's private behaviour. Implicit in the principle is a strict demarcation between public life which is the business of the state, and private life which is the concern of the individual and the family. That line of demarcation is fundamental to Conservatism and to a free society.

As was seen earlier, the Conservative Party can fairly claim to have acted upon Popper's principle before it was promulgated. Disraeli was more alive to the social evils of his day than were his political opponents. Neville Chamberlain, as Minister of Health, carried out an extensive programme of social reform in the 1920s, and steady progress was made throughout the 1930s, so that by the beginning of the war Britain had the most advanced social services in Europe. During the thirteen years, 1951–64, the standard of living of the people was transformed out of all recognition. According to Mr Frank Field of the Child Poverty Action Group, the poor were worse off at the end of the Wilson administration in 1970 than they had been in 1964. During Mr Heath's Conservative Government the poor fared better, and Sir Keith Joseph produced a number of valuable schemes to help the disadvantaged.* In a secret Cabinet paper in

---

*Probably Sir Keith's most imaginative innovation was the Family Income Supplement, which gave a state supplement to low-wage earners with families. This is somewhat akin to what the Speenhamland Magistrates did in 1794, when they subsidized the wages of agricultural workers out of the rates. Both expedients show a fine and proper acknowledgement that humanitarianism should triumph over economic dogma.

1976, which was leaked to *New Society*, the Secretary of State for Social Services, Mr Ennals, admitted that families with children were receiving substantially less support under Labour than they had received under the Tories.[24]

Yet plainly the powers of the state have been extended too far. The justification of state help and welfare is that it should enlarge freedom by diminishing poverty and by increasing security. Too often, now, it diminishes freedom and merely increases bureaucracy. Paternalism is strongly in the Tory tradition, but paternalism if it is to be beneficent depends, as it were, upon the father paying. In other words state paternalism can be justified when it results in the better off helping the poor. But when a great deal of the money that is transferred comes from the less well-off, the situation is very different. Paternalism becomes fairly fraudulent, when it is, as it were, the children who are paying. And with taxation at its present height and extent, that is what is happening. Income tax is now paid at levels of earnings below those which qualify for supplementary benefit. The starting rate of income tax in Britain is the highest in the world. At the end of Conservative rule in 1964 a man on average earnings paid less than one-tenth of his income in tax and social security contributions. In 1976–7 he paid almost a quarter.

There are many other threats to freedom posed by excessive state interference. Very high taxation is itself a threat to freedom. Socialists like high taxation. Mr Douglas Jay became lyrical on the subject in his book. 'As surely as there will always be an England', he sang, 'there will always be direct taxation.'[25] Mr Healey aroused the Labour Conference to a frenzy of excitement in 1973 by gloating over the prospects of squeezing the rich until they howled. Many Socialists are, as Leo Amery said of Snowden, Socialists in the sense that they hate the rich.[26] But now Socialist taxation penalizes people who are far from rich and who would not dream of offending Mr Jack Jones by venturing as far as Ascot races. Unlike Socialists, Conservatives regard taxation as a disagreeable necessity, and a diminution of freedom; in consequence their constant aim is to reduce it.

Labour's hostility to the spread of home ownership, the increase of bureaucracy, and the Labour Government's attitude to the press and to the rule of law are additional Socialist invasions into the country's liberties. At a meeting with newspaper editors, the Minister of Labour, Mr Booth, evidently thought that the flow of news was on a similar plane to the flow of sewage.[27] And the Labour Government, in obedience to an imperial edict from Transport House, insisted upon passing a law which endangers the freedom of the press. Again Mr Michael Foot, who was the guiltiest man over the press law, had no qualms about making a scurrilous attack on a Judge in the House of Commons. Labour's contempt for the rule of law was revealed by the Clay Cross business, while the then Deputy Leader of the Party, Edward Short, declared that it was not his duty to urge people to obey the law.[28] Early in Roosevelt's New Deal, when an opponent suggested that one of the Government's schemes might be unconstitutional, a Governor cheerfully replied, 'Hell, what's the constitution between friends?'[29] That sums up Labour's attitude to the constitution and the rule of law.

That a government should feel free to abuse the rule of law and the constitution is of course repugnant to Conservatives. There can be no liberty and no security without law; and a Government has an even heavier obligation to act in accordance with law than have individuals. The impartial administration of the law and its strict observance by Governments are cardinal to Conservatism.

The power of the state should be used not to coerce its citizens but to prevent their coercion by anybody else. Sadly no Government of this country can at present carry out that duty. Hume commented in the eighteenth century on the extraordinary coexistence of the rule of law and the practice of press-ganging men into the navy. 'The wild state of nature', he wrote of the press gang, 'is renewed in one of the most civilised societies of mankind, and great violence and disorder are committed with impunity.'[30] No less extraordinary is the spectacle of twentieth-century Britain, where the whole community is subject to the laws except for the trade unions which are above them. Probably the greatest of Sir Harold Wilson's disservices to this country was his *volte face* on trade-union reform and his unscrupulous support of unconstitutional opposition to the Industrial Relations Act. As a result, the opportunity to bring the trade-union movement within the rule of law, which would in fact benefit trade-unionists themselves as much as the rest of the community, has for the time being been lost.

With the state unable to protect the people from coercion, and with the Government when under Socialist control itself a threat to freedom, the defence of liberty is more than ever the task of the Tory

Party. Crucial to that defence is the recognition, as Benjamin Constant observed, that 'there is a part of human life which necessarily remains individual and independent and has the right to stand outside all social control. Where', he added, 'the independent life of the individual begins, the jurisdiction of the sovereign ends.'[31] One of the advantages of the Tory distinction between trying to improve the world, that is to say trying to improve social and economic conditions, and not presuming to try to improve the individual, is that it clearly confines state interference to public life and rigidly excludes it from private life. There can be no 'thought' police. The totalitarian allows no such distinction, and for the non-totalitarian ideologue or the starry-eyed social engineer the distinction is blurred almost out of existence.

Implicit in the distinction are two ideas. First there can be no such thing as a 'political' crime. What a citizen thinks or says, provided it is not liable to cause a breach of the peace (or to stir up racial or sexual antagonism),* is no concern of the Government. Secondly sin and crime are two very different things. For Conservatives there are several reasons for this. They agree with Spinoza that 'he who seeks to regulate everything by law is more likely to encourage vice than to smother it'.[32] That is the practical point. To prohibit abortion, say, merely drives it underground and makes it more dangerous medically, as well as legally, for those women who decide to have one. Censorship is nearly always ridiculous. In the early 1860s the Russian censorship banned Hobbes and Spinoza, but permitted Marx.[33] In Britain, Tolstoy's *Resurrection*, probably the greatest religious novel ever written, was at first banned by W. H. Smith and some other booksellers.[34]

There is another practical point. The extension of law into what should properly be private life degrades the law and lowers public respect for it. Prohibition in America may have been, as President Hoover said, 'an experiment noble in purpose', but it was an experiment disastrous in practice, vastly increasing the number of

*The forbidding by the Sex Discrimination Act of advertisements for waitresses, postmen, etc., may or may not be an infringement of liberty, but it is certainly silly and an invitation to ridicule. A recent House of Commons report talked about waitpersons. However, feminism was occasionally taken further in the nineteenth century. In 1891, *Fabian News* announced, 'Frank Podmore has married Miss E. O. Bramwell and *vice versa*.'[35] And in America Mrs Belmont once wrote to Julia Ward Howe: 'Call on God, my dear, She will help you.'

law breakers and turning liquor-running into a major industry.*

A third more general point is that there is a positive good in the state and the law refraining from entering private life. The typical ideologue, of course, does not recognize privacy any more than he recognizes any other freedom but that of obeying his orders. Babeuf quotes Robespierre as saying 'true lawgivers ought not to subordinate their laws to the corrupt morality of the people . . . but they ought to be able to restore the morality of the people by their laws . . . and . . . to impose them upon men'.[36] That is the authentic voice of tyranny. For the libertarian and the Christian, on the other hand, as Lord Hugh Cecil, Lord Hailsham and others have pointed out, compulsory morality is a contradiction in terms like compulsory freedom. More important politically, a society will not long remain free if its citizens are ordered about in their private lives. The more freedom they have in their private lives, the more likely is political freedom in the state to be strengthened. Private freedom should foster public freedom. Private regulation fosters public regulation.

Burke in his *Reflections* adjured us to look to 'the little platoon', and generous benevolence is much more often found in small collectivities than in large. Private affection spreading out from the family into public affection is a far more probable progression than its reverse. Certainly a morality imposed from above will not be observed, and it will lead to tyranny. Conservatives agree with Dostoyevsky that 'if there are brothers, there will be brotherhood. If there are no brothers, you will not achieve brotherhood by any "institution".' If you erect an institution and carved *Liberté, Egalité, Fraternité* upon it, Dostoyevsky warned in his 'Pushkin Speech', you will necessarily be driven 'to add to the three *constituent* words the fourth also: *ou la Mort. Fraternité ou la Mort*: and brother will begin to chop off the head of brother in order to attain brotherhood by means of a "civic institution".'[37]

Conservatives believe that there is brotherhood in the nation, but they are not tempted to impose a false brotherhood by force. While not agreeing with Lord Melbourne's complaint that things have 'come to a pretty pass when religion is allowed to invade the sphere

---

*Mr Emory R. Buckner who was appointed a federal District-Attorney for New York during prohibition announced that he was giving up alcohol for the duration of his appointment.[38] This showed more respect for his office than for the law.

of private life', they unswervingly defend private life against the state.[39] There is, moreover, the Tory instinct for enjoyment, typified by Hume. While Tories respect the moral law and try to obey it, they are aware that they and other people do not always live up to its highest standards. They take the world as it is, and try to enjoy themselves as best they can. Pleasure is not a sin. Cocktails are now out of fashion, but H. L. Mencken expressed a good Tory sentiment in his litany: 'From persons who know the difference between "will" and "shall" but don't know the difference between a Manhattan and a Martini – kind fates, deliver us.'[40] Naturally, if people are allowed to enjoy themselves, their amusements will not always gain the approval of everybody else. Moralists are entitled to their disapproval, but they are not entitled to turn it into law and to impose it on everybody else. On the whole, people who enjoy themselves do less harm than high-minded people who wish to curtail other people's pleasures. Tories are wary of what Burke called 'metaphysical knights of the sorrowful countenance'.[41] No doubt it is possible to be a Tory puritan. It is possible to be almost anything and also a Tory. But while puritans are often estimable people, they are seldom Tories. What Norman Douglas called 'Anglo-Pecksniffian principles' are no part of Toryism.[42]

In America, according to H. S. Commager writing twenty years ago, it is those 'who extol private enterprise in the economic realm who are the mortal enemies of private enterprise in the spiritual and the intellectual realms'.[43] That is not true in Britain. Tolerance of human frailties and a dislike of moralizing cant, particularly when it is sicklied over with alleged concern for the country's security, should be Tory characteristics. They necessarily flow from the fundamental Conservative beliefs that human nature is not perfectible and that government has no business to seek to alter it. The Tory belief in enjoyment and in the private sphere of life reinforces the Tory defence of private property. Privacy can scarcely be defended if there is no private property, and the element of security and independence given by the possession of private property naturally increases the citizens' capacity for enjoyment.

Conservatives, then, take life as they find it, while always seeking to ameliorate its harshness. For Conservatives, the key question is 'How?' They aim to build on what exists, and they ask how we can improve what we have. For Socialists and all ideologues the key question is not 'How?' but 'Why?' Why is X better off than Y? Why should Z be able to do that when I cannot? Why are not men better than they are?

To ask 'How?' is the approach which leads to action and possibly reconciliation. To ask 'Why?' is to stir up resentment against fellow men, nature and possibly God; it very likely leads to self-pity and, possibly because of self-hatred or merely hatred of others, it is liable to lead to grandiose schemes of reform to be imposed on back-sliding fellow citizens. Burke's gibe that Rousseau was 'a lover of his kind, but a hater of his kindred' is famous.[44] Tolstoy was vastly superior to Rousseau as a man, as an artist, and as a thinker, but his wife wondered if he tried to justify his 'lack of any profound love by pretending to love the whole universe'.[45] Dostoyevsky's Prince was in no doubt that 'abstract love of humanity is nearly always love of self'.[46]

Conservatives are not afflicted with an abstract love of humanity. Their affections are more restricted and hence more intense. Their field of operation is limited, and therefore their work is more effective. They proceed empirically, while always remembering that society is not a laboratory for social experiments. Burke and Coleridge differed from most of their contemporaries because they rejected their shallow *a priori* psychology. Instead they tried to proceed from observed facts of behaviour. Similarly, today, Tories do not try to counter Marxism by counter-speculation about class, labour, capital, etc. Facts are more telling than abstractions. They content themselves with pointing to the undoubted truths that private-enterprise economics are much more efficient than Socialist economics, and that while freedom is the likely outcome of a free-enterprise economy, tyranny is the inevitable outcome of a fully Socialist state.* Free from utopian fantasies, and lacking any revelation or deposit of faith, Tories are not blinded by delusions of an idealized past or a future paradise. They can look at the present as it is, and then in the light of experience seek to improve it.

The themes developed here avail the party and the country little, unless they are developed in conjunction with the theme of a national party. If the Conservative Party were not a national party, it would become a quite different animal. It would never win elections, and the cause of Conservatism would go by default. With Labour firmly ensconced among the working classes, though it never gains more

---

*This is discussed at greater length in the next chapter.

than two-thirds of their vote, the Conservatives have no alternative
to seeking support throughout the country. The middle classes are
not numerous enough to return a Conservative Government. Besides, as we have seen, it is the essence of Toryism to be national and
to seek the unity of the nation; and the party would be betraying its
history and its *raison d'être* as well as destroying its electoral prospects, if it became anything else.

Patriotism, being a national party, 'one nation', are all parts of
the same ideal. A party which represents merely a sectional interest
has no special claim to be considered patriotic. A party which puts
forward policies that blatantly favour only one section of the community plainly does not believe in 'one nation' and plainly is not a
national party. The Tory Party is not so foolish as to claim that its
supporters are necessarily more patriotic than those of other parties.
But it does justly claim to put the national interest before that of any
sectional interest, such as an abstraction like the working class, and
before any ideology such as Socialism.

The Tory Party is not a national party by divine right. To be and
to remain a national party is something that has to be constantly
worked for. There is a natural tendency for any party to become
sectional, to come too much under the influence of its most active
supporters, and therefore to become a vehicle for the furtherance of
their interests. The Tory Party has not always been successful in
resisting such influence. The induction of the Whigs into the party
in 1886 brought a great influx of commercial power and riches, and
weakened the Tories' traditional principles.[47]

Today, the increase of 'democracy' in the Tory Party as in all
other parties could threaten to make the party more responsive to
the needs and wishes of its active partisans, at the expense of making
it less responsive to the needs and wishes of the nation as a whole.
Political parties, as Professor Hirschman has remarked, tend to be
influenced 'especially when they are out of power by their present
activist members' rather than by the need to gain additional support.[48] So far the Conservative leadership since the party's two defeats
in 1974 has resisted such a development, but unless it continues to do
so far more successfully than its opponents, the future of the Tories
as a governing party will be in jeopardy, and the two-party system
will become even harder to defend. Partly as cause, and partly as
effect, the major parties have become more inward-looking at the
same time as the two-party system, which means the sharing of

governmental power between them in varying proportions, has been steadily losing acceptance.

The Tory Party's emphasis on its national status and its belief that the national interest must override sectional interests makes imperative its own avoidance of identification with any sectional interest. This would be vital at any time, but it is especially vital now that society is breaking more and more into sectional interests. If the party is to be able to control the sectional interests now threatening the country, it must be plainly seen not to be itself one of those interests. It must be plainly seen to be above them because it has retained and strengthened its 'one nation' character. The Tory Party's national character does not inhibit it from undoing the damage Labour Governments have done, for example, to the middle classes. But in doing that it must shun not only all extremism, but also doctrines that are the mirror image of those of its opponents. Otherwise it will no longer be a national party. And if that will not make it, as Disraeli thought, 'nothing', it will make its steady decline largely inevitable.

Clearly not all Tory policies can gain general acceptance. But those which can be made to appear sectional or to threaten the interests of particular sections of the community must be balanced by policies which are unequivocally national.

To stress patriotism does not preclude sensible internationalism. The party's attitude to the EEC demonstrated that. Indeed, the furthering of the national interest is the only sound basis for the transaction of international affairs. If the national interest is deposed from being the prime determinant of a country's foreign policy and some other criterion is substituted, international behaviour is not improved. Nations like individuals behave best when they are sensibly furthering their own interests. Individuals allow themselves to be much less scrupulous when they think they are serving a cause than when they are merely acting for themselves. Similarly governments or countries which believe they embody a cause think that that cause absolves them from the normal rules of international conduct. Burke talked of 'the homicide philanthropy' of revolutionary France.[49] In the twentieth century 'homicide philanthropy' has become a prevalent disease.

Besides, the relegation of national interest and the promotion in its stead of morality or internationalism usually means in practice merely the substitution of the interest of a pressure group for that of

F

the nation. This can be seen clearly enough in the attitude of various groups in Britain to the sale of arms to different countries. And while some dictatorships are noisily denounced on ideological grounds, others are silently applauded. Many British people have a strong instinct for morality overseas. This handicaps the conduct of British foreign policy without noticeably adding to the world's stock of morality. The countries or factions these well-meaning people support are commonly at least as aggressive and ruthless as those they criticize. What seems humanitarian in Great Britain is usually pretty lethal on the spot.

Patriotism and the national interest are thus the best guides in international behaviour. Of course things often go badly wrong, as they did at Suez. But while that adventure can be criticized on many moral grounds, it can be criticized no less harshly for being disastrous to British interests in the Middle East. Suez does not therefore rebut the general contention that intelligent self-interest is the right guide in international affairs. No sensible British statesman believes that the British national interest can be pursued irrespective of the interests of other countries, of the moral feelings of the British people, or of the general international interest.

Leaving aside the economic arguments for entry into the EEC the political arguments to most Conservatives were overwhelming. Europe nearly destroyed itself by two great European civil wars in this century. Before 1914 Europe was the centre of the world. The two great wars handed the hegemony of the world to the United States and Russia. A development of Europe which made a third European civil war impossible or highly unlikely, which made Europe more capable of defending itself against the Soviet threat, and which gave back to Europe some control of its destiny, was as Churchill saw a vital European interest. 'We shall only save our-ourselves', Churchill told the Congress of Europe in 1948, 'from the perils which draw near by forgetting the hatreds of the past, by letting national rancours and revenges die, by progressively effacing frontiers and barriers which aggravate and congeal our divisions, and by rejoicing together in . . . the true inheritance of Europe . . .'[50]

The unity of Europe was also a vital British interest, but for a variety of reasons Britain from the end of the war to the early sixties missed the opportunity of helping to shape European integration. Yet even if European integration had not been in British interests, once the EEC had been set up and proved successful it would have been in Britain's interest to join it. No doubt some theoretical loss of sovereignty was involved. But in the post-war world the institutions of the nation state were no longer enough to safeguard national interests. And to Conservatives and most other people, the reality of power and influence is more important than abstract and legalistic speculation. Except during the first Elizabethan Age, Britain has in her greatest days always been closely associated with other countries through European alliances and coalitions and through the British Empire. In a world of super-powers Britain could by herself have little influence. America and Russia would have dealt with the E E C not with Britain. As a member of the Community we could influence the Community; outside the Community we should have been influenced by it. The point was well put by Mr Wedgwood Benn during his short pro-European phase in November 1970: 'Of course we can stay out and stand alone, but we will still find that European, American and Russian decisions will set the framework within which we would have to exercise our formal parliamentary sovereignty.'[51]

Besides, the alarming growth in Russian military power constrains those who believe in freedom to do all that they can to strengthen the cohesion and the defences of the West. Admittedly the Treaty of Rome does not mention defence, but as Churchill said, 'it is impossible to separate economics and defence from the general political structure',[52] and increasing Western unity is bound to enhance the military as well as the political and economic strength of the West.

The European policy of the Conservatives has therefore been a good illustration of how sensible national policies are not hostile to internationalism. It also showed how the courage and consistency of, above all, Edward Heath could overcome public fears and doubts. In contrast the Labour Party has in Opposition twice fed those fears and doubts, and it has then in Government twice been forced to do a ragged right about turn and become pro-European. It has not put British interests first and it has not been internationalist: an ignoble conjunction of negatives.

Conservatives have long regarded their party as the national party, but they have not always thought that the national interest would be served by its being in office. In the 1830s much of Peel's efforts were devoted to helping the Whig Government frustrate its Radical supporters rather than to seeking the return of a Conservative Government.[53] Disraeli and Derby saw well enough that

Palmerston as Liberal Prime Minister in the early sixties was doing their work for them. Disraeli's successor, Salisbury, thought that the principle upon which Palmerston's Government had been carried on – the combination of Liberal profession and Conservative practice – was in accordance with the inclination of a large proportion of the educated classes.[54] Salisbury was more concerned with the Conservative cause than with the Conservative Party. After the passing of the Second Reform Bill the Conservatives, he believed, should support the moderate Liberals and make it possible for them to cooperate with the Conservatives even if that involved accepting Whig leadership.[55] And at least until he became leader of the party, Salisbury cared more about the preservation of Conservative principles than about the electoral prosperity of the Conservative Party.[56] In similar vein, Neville Chamberlain once wrote of 'old fogies . . . regarding the party as an end in itself, instead of an instrument for attaining ends of national importance'.[57]

Other Conservative leaders have also been prepared to put the national and the Conservative cause before that of the party. But they did not go so far as to want government by the other party (though during the 1945 election Eden thought he had no party politics and half hoped to lose),[58] and Macmillan thought four years later that the Conservative defeat in that election had saved the party.[59] They merely believed that the cause would be better furthered by coalition rather than party rule.

Disraeli's remark that 'England does not love coalitions' is scarcely borne out by the history of the Tory Party or by what is known of the views of the British people. Indeed he himself made the remark immediately after he had tried to form a coalition with Cobden and Bright. Salisbury joined with the Liberal Unionists in 1886, and they were members of his second Administration. Balfour was a member of that Government and then succeeded Salisbury as head of it. He seriously considered Lloyd George's proposal for coalition in 1910. The party system was not serving the country well, but the plan came to nothing owing to the objections of the Tadpoles and Tapers in the party. Balfour was later a member of both Asquith's and Lloyd George's wartime coalitions. In the circumstances of war, Balfour's successor, Bonar Law, had naturally agreed to taking the party into a coalition. His successor, Austen Chamberlain, wished to perpetuate the wartime coalition, and like Churchill and Birkenhead, he hoped for fusion with the Lloyd George Liberals and the formation of a centre party. Though this lost him the leadership of the Tory Party, he was in 1929 still hoping for a merger with the Liberals.[60]

In contrast Baldwin's political career was largely founded upon opposition to the Tories sticking to Lloyd George in 1922. Yet he was very willing to bring the party into a National Government in 1931 and to leave the premiership to Ramsay Macdonald. Neville Chamberlain, like Baldwin, was a minor member of Lloyd George's coalition and a key member of the 1931 and 1935 National Governments. Churchill flirted with some Labour elements in the thirties in the hope of forming an alliance against appeasement, and he would have liked his wartime coalition to continue after the war. In the early fifties he spoke for Lady Violet Bonham Carter, the Liberal candidate for Colne Valley in the 1950 election, he offered the Liberal leader, Clement Davies, a post in his 1951 Cabinet,[61] and he favoured electoral reform which would have benefited the Liberal Party. Macmillan and Eden were both members of Churchill's great wartime coalition, and finally Mr Heath offered the Liberals a coalition after the election of February 1974.

With the exception of Sir Alec Douglas-Home, therefore, every Conservative Prime Minister since Peel has at one time in his political career formed, considered forming, joined, or attempted a coalition with other parties. Even allowing for the necessities of war, this surely shows a considerable propensity towards coalition. Bolingbroke would have approved. Past experience is not, of course, an argument for a coalition now. Coalitions, as Lord Hailsham has said, are born not made. In addition, the party mould is now so rigid as to make coalitions less likely than before. But if the occasion did arise, no doubt the Tory Party would form or join a coalition and would probably benefit. After all, the previous coalitions helped the Conservatives, though that was not the reason for their formation. In the past, Tory leaders put the national interest first, or identified the national interest with that of the Conservative Party, and doubtless they will do the same in the future.

In any case, there is seldom likely to be a divergence between the interest of the Tory Party and Conservatism or the Conservative cause. Conservatism is concerned with people not abstractions, with issues not ideologies. And this preference for the concrete over the abstract or the ideological obviously extends to a preference for the interests of the Conservative Party over the promotion of some imaginary Conservatism or the preservation of some allegedly cardinal Conservative principle. This emphatically does not mean that Conservatism is mere pragmatism. Certainly, since Peel, most party leaders have had as a paramount aim the preservation of the unity of the party. Salisbury thought Disraeli's 'only final political principle was that the party must on no account be broken up'.[62] Carnavon said much the same thing about Salisbury.[63] Balfour talked of Peel's 'unforgivable sin'.[64] Bonar Law even thought that it was more important to keep the party together than to win the next election.[65] Yet party unity is only an ignoble aim if it is achieved at the expense of the national interest, as it was in the Labour Party during the Wilson years. 'Party conflict and party government', as Churchill observed, 'should not be disparaged. It is in time of peace, and when national safety is not threatened, one of those conditions of a free Parliamentary democracy for which no permanent substitute is known.'[66] 'Party' is fully defensible, so long as it is always regarded as a means to an end, not an end in itself.

This has not been achieved by Labour. How can it be achieved by the Tory Party? Many Conservatives are still religious, but religion has probably become too weak, at least for the present, to be able to perform for Conservatism the task that Lord Hugh Cecil thought vital: to stop the Conservatives appealing to as many people as possible for votes, or alternatively to stop them merely furthering their own selfish interests. To give people what they want seems to me a political virtue not a vice, unless the giving is accompanied by the telling of lies about the probable consequences. Yet some means of purification is needed for every party. In the absence of religion, patriotism seems the right and indeed the only possible candidate for the Tories. 'What's good for General Motors may be good for the USA,' Mrs Thatcher has said, 'but nothing that's bad for Britain can ever be good for Conservatives.'[67] The Conservative cause is the national cause. Anything that is good for the country is good for Conservatism. Admittedly the national interest does not always provide a clear and infallible guide for political action. But then there is no such guide for politics, any more than a code of morals can provide a clear guide to the correct moral action on every occasion. People who believe in freedom cannot free themselves from responsibility by resorting to rigid rules.

In pursuing the national interest at home and abroad, the Tory Party has several advantages over its principal opponents. It is not

tied to a sectional interest, and it is not a class party. In so far as
these categories still have meaning, it gets about half its vote from
the working and half from the middle class. Its belief that politics
should be looked at in a national not a class context is shared by
most of the country. It has no totalitarians in its midst. There is no
equivalent on the Right of the Conservative Party of the Marxists,
Communists, Trotskyites, Fellow Travellers, New Left, International
Socialists, many of whom have penetrated the Labour Party. In
addition, the Labour Party is divided between those who still believe
in Socialism, and those who no longer believe in it but try to conceal
their loss of belief by using the word a great deal. The Conservative
Party is in no sense wedded to an ideology, and has no feelings of
guilt about the lack of one. This freedom of the Tories from dogma
makes it easier for them both to discern the national interest and to
pursue it.

Conservatives know that the country can only be well governed
from the centre. Almost by definition, the country will be divided if
it is governed from anywhere else. Certainly a nation of 56 million
people cannot be fully united on a narrow dogma. Any party seeking
the support of a majority or a near majority must cover a wide range
of opinions. The exclusive stress of any part of Toryism other than
balance and moderation is in the theological sense heretical. Balance
and moderation are integral to Toryism; and heresies are born in
Père Congar's words 'of deductions pursued in a unilateral sense'.[68]
They express part of the truth, but they are not held in check by the
other necessary parts of the truth. Yet the Conservative Party is not
a church or a branch of theology. It has seldom gone in for heresy-
hunting. It knows that its unity depends on its permitting a wide
diversity of opinion, and that that unity is far greater than that
of its opponents. The party is more tolerant than Labour, and
it has less to be tolerant about: the distance between the various
wings of the party is much smaller than the distance in the Labour
Party.

The Tory Party, like the Church of England, seeks the *Via Media*,
and all the evidence suggests that that is what the British people
want. Such a middle way excites the contempt of fanatics on both
sides. But there is little fanaticism on the Right in Britain, at least in
the Conservative Party. Hooker thought there were two things that
troubled the late sixteenth century: 'One that the Church of Rome
can not, another that Geneva will not, erre.'[69] Socialists believe in the

infallibility of Socialism; Conservatives do not similarly believe in the infallibility of capitalism.

'It is now often said', Dr Hayek wrote in *The Road to Serfdom*, 'that democracy will not tolerate capitalism. If capitalism means here a competitive system based on free disposal over private property, it is far more important to realise that only within this system is democracy possible.'[70] The second proposition is certainly true, but what if the first proposition is also true? If the people will not accept capitalism as such, it will do little good to tell them nothing else is compatible with democracy. Confronted with such a choice, they may well opt for the non-democratic alternative. In his book *The Middle Way*, Harold Macmillan expressed his belief that 'if capitalism had been conducted all along as if the theory of private enterprise were a matter of principle', and all intervention by the state had been resisted, 'we should have had civil war long ago'.[71] In other words the Tory Party has always to modify the economic system so as to make it acceptable to the electorate, while ensuring that those modifications do not spell the end of democracy. Conservatives are profoundly aware that private enterprise is incomparably preferable both economically and politically to Socialism, which is not compatible with political freedom. Yet they are not blind to the imperfections of free enterprise and the market, and they are ready and willing to remedy them. They do not believe that the profit motive will solve all economic problems. There is no Tory equivalent of the Labour Party's Clause 4.

For the Tory Party, then, to persevere in its task of seeking a reconciliation between capitalism and Socialism may to some be reminiscent of the Heaven and Hell Amalgamation Society that existed in the nineteenth century.[72] Yet to find a way of reconciling the British people's desire for peace and security with their desire for increased welfare and economic well-being is a continuance of the Tory Party's mission to unite the nation. The trouble is that at least since the war the British people's anxiety for peace and security has been much stronger than their urge to create the wealth which would have given a firm foundation to that security. Had the entrepreneurial spirit, the Protestant work ethic and other fuels of capitalism remained a more powerful force in Britain since 1945, this country would not have fallen, economically, so far behind its neighbours. Those virtues can and must to some extent be revived. One of the main Tory tasks is to restore enterprise and vitality to the country's economy. Otherwise Britain's decline will continue and accelerate, notwithstanding North Sea oil. Yet, as Burke said, 'there is no such thing as governing a people contrary to their inclinations'.[73] He was writing before modern dictators with their apparatus of a totalitarian ideology, secret police, one-party government, and strong armed forces with modern weapons, had shown that it is indeed possible to govern a people contrary to their inclinations. But what Burke said is still true of a free society, and the inclinations of the British people seem to lean strongly towards a middle way.

Both by history and by temperament, the Tory Party is well fitted to pursuing the middle way. Tranquillity and continuity are perennial Tory objectives. Also the longing for security is deeply embedded in British history and is thoroughly Tory. And while encouraging a more entrepreneurial and pioneering approach, the Tory Party must not copy the mistake Liberals made of thinking that everybody is ready to reform himself by self-denial into a capitalist overnight. The spreading of property may achieve that, gradually, but at present there are too few Lord Nuffields in our factories or anywhere else. Meanwhile the Conservatives must not abandon their representative function. Parties must attune themselves to the electorate; they cannot rely on the reverse process. Besides, the Conservative Party is necessarily restricted by the prevailing tendencies of the time; otherwise Conservatism would be either reactionary or revolutionary, which would be ridiculous. A party which rightly sees itself as the national party must seek to represent the nation. If it does not, it abandons its national character and begins to resemble a pressure group.

Conservatives are more concerned with life than with theory. Especially in an age when theorists and theories are more easily come by than people who actually do things, this is a valuable corrective. But men, especially the young, do not live by bread alone. The Conservatives' knowledge of human nature makes them fully aware that people will not for long be satisfied with mere common sense. The present cult of Marxism in the West is just another confirmation of that. 'There is nothing so tragic in life', said Benjamin Franklin, 'as the murder of a beautiful ideal by a gang of facts.' What is much more tragic, however, is the refusal of the ideal to lie down after it has been so murdered. But the truth is that often it does not. And it is a defect of Toryism not to be able sufficiently to cater for man's appetite for ideals. Certainly it is the function of Tories to bring common sense to bear, to look at theory in the cold light of practice, to scrutinize ideals and schemes with great care, and to provide a capable and just administration of affairs. Yet, when all is said, there has often in post-war Toryism been an excessive lack of idealism. There is more to politics than good management and smooth-running business efficiency. A solely down-to-earth or materialistic appeal is not compelling. There must be idealism and inspiration as well. Managers are useful, but they are not enough. No doubt Enoch Powell is right to say politicians should not be preachers. Preaching, as Harold Macmillan might have said, is the job of archbishops. Equally, politicians should not be mere managers. Their place is midway between the counting house and the pulpit. And over the last fifteen years or so Tory politicians have strayed too far towards the counting house. Since the war the Tory Party has often failed to give its usually popular policies an aura which carried an appeal to people's hearts as well as their heads.

There are of course respectable reasons for this. Our affairs were in general so deplorably badly managed by Sir Harold Wilson, that a Conservative emphasis on competence and efficiency was natural and necessary. Again Toryism is bound up with national success if not national greatness. Salisbury said Conservatism could be defined as 'the policy of a party which preaches confidence',[74] and the last decade has not been the most congenial time for that particular text. The loss of the Empire opened a gap in Toryism, and nothing has been put in its place.

Yet surely there are still available themes and ingredients of Conservatism sufficient to make an appealing whole: leadership, security (both national and personal), authority and freedom, consensus and constitutionalism, national unity encompassing diversity not uniformity, a tempered attitude to free enterprise, state welfare as an aid not a burden, common sense not party dogma. These are not merely Conservative aspirations. They are shared by the bulk of the British people.

Soon after becoming Prime Minister, Baldwin said he wanted 'to be a healer',[75] and at home he largely succeeded. Later, he said he would like to be the leader of those who did not belong to any political party.[76] Those are the right ambitions of all Conservative leaders, and the success of the Tory Party is dependent upon their achievement. 'From extream to extream, from East to West,' said John Donne, 'the angels themselves can not come, but by passing the middle way between . . .'[77] Conservatives are content to follow the angels.

4. The British Social Democrats

Do not attempt to do us any more good. Your good has done us too much harm already.
Sheikh Muhammed Abduh, an Egyptian in London in 1884[1]

Having seen what was done in the name of fraternity, if I had a brother, I should call him cousin.
Metternich[2]

A great lover of the plain people, but always stopping short of a suicidal fondness.
H. L. Mencken on Senator Hiram Johnson[3]

There is much in British Social Democracy which is admirable and which Conservatives can accept. The Social Democratic emphasis on the elimination of poverty and on the protection of the environment are entirely agreeable to Conservatives. So is their emphasis on the need for economic growth. Above all, British Social Democrats or revisionists do not believe in Socialism. Given the Socialist record round the world, this is both fully understandable and a matter for congratulation by non-Socialists. Yet the failure of the revisionists to draw the correct conclusions from their loss of belief, and their insistence upon calling themselves Socialists, have had unfortunate consequences both in theory and practice. So, regrettably, they can be given only one and a half cheers.

In his last considered pronouncement on the subject, a lecture on Social Democracy delivered in Costa Rica in 1975, Anthony Crosland denied that there is some ideal Socialist society of which blueprints can be drawn.* Instead, to him, Socialism described 'a set of

*This chapter was originally finished before Mr Crosland's untimely death. I have removed the personal references to him. But he was by far the most prominent and articulate of the theorists of Social Democracy, and a critical

values, of aspirations, of principles which Socialists wish to see embodied in the organisation of society'.[4] This denial of dogmatism was welcome so far as it went, but it was surely a little too bland. For Socialism has traditionally meant a great deal more than a 'set of values' etc., and it still does mean much more than that to many of the Social Democrats' colleagues in their own party.

'Socialism', wrote the British Socialist, Joseph Clayton, in his book *The Rise and Decline of Socialism in Great Britain 1884–1924*, published in 1926, 'was a proposal to end this struggle of classes . . . by the reorganization of the community on a cooperative basis'.[5] The essence of Socialism was the substitution of cooperation for competition, and this magical transformation would, Socialists believed, be achieved by the elimination of private ownership of the means of production and the substitution of public ownership. Nationalization in Britain has palpably not substituted cooperation for competition in the industries in which it has taken place. And all but the wilfully blind know how 'cooperation' is achieved in Communist Russia, and how non-cooperation is punished in psychiatric clinics and the Gulag Archipelago. But in abandoning the objective of a fully Socialized economy, Social Democrats are not merely opening their eyes to disagreeable reality, they are also abandoning Socialism. For, while a fully Socialized economy clearly does not produce cooperation but produces results that are much more unpleasant than any form of competition, equally clearly there is no other political method of getting rid of competition and replacing it with cooperation. The Social Democrats accept this, yet go on calling themselves Socialists. They are doctrinaires without a doctrine. Having abandoned the key element in their creed, they cling all the more tenaciously to subsidiary parts. Yet branches cannot live once they have been cut from the bough. What may be theoretically appropriate when the avowed objective in the achievement of a society where cooperation will reign, is unlikely to be even theoretically appropriate for a society where competition is recognized to be essential.

After the relief of poverty, which is common ground between the parties, the essential 'values' of Socialism enumerated by Mr Crosland were a belief in 'equality', and 'strict social control over the environment'.[6] This third object is also common ground between the parties,

---

examination of his writings is unavoidable in any study of the British Social Democrats.

though there are differences over method. Evidently, therefore, it is only because of the second 'value' that everybody is not a 'Socialist'.*

'By equality' the Social Democrats 'mean more than a merito-cratic society of equal opportunities, in which unequal rewards would be distributed to those most fortunate in their genetic endowment or family background. We also mean more than a simple redistribution of income. We want a wider social equality embracing the distribu-tion of property, the educational system, social class relationships, power and privilege in industry – indeed, all that is enshrined in the age old Socialist dream of a "classless society".'[7] Making due allowance for rhetoric, the revisionists are still envisaging the Socialist objective, happily oblivious of the fact that they have abandoned the means of achieving it.

Having discarded traditional Socialism, the Social Democrats try to put 'equality' in its place. What the far-left-wing Mr Ralph Miliband calls 'the amplitude of its egalitarian rhetoric'[8] is the core of revisionism. Yet as the passage quoted above brings out clearly, the revisionists are far from certain what they mean by equality. Indeed in his book of essays, *Socialism Now*, Mr Crosland declined even to discuss the question, 'How much equality ultimately?'[9] Mr Douglas Jay in his book, *Socialism in the New Society*, does give us some guidance. 'Equality', he tells us, 'is the specifically Socialist aim. But what', Mr Jay goes on, 'does equality mean?' His answer in the economic world is 'not literally "equality"; but the minimum of inequality . . .' Curiously Mr Jay puts inverted commas round the word where it means literally equality, that is to say equality,

*In one sense, the word 'Socialism' has long had a very wide meaning. 'I have learnt,' Joe Chamberlain said in 1885, 'not to be afraid of words that are flung in my face instead of argument . . . The Poor Law is Socialism; . . . the greater part of municipal work is Socialism; and every kindly act of legislation, by which the community has sought to discharge its responsibilities and obligations to the poor is Socialism.'[10] And every schoolboy knows of Harcourt's remark ten years later that 'We are all Socialists now'. But that is largely to rob the word of useful meaning. 'Socialist' in that sense includes all political parties, and the Social Democrats are more restrictive in their use of the word. Yet once the use of the word is restricted, there is surely a case for restricting its use to its traditional meaning. Socialism does not just mean social reform. It means amongst other things the virtual abolition of private property and its transfer to the state. And since the Social Democrats mean by the word something quite different from what it has traditionally meant, it would be less confusing to themselves and to other people if they always stuck to the description 'Social Democratic' and left 'Socialist' to their more left-wing and truly Socialist comrades.

instead of when it does not mean equality, but merely 'the minimum of inequality' which Mr Jay thinks undesirable. Not surprisingly, therefore, Mr Jay prefers the phrase 'social justice', 'since it expresses the true aim far more accurately than "equality" ', which Mr Jay tells us 'many people, strangely enough, interpret as actually meaning equality'![11] But this Wykehamist ingenuity merely substitutes one problem for another, since as Angus Maude has pointed out 'it is almost impossible to define social justice objectively'.[12]

On the whole, however, the Social Democrats have no inhibitions about using the word 'equality' however much it may be mis- interpreted. It recurs constantly throughout their writings and is the main plank of their policy. In continually demanding more equality, while refusing to specify how much, the revisionists are like a general continually ordering his troops to move east irrespective of whether the terrain is flat or mountainous, fertile or barren, well drained or swamp, and ignoring the casualties they suffer or inflict and the amount of equipment they lose. But then ideologists do not make good generals.

The revisionists' claim that 'Socialism is about equality' is histori- cally inaccurate. Only a very few Socialist writers, such as Babeuf, have put equality as their main objective. Even Marx maintained that under Socialism *'equal* right . . . recognises no class differences . . . but it tacitly recognises unequal individual endowments and thus productive capacity as natural privileges. *It is, therefore, a right of inequality, in its content, like every right.*' Only when abundance had been achieved under Communism, the 'higher stage' of society, would each receive 'according to his need'.[13]

The meaning attached to equality has widely varied. Thus Aristotle thought justice meant 'not equality for all, but only for equals'.[14] The difficulty is that men are manifestly not equal.* In some ways of course the differences between them are less important than the similarities. Most people accept that all men are equal in the sight of God, which takes us back to Coleridge's idea that no man should be treated as merely a means to an end. In this sense the phrase 'all

---

*There is another difficulty, as Bertrand Russell pointed out. If men and ani- mals are descended from the same ancestors, and if during evolution there were creatures on the borderlines between humans and animals, at what stage did man or his semi-human ancestors all begin to be equal? Should the ape be regarded as equal to man? If so, thought Russell, 'Why stop with apes?' There was no logical argument for opposing 'votes for oysters'.[15]

men are equal' means all men are men and should be treated as such. Even though men are not equal, they should generally be treated as though they were. Therefore there must, for example, be equality before the law. This is a fair and civilized principle.

But to impose economic equality is a very different thing. Since men are unequal, they can only be made equal, economically, by being treated unequally. This is likely to be neither fair nor civilized. And it can only be achieved by strong governmental action, which plainly diminishes the liberty of the citizen. The Social Democrats' attitude to freedom will be discussed shortly. In their yearning for equality there is much genuine idealism; yet there is also often a good deal of envy of those who are better off as well as much guilt about those who are worse off. 'Envy', as Bacon said, 'never makes holiday.' The revisionists are inclined to be scathing about the middle classes, while remaining, at best, indifferent to the hardships, which many middle class people, particularly those on fixed incomes, have been caused by inflation. According to them, the middle classes 'moan endlessly over Sunday morning sherry' about their lost and threatened privileges.[16] But in adopting the stern tones of the moralist, the Social Democrats seem to be generally unaware of the vulnerability of their own position. After all, the life style of most of them is as far beyond the means of the great majority in Britain as is what Mr Crosland oddly called 'the grossly excessive sumptuary spending of the wealthy classes'[17] beyond the means of many Social Democrats.

Most people are delighted that the Social Democrats should enjoy the good things of life, but they are not quite sure why their standard of living should be the ceiling for everybody else. These somewhat sybaritic Savonarolas talk about the 'Socialist rejection of the claims of the wealthy to a wholly unacceptable degree of privilege';[18] evidently it is taken for granted that their degree of privilege should be wholly acceptable to Socialists and non-Socialists alike. 'Levelling', as Carlyle put it, 'is comfortable, as we often say: levelling, yet only down to oneself'.[19] Second homes, for instance, are permissible for Social Democrats, indeed almost compulsory. But they must be fairly discreet. Tennyson said Browning would die in a white tie.[20] British Social Democrats will die in a black one.

There are, however, more important objections to the egalitarianism of the Social Democrats than any discrepancy between their theory and their practice. Even if they all lived in a garret on a diet of

beer and biscuits, their obsession with equality would still weaken
and warp their politics. If equality does not mean 'equality' but
something that the Revisionists find more convenient, there can be
no agreement on what that something is even among the revisionists
themselves, let alone among everybody else. The rigid criterion of
complete equality is easy to understand, though as Hume pointed
out, its imposition would inevitably produce both poverty and
dictatorship. But once what Babeuf called 'real' equality[21] is abandoned, there is no other criterion which will achieve acceptance.
This is, as Hume again pointed out, due to man's inability to judge
merit and to 'the self-conceit of each individual'.* The attempted
imposition of any such modified equality will therefore create more
jealousies than it removes, and is likely to be almost as disastrous to
freedom and prosperity as the attempted imposition of equality in
the full meaning of the word.

Besides, good Social Democrats are presumably concerned not
merely with equality in one country. Most of them rightly pay much
attention to Britain's growth rate, believing that their aims cannot be
realized unless the British economy grows at a reasonable speed.
British revisionists are no longer quite 'the moral imperialists' they
used to be. But they still have a high opinion of their moral qualities
and regard themselves as setting an example to Social Democrats in
other countries. George Orwell wrote before the war of 'the equivocal position of Britain, with its democratic phrases and its coolie
empire . . .' The Social Democrats today are in an equivocal position
with their desire for increased wealth here in order to achieve further
equality, which will at the same time ensure less equality between
Britain and the underdeveloped world.

But there is a more immediate practical problem. Revisionists
from time to time ask if recent developments have made the Marxist
analysis valid,† and they decide correctly enough that they have not.
Yet they never ask if recent developments have destroyed their own
thesis. The Social Democrats and the Labour Party have now been
in office for ten of the last thirteen years. The results have not been
exactly spectacular, and a little self-questioning would surely be
appropriate. But it has not been forthcoming. The Social Democrats
are as fundamentalist about revisionism, as are the left wing about

*See above, Part II, Ch. 3.
†See, for example, Crosland, *Socialism Now*, p. 27.

nationalization and Clause 4. Whatever else must be revised, it is not revisionism. And the reason for this is presumably as Kautsky said of the Belgian revisionists in 1902, 'They have nothing to revise, for they have no theory.'[22] Much of the Manifesto Group's recent pamphlet, 'What We Must Do, A Democratic Socialist Approach to Britain's Crisis', is unexceptionable, but both its Socialism and its intellectual content are minimal.

Mr Crosland was however frank about the economic failure of the first Wilson Government. 'Nobody', he wrote, 'disputes the central failure of economic policy. In 1970 unemployment was higher, inflation more rapid and economic growth slower, than when the Conservatives left office in 1964.'* But apparently this failure was entirely caused by the attempt to defend an unrealistic exchange rate for sterling;[23] and so other deeper reasons for failure, such as defects in Social Democracy, need not be sought.

Here we return to the central problem of British Social Democracy. By their revisionism they accept the continuance of a competitive society; but by their clinging to the relics of their creed and by claiming that these relics are Socialism, they make it difficult for competition to work. 'We shall not get the allocation [of resources] we want',

*The use of the word 'nobody' here seems a little sweeping. The leader of that Government has not been prominent in proclaiming its failure. In his foreword to his massive apologia *The Labour Government 1964–1970*, Sir Harold Wilson does not mention unemployment, inflation or growth. The word 'transformation', however, occurs twice, and we learn of 'an expansion in the social services, health, welfare and housing, education and social security, unparalleled in our history'. Apparently the Wilson Government 'achieved far more than most would have expected'. And everything, it seems, that the Prime Minister did and said throughout his tenure of 10 Downing Street was 'part of a coherent political strategy'. Mistakes, such as the condemnation of India as aggressive, or the remark that Rhodesia would be settled in 'weeks not months', or 'l'Affaire Soames' were not, needless to say, Wilson's fault but the fault of incompetent or ill-intentioned officials.[24]

The Wilson memoirs evidently resemble those of the Byzantine Emperor, John Cantacuzene, of which Gibbon writes that 'he presents not a confession, but an apology, of the life of an ambitious statesman. Instead of unfolding the true counsels and characters of men, he displays the smooth and specious surface of events, highly varnished with his own praises and those of his friends. Their motives are always pure; their ends always legitimate; they conspire and rebel without any views of interest . . .' According to Richard Crossman, however, Wilson was 'the only conspirator' in the Labour Cabinet.[25] But that seems harsh and improbable. And, to be fair, Wilson does not actually say, as does Cantacuzene, that his triumphs were due to 'my sublime and almost incredible virtue'.[26]

the revisionists tell us, 'without a certain view of taxation and public expenditure, and of social control and collective responsibility. And we shall not get that without a healthy rate of economic growth.'[27] Their 'certain view' means ever higher taxation, ever increasing public expenditure, more state control, and more Socialist interference. They are thus capable in the same paragraph of expressing a wish for growth, and adopting an attitude which will prevent it.

By common consent the economic stick has been largely removed. While improved social benefits are no substitute for a job to those who want to work, they at least reduce the hardship of unemployment. The Social Democrats now want to get rid of most of the carrot too. Income differentials in Britain are now less than in almost any other comparable country and much less than in Soviet Russia.[28]* Yet instead of wondering if this is not an important cause of Britain's poor economic performance, the Social Democrats wish to compress the differentials still further.† A competitive economy cannot work well if adequate rewards are withheld from those who do difficult and responsible jobs, from those who are prepared to take risks with their money, and from those who have to undergo long training before they can gain the necessary qualifications to practise their profession or occupation.

Unfortunately the dogmatism of the Social Democrats blinds them to these obvious facts. Yet they may even now be forced to recognize reality. The skilled and energetic are already leaving these shores in increasing numbers for less envious societies where the rewards are more commensurate with their work and skills. And the more equality is striven for by the Social Democrats, the larger the exodus will become. What then are the Social Democrats to do? They could, as it were, build a Berlin Wall round this country and forbid people to go abroad without their permission. But that would soon create an emigration racket alongside the present immigration racket; and even Mr Jones, Mr Foot and Mr Benn might think such

*In *The State and Revolution*, written just before the Bolsheviks seized power, Lenin wrote that in the 'first phase' of Communism 'the whole of society will have become a single office and a single factory, with equality of labour and equality of pay'. But the first phase has never been reached, and fourteen years later Stalin admitted reality when he said their task was 'to put an end to the instability of labour power, to abolish equalitarianism, to organise wages properly, and to improve the living conditions of the workers'.[29]

†Social Democrats of course consider differentials that are insisted upon by trade unions to be special cases.

a policy impracticable. Secondly they could continue to let people leave. They would tell us that those who departed lacked patriotism. But they would be well aware that the exodus would help the creation of a socialist state, on a poor Eastern European model, since it would lead to further economic decline. Thirdly, the revisionists might admit error, and go into reverse on egalitarianism in order to keep valuable members of the community at home. But that would be to let the bottom out of Social Democracy. Hence the second policy of economic decline is likely to be preferred to one of recantation and amendment.

The revisionist obsession with equality does not even have the justification that greater equality will benefit the poor. They admit that it won't.[30] But that, Mr Crosland thought, was not the point, since 'the argument for more equality is based not on any direct material gain to the poor, but on the claims of social and natural justice'.[31] This is surely the converse of the puritan attitude to bear baiting as described by Macaulay. The Social Democrats are in favour of equality not to help the poor, but to give pain to the rich. In fact, because of its damaging effect on the economy, greater equality hurts the poor as well as the rich and indeed everybody else in the country – except perhaps Government Ministers who are sometimes insulated against financial decline.*

The revisionists' equality, then, does not help the poor. Nor is it wanted by the country. The objectives of the Social Democrats can only be achieved by higher public spending, higher taxation and greater control. But these, they concede, 'are by no means popular with the British public'.[32] Mr Crosland admitted that 'our socialist claims on the increment [achieved by the growth in the economy] are not always the same as those of the mass of our supporters. While', he added, 'we rightly say that equality and higher public expenditure are what divide us from the Tories, they may reply that their priorities are more jobs, lower prices, lower taxes or the suppression of crime.'[33] So equality, it appears, divides the Social Democrats not only from the Tories, but from their own supporters as well.

According to revisionists 'the ethical basis . . . for greater equality

---

*In the Federalist papers, Hamilton thought a representative assembly could 'make no law which will not have its full operation on themselves and their friends, as well as on the great mass of the society'.[34] Mr Healey's legislation on fringe benefits seems to refute him.

is that it will increase social contentment and diminish social resentment'.[35] For more than twenty years the Social Democrats have been preaching the need for greater equality, and when in government they have tried to achieve it. But their campaign has not in fact increased social contentment or diminished social resentment. The Social Democrats have employed what Burke called 'the old evil counsellor, envy',[36] and he has done his work. Not surprisingly, the systematic inculcation of envy has multiplied envy and social resentment. Social mobility in Britain does not seem to be less than in other countries.[37] Yet there is probably less social contentment in Britain today than in most comparable countries, and almost certainly less than there was in Britain twenty years ago. The Social Democrats' ethics are as dubious as their economics.

Social Democrats thus make equality their central objective and make the, historically, dubious claim that equality is what Socialism is all about, when they mean by it not full equality but something vague which they dare not define, because it is indefinable; when it is a purely insular pursuit; when it prevents the efficient running of a competitive economy which they say they accept; when it drives abroad thousands of our most talented citizens thus making our frail economy more fragile still; when it weakens rather than strengthens social cohesion; when it hurts rather than helps the poor; and when it is desired by neither the country nor by Labour supporters. The demand for ever greater equality is in these circumstances surely a supreme example of placing the pretensions of abstract theory above the dictates of experience and common sense. To its devotees, revisionism and equality have become as much a sacred text as Marxism is to the old believers.*

'In many instances', Robert Michels suggested, 'reformism [it would be called revisionism today] is no more than the theoretical expression of the scepticism of the disillusioned, of the outwearied, of those who have lost their faith; it is the socialism of non-socialists with a socialist past'.[38] Regrettably the socialism of non-socialists, or perhaps the non-socialism of socialists, is in practice as dogmatic as the socialism of socialists. Because they have always to prove their socialist credentials to their more left-wing comrades, they do not dare abandon their doctrinal approach. If the Social Democrats,

---

*In his memoirs, Hugh Dalton quotes Josiah Wedgwood as saying that 'Labour men always find it exceedingly difficult to change their mind'.[39] Under Sir Harold Wilson, the Social Democrats did not experience this difficulty.

having sloughed off the more obvious implausible doctrines of Socialism, had concentrated upon their primary aim of relieving poverty, they might have achieved much. But that would have looked too modern and radical to the fundamentalists. Therefore the quest for equality had to be made the primary aim, so that revisionism could still be called Socialist.

All this is of course contrary both to the Conservative concern to avoid abstractions, and to the Conservative principle of removing misery but not seeking to impose happiness. If the poor are made better off, which is a Conservative aim, progress has clearly been made towards the elimination of poverty. Almost certainly, too, greater equality will also have been achieved. In contrast, when as with the Social Democrats equality is the overriding objective, the poor may well end up worse off. There will then be less equality, and probably virtually everybody will be poorer.

The Conservative approach, as we have seen, is to abolish poverty, which is a continuing struggle since poverty is relative. Conservatives believe that the rich should pay their share of the expenses of the state, which is obviously a higher share than that of the poor. But they do not believe that the rich should be taxed in order to assuage Socialist spleen. The whole drift of Mr Healey's new taxes on the better-off is to appropriate their money for the state, thereby turning capital into income, instead of for other individuals. The Conservative aim is a property-owning democracy, in which as many people as possible own property; the Socialist aim is the concentration of property in the state, which spells the end of democracy. Further, Conservatives do not consider it defensible that Mr Healey, Mr Jones or Mr Benn should determine the level of wealth the individual is allowed according to what they think suitable or convenient at any given time. The prejudices of Mr Healey, Mr Jones and Mr Benn are no doubt interesting and important to themselves, but they are not principles of taxation.

Conservatives also favour the diffusion of power. The Social Democrats because of their obsessional egalitarianism have to further its concentration: equality can only be imposed by increasing state power. Hence the Social Democrats' primary objective embraces an obvious threat to freedom. The Social Democrats try to escape the dilemma by conveying that liberty and equality are much the same thing – 'our creed', said Mr Crosland, is 'equality with liberty'[40] – and that the two things cannot be separated. Today 'you cannot', writes Mr Jay, 'have freedom without equality . . .'[41] None of this, of course, is true. 'Everything', Sir Isaiah Berlin has said, 'is what it is: liberty is liberty, not equality or fairness or justice or human happiness or a quiet conscience.'[42] And Sir Karl Popper gave up Socialism because he recognized that 'freedom is more important than equality; that the attempt to realise equality endangers freedom; and that, if freedom is lost, there will not even be equality among the unfree'.[43]

The Social Democrats do not – cannot – admit that liberty and equality are irreconcilable. If they did, they would have nothing left. Similarly they have to gloss over the dangers of concentrating power in the state. 'To paint General Motors or ITT as bastions of individual freedom against an over mighty state', they sneer, 'is perhaps a little far fetched.'[44] Yet the mere fact that these concentrations of power are not the state and provide countervailing power to it is an aid to freedom.

'We want', Anthony Crosland laid down, 'democratic control over *all* concentrations of power.'[45] This shows a surprising disregard of much political theory and most political practice. Mr Crosland quoted de Tocqueville on 'the gradual development of the equality of conditions' being apparently inevitable. But he did not quote any of de Tocqueville's warnings about equality's threat to liberty. De Tocqueville believed for example that 'the vices that despotism engenders are precisely those that equality fosters' and he remarked that 'equality awakens in men several propensities extremely dangerous to freedom'.[46] Mr Crosland apparently meant by 'democratic control over all concentrations of power' increased control by the Government. But the idea that giving increased power to government without constitutional safeguards is likely to extend liberty is surely as primitive a piece of political thinking as the idea that the dictatorship of the proletariat is likely to lead to democracy.

Instead of worrying so much about 'democratic control', the Social Democrats should be worrying about providing greater freedom for the British people. If everybody, because of the egalitarianism approved and imposed by the Social Democrats, has to use the same medical service, to use the same school service, and to use an increasing number of monopolies created by the revisionists' egalitarian zeal, the citizen will be increasingly regimented by the monopolists and increasingly at their mercy. If on the other hand, there is someone else the aggrieved citizen can go to, his freedom is enlarged, and the power of the bureaucrats, the monopolists, and the public-sector unions is correspondingly diminished.

This was graphically demonstrated in a recent article by Professor A. H. Birch. When his son and other children were being bullied by their teacher at a primary school, nothing at first could be done because the National Union of Teachers did not allow teachers to be dismissed. But after three families transferred their children to a private school and protested strongly to the education authority, some action was taken. 'For the sake of our children', Dr Birch comments, 'none of us would have felt able to protest like this had we not been able to take them elsewhere.' Similarly, after Dr Birch himself had had a serious operation, he like the other patients was being very badly nursed. Eventually he decided to be transferred to a private ward and have a second operation without help from the taxpayer. His wife then complained to the surgeon and there was an immediate improvement. But, Dr Birch emphasizes, 'my wife and I could not have taken this action – which benefited all the patients – unless private hospital facilities were available to which I could be transferred. The other patients in the ward knew well enough what was happening, but none of them dared to complain.'[47] Regrettably the Social Democrats in their mindless pursuit of uniformity and equality are blind to the dangers to freedom. They cannot see that alternatives to the state system are of far greater benefit to the citizen than so-called 'democratic control' and carry none of its dangers.

The Social Democrats' disregard of freedom is probably explained at least in part by their declining position in the Labour Party, and by the greatly improved position of those in the party who care nothing for liberty. When about twenty years ago the Social Democrats first complained that the party was more dogmatic and old-fashioned than its Continental counterparts, Hugh Gaitskell's courageous leadership seemed about to bring Labour into the modern age. The Clause 4 controversy, during which Sir Harold Wilson stood against Gaitskell for the leadership, prevented all that. And by the time, in his lecture in Costa Rica, Mr Crosland made the complaint that 'amongst the European socialist parties, the British Labour Party is unique in the doctrinal energy which it still devotes to the issue of public ownership',[48] the situation had changed substantially for the worse. Instead of advancing with the Continental parties, Labour has retreated. Parts of it have gone into a Marxist

second childhood. There is probably a greater desire in the Labour
Party today to nationalize everything in sight than at any time in the
party's history. The process has been arrested for the moment by the
IMF and our international creditors. But whereas up to 1970 the
Labour Party was firmly in the British empirical democratic tradi-
tion, that has not been so during the last few years.

The Social Democrats' response to these ominous developments
has been cautious rather than courageous. They have been careerists
not crusaders. Although they have no enthusiasm for yet more state
monopolies,[49] in practice they always go along with any extension of
nationalization, blandly explaining that it can be justified on its
merits. Mr Roy Jenkins, Mr Lever, Mr Thompson and some of
their followers resigned their Shadow posts, because of Wilson's
behaviour over Europe. Some of the others made the convenient
discovery that Europe was not an important issue. Even those brave
enough to resign voted solidly and consistently against the Bill that
took us into the EEC. On the other betrayals by Sir Harold Wilson
of his own Government's policies, such as attacking the Industrial
Relations Act and the Conservative prices and incomes policies, the
Social Democrats obediently followed the party majority. Plainly
politics was not a matter of principle.

In the autumn of 1973 when it was already plain that the party had
moved sharply to the Left, Mr Crosland concluded 'that a move to
the left is needed'.[50] In opposition, the Social Democrats had no
doubts about the need for an incomes policy. 'Labour', we were told
in 1971, 'must stand adamantly for an incomes policy,' and
Labour's lack of one was deplored in 1973.[51] Whereupon the Social
Democrats fought two elections in 1974 against an incomes policy;
only after the disastrous wage inflation of 1974 and 1975 did they
come full circle for the second or third time and once again support
such a policy. In opposition the Social Democrats had lamented that
'even the rule of law is challenged by some Labour councillors and
trade unionists, though historically – and let no Socialist ever forget
this – the law has been the means by which the weak obtained
redress against the strong'.[52] Their attitude to the Clay Cross councillors altered sharply when Labour came to power.

And all this took place against a background of a Labour Party
becoming more extremist, more Marxist, more contemptuous of the
rights of others, more trade-union dominated, and more unscrupulous in its political behaviour. Yet hardly ever did the revisionists

stand up for the sort of Labour Party they once believed in. By any standards, their record over the last few years has been one of ignominy and cowardice. A conviction had only to become unpopular for it to be abandoned. A Wilsonite somersault had only to be mooted for the Social Democrats to jump on to the trampoline eager to show their paces. Once a lurch to the Left became expedient, immediately the Social Democrats said it could be justified on its merits. A fundamental policy had to be changed? That presented no problem: the issue involved was never really important.

Yet despite all this the British Social Democrats surprisingly remain, for some, the knights in shining armour of British politics. Their armour is indeed highly polished; unfortunately the last thing they ever do in it is to fight. Carlyle's verdict on Barère was, 'Truth may lie on both sides, on either side, or on neither side; my friends, ye must give and take: for the rest success to the winning side. This is the motto of Barère.'⁵³ It is not the motto of the Social Democrats. But it comes uncomfortably near to describing their behaviour since 1970.

Yet it is often taken for granted that Socialist morality is somehow higher than Tory morality; or to put it rather differently: Socialism is moral, and Conservatism and free enterprise are immoral. This widespread if erroneous impression is of great electoral value to the Labour Party, and it is worth examining.

Presumably nobody in his senses, with the possible exception of the Bishop of Southwark, would argue that Russian Communist society is more moral than Western capitalist society. Even if we leave out of account Russian behaviour over the Nazi–Soviet Pact in 1939, the Russian invasion of Poland, the Baltic States and Finland, and after the war Russia's despotism throughout Eastern Europe, her invasions of Hungary and Czechoslovakia and other excesses, there is still ample material left. Stalin's treatment of the Kulaks at the end of the twenties; the monstrous purges of the thirties; the labour camps which make Dostoyevsky's House of the Dead sound like a haven of civilization; the absence of freedom, law and justice; the persecution of religion; the incessant activity of the political police – not even the most perfervid Soviet admirer can find anything remotely parallel to any of this in Western Europe or the United States. Of course there are excrescences in Western society, such as unemployment, inflation, racial tension, which are open to heavy criticism. But they are surely mere fleabites of evil in comparison with the mass organization of evil that is the Soviet Union. According to Alexander Solzhenitsyn, from 1917 to 1959, excluding the Second World War, Socialism cost the Soviet Union over sixty million lives.[54] Over the same period the political executions 'were at least fifty times as numerous as over the last half-century of Tsarist rule, and the maximum number of political prisoners at any one time was at least seventy time as great, as the highest Tsarist figure of 183949.[55] In the United Kingdom, if Ireland and the IRA are excluded, only eight people have been killed in political or industrial riots in the 130 or so years since 1842.[56]

A British Communist or fully Socialist state would, one hopes, be less ruthless and bloodthirsty than Soviet Russia. It would presumably be like one of the Eastern European so-called People's Democracies. It would certainly be a dictatorship. If all political and economic power is in the hands of the state, tyranny can be the only outcome. There would be no freedom and no rights except for members of the Communist Party. Tyranny is not moral.

Clearly, therefore, the morality of the free-enterprise states is infinitely superior to that of the Communist states; and the Far Left in England would do well not to talk of morality. There remains the question whether in spite of this, the morality of British Social Democracy is in some way superior to that of British Conservatism. Mr Douglas Jay has no doubts on this score. Under the Labour Government of 1945–51, he tells us, 'a social conscience' was rife in the country and a 'deep tide of British idealism' washed 'selfishness' away from these shores. Presumably the selfishness was washed away to America, which in its capitalist selfishness then produced the Marshall Plan that enabled the idealistic British Government to pay for its welfare state with American money and to roll along from one economic crisis to another. The black market and the legion of 'spivs' in Britain at that time similarly demonstrated the prevalent idealism fostered by the Socialists.

In the same key Mr Jay writes of 'the efforts of the British Conservative Party to revive selfishness and stifle social conscience since 1951', and of 'the thick coating of snobbery and self seeking smeared over the surface of life by ten years of Tory Government'.[57] Mr Jay wrote this before Britain's two great ages of selfless idealism, socialist altruism and high political principle were inaugurated by the two arrivals of Sir Harold Wilson and his entourage in 10 Downing Street. We have not yet had his eulogies of them. But Mr Jay evidently does not fully realize that his abandonment of Socialism and acceptance of competition necessarily involves what he calls selfishness.

To appreciate that a competitive society entails what Mr Jay calls selfishness and then to try to ensure that that 'selfishness' also serves the common good is surely better than to denounce it on grounds which in view of the Social Democrats' acceptance of competition are invalid, and then to seek so far as possible to inhibit it from generating wealth. Mr Jay seems to think that a sluggish and incompetent competitive society is somehow more moral than an energetic and successful one. 'An Englishman', Shaw said, 'thinks he is moral, when he is only uncomfortable.'[58] And in fact the chief sufferers from an inefficient economy are the poor.

Besides, we should be wary of accepting at its face value the idea that making money is especially 'selfish'. After all somebody has got to make money before the Social Democrats can take it away. Anybody who gives his own money to charity or like Stanley Baldwin gives a substantial part of it to the state is plainly being unselfish and moral. Yet it is hard to see how the creators of wealth who retain the untaxed part of it are somehow more immoral and more selfish than the distributors or users of other people's wealth. Somebody has got to earn enough to pay for the army of politicians, social workers, teachers, and others who do not sully their hands by engaging in 'selfish' trade or industry. If free enterprise is in some way selfish and immoral, then a great many people are living on immoral earnings.

But of course, as Churchill once pointed out, 'the idea that all service is valueless unless disinterested is a fallacy. Mutually advantageous exchange of goods and services between communities is the foundation alike of the prosperity and peace of the world.'[59] This is just as well, since very little service is wholly disinterested. Civil servants no doubt should be disinterested in their pursuit of the public interest. But Whitehall has its own private interests. In any case there would be little public interest for civil servants to pursue, were it not for the economic efforts of people in the private sector of industry. And now that civil servants are so well paid and pensioned, their activities cannot be said to be more moral or disinterested than the activities of those who pay their salaries and pensions.

Conservatives favour a society in which there is an ever growing number of people with property of their own, living their lives in their own way in freedom, doing the best they can for themselves and their family, a society in which those who cannot look after themselves are protected by the state. Socialists favour a society in which everybody uses the same services provided by the state, there is no freedom of choice, and everyone has less for fear that anyone has too much. Socialists believe in providing, in Mrs Thatcher's phrase, 'pocket money'[60] for the people; Conservatives believe, in Gladstone's phrase, in letting money fructify in the pockets of the people. Putting the matter at its lowest, the Conservative ideal cannot be said to be less moral than the Socialist. So much for theory.

In practice, there have, notoriously, been a number of land scandals in the last few years. Yet Sir Harold Wilson's differentiation between land 'speculation' which was vicious and Conservative, and land 'reclamation', which involved his private office and was therefore Socialist and virtuous, should perhaps be regarded more as a trailer for his resignation honours list than as a serious ethical or environmental distinction.* Notoriously, too, there are occasional scandals in the City or in industry. In a famous phrase Mr Heath referred to 'the ugly and unacceptable face of capitalism'. Of course some business men do harm, but then so do some people in every walk of life. Social Democrats harshly admonish offenders in the business world and talk about 'the avarice, cupidity and lack of patriotism of the Lonhro directors'.[61] But do Social Democrats think those disagreeable characteristics have been lacking among their trade-union allies during the last few years? On any objective standard trade-union behaviour has been far worse than that of industry or the City. No baron in the fifteenth century acted with such arrogance or with such sublime indifference to the national interest as have Mr Scargill, Mr Buckton and many other trade-union chieftains. The interests of individuals have been as ruthlessly disregarded by trade unions as the interest of the public; inconvenience, discomfort, hardship and misery, to say nothing of great economic damage have been caused by trade-union leaders' ruthless use of the strike weapon in pursuit of their own interests. All this is often accompanied by considerable intimidation. Business morality may occasionally be deficient; all too often trade-union morality seems non-existent. And the fact that inexcusable trade-union action against the public is often accompanied by unctuous sentiments of the 'this hurts us more than it will

*Mr Joe Haines and Mr Bernard Donoughue wisely advised that Wilson's sentence about reclamation should be struck out. Their advice was rejected.[62]

hurt you' variety merely adds hypocrisy to selfishness. Finally, a Labour Government is not particularly unselfish or moral, as the Crossman Diaries make sufficiently clear.

Hence Social Democratic pretensions to greater moral virtue is mere posturing. There is nothing moral or unselfish about preaching but not practising egalitarianism. There is nothing moral or honest about denouncing business wrongs but keeping silence over trade-union wrongs. The impression of Socialist virtue is conveyed by a crude sleight of hand. Socialism, by which is meant cooperation, is theoretically more moral than capitalism, by which is meant competition. The Social Democrats have given up cooperation, because it is unobtainable, and they have accepted competition. But they still feel free to criticize the operation of competition from a standpoint they have given up. Having willed the end of competition, they refuse to will the means. This is mere intellectual dishonesty, and Socialist or Labour morality is in practice not superior to free enterprise or Conservative morality.

But of all the equivocations of the Social Democrats their alliance with the Left is the most glaring. They are remarkably careless of the company they keep. J. R. Clynes, a former Labour leader, said in the twenties that 'a Communist is no more a left wing member of the Labour Party than an atheist is a left wing member of the Christian Church'.[63] The Social Democrats not only tolerate atheists in their Church, they have accepted some of the atheists' creed. In all levels of the Labour Party there are now many people who are not democrats in the Western sense and whose affinities lie with Eastern rather than Western Europe. One can well imagine the public outcry there would be if within the Conservative Party at all levels there was an increasing powerful body of men whose real sympathies lay with the National Front. The British Labour Party is the only party in Europe which is so open to all comers from the Left. On the Continent such people join the Communist Party. In England they join the Labour Party, and with the concurrence of the revisionists push it towards full Socialism.

' "Socialist Democracy" ', Alexander Solzhenitsyn has said, is about as meaningful as talking about ' "boiling ice" '.[64] A mixed or free economy is indeed a necessary condition of freedom; and the nationalization of the means of production, distribution and exchange, in other words a fully socialist state, spells dictatorship. Those propositions are supported by all experience and by common

sense. No Socialist country in the world is free. Wherever free enterprise has been eliminated, dictatorship has followed.

Common sense shows us why this must be so. If the state is the
only employer, who can defy it? 'In a country where the sole employer is the state', said Trotsky not without experience, 'opposition
means death by slow starvation'.[65] And indeed if the state is the only
employer, there can be no free trade unions. If all employees are
employees of the state, trade unions, as Lenin, Trotsky and Stalin
all agreed, must become mere tools of the state. There was therefore
nothing untoward in Mr Shelepin, a former head of the Soviet
secret police, becoming the boss of the Russian so-called trade
unions. But in entertaining him in England, members of the TUC
were showing either a deplorable ignorance of the Russian constitution or a cynical contempt for free trade unionism.

If all economic power is concentrated in the state, there can be no
countervailing power, and without countervailing power there can
be no restraint on the Government and therefore there can be no
freedom.* An all-powerful state is an all-powerful state. It is as
simple as that.

These truths are not the result of a Russian perversion of Marxism
or of a Stalinist perversion of Leninism. The nineteenth-century
anarchist, Bakunin, said of Marxism: 'Those previous workers
having just become rulers or representatives of the people will cease
being workers; they will represent not the people but themselves . . .
He who doubts it does not know human nature.'[66] Writing in auto-
cratic Russia, Tolstoy made the same point: 'Even if that which
Marx predicted should happen, then the only thing that will happen
is that despotism will be passed on.'[67] Similarly the seeds of the
Stalinist and post-Stalinist dictatorship were sowed by Lenin. Long
before Lenin attained power, the Russian Marxist, Plekhanov,
accused him of 'confusing the dictatorship of the proletariat with the
dictatorship over the proletariat';[68] and Trotsky predicted that the
party would be replaced 'by the organisation of the party, the
organisation by the central committee, and finally the central committee by the dictator'.[69] Finally, as Mr E. H. Carr makes plain, it
was under Lenin that the terror became 'a deliberate instrument of

*There can of course be competing power centres within the state apparatus,
such as the party, the secret police and the army. But presumably even the most
enthusiastic Socialist would scarcely argue that the KGB or the Gestapo were
bulwarks of freedom.

policy'.[70] Nor can Trotsky be absolved. He was as heavily implicated as Lenin. When the Kronstadt sailors rebelled and demanded proper elections, it was the man they called 'the bloody field-marshal Trotsky' who crushed them.[71]

Nobody, therefore, has any excuse for not knowing what full Socialism means. In favouring it, the Far Left of the Labour Party are well outside the British political empirical tradition. The true line of demarcation in politics, as Professor Talmon has pointed out, is between absolutism and empiricism.[72] An all-embracing and all-solving creed is incompatible with liberty, because the creed reduces politics to mathematics or science. If a teacher of mathematics at a university found that one of his pupils insisted that 2 and 2 made 5, he would not say 'that is an interesting point of view which we must now discuss'. He would say 'that is rubbish, you are a mathematical idiot and you had better go off and read sociology'.

Marxism is like that mathematics teacher. It purports to be scientific, and disagreement is therefore impermissible. It knows all the answers, and no other answers are tolerated. There is only one truth, and Marxist–Leninism is its prophet. But politics are not mathematics, and human beings are not numbers. And any attempt to treat them as such, and any claim by leaders to be in possession of an all-embracing truth leads infallibly to tyranny. Marxism therefore contains a double guarantee of dictatorship. Objectively, as the Marxists say, it creates economic and political conditions which produce dictatorship; and secondly it produces leaders who are natural dictators. A left-wing critic, Djilas, has pointed out that a defect of Marxism is the absence of a theory of political liberty.[73] But to talk of Marxism lacking a theory of political liberty is like talking of fascism lacking a theory of political liberty.

The Social Democrats know all this. In his major work, *The Future of Socialism*, Mr Crosland wrote long ago that 'Marx has little or nothing to offer the contemporary Socialist . . . his prophecies have been almost without exception falsified, and his conceptual tools are now quite inappropriate'.[74] Yet the Social Democrats remain the willing aides of Labour's anti-democratic Far-Left wing. Their acquiescence in what has happened to the Labour Party over the last few years has forced them continually to justify things which they know to be wrong. By their continued presence in the party they have given an aura of respectability to the Socialism in which they do not believe, thus hastening the arrival of a society to which they are opposed. Certainly after a year or two in office Labour pursues more Conservative policies, which have been made unavoidable by the failure of its earlier Socialist policies. Yet the change is the result not of doughty fighting by the revisionists but of the dictates of foreign bankers and oil sheikhs. In any case the general march is towards Socialism.

And one wonders if there is any point at which the Social Democrats will cry 'enough'. Will they always be content to stay in harness with what Churchill called 'the subversive and degenerate elements'[75] in the Labour Party, even though those elements are much more powerful than they have ever been before? For the moment, at least, the answer seems that they will put up with anything rather than drive out the Far-Left wing or themselves leave the party. Yet they cannot claim to be ignorant of where they are going. The final Socialist port of call has after all been reached by other countries – though by none of them voluntarily. Nor can they deceive themselves that the voyage will necessarily be long. They know that there are rocks ahead, but they remain members of the crew of a ship which is steering straight for them. It is this more than any differences about equality and state control, fundamental though those are, which differentiates British Social Democrats from many Centre or left-wing Conservatives. Social Democrats are prepared to risk the loss of Britain's free institutions; Conservatives are not.

So Conservatives cannot rely on the help of the Social Democrats in upholding British institutions and defending British liberties. The revisionists are themselves a threat to those institutions and those liberties, firstly because of their alliance with the Left and secondly because of the flaws in their own creed. So long as they concentrate on the question '*why* have some got more than others?' instead of on the question '*how* can we make things better for all?' their idealism will be wasted, and their energies misdirected. Their folly in making a god out of the abstraction, equality, in order to prove themselves good Socialists after all, puts them on the wrong side of the barricades of freedom.

Conservatives must, then, be relentless in exposing the flaws in Social Democracy. But they must not be contemptuous of the challenge it presents. They cannot merely oppose the false easy certainties of Socialism with the false easy certainties of capitalism. The British are profoundly undoctrinaire; they want the benefits of both free enterprise and Social Democracy. From opposite sides of the

G

House, and in opposition to each other, Conservatives and revisionists could have together worked out the acceptable compromises which were reached when the two-party system was functioning properly. Recent developments in the Labour Party and the decline of British Social Democracy have now made that impossible. The Conservatives must do it by themselves. But the compromise must not only embody the political and economic realities; it must include a moral element as well. However perverted it may now be, Socialism contains, as Baldwin realized, a moral challenge, and that challenge must be met.

5. The Constitution

Present interest makes men forgetful of their posterity.
David Hume[1]

He that will not apply new remedies must expect new evils, for time
is the greatest innovator.
Bacon[2]

Reasonable men will look upon the general plan of our Constitution,
transmitted down to us by our ancestors, as sacred; and content
themselves with . . . rectifying the particular things which they think
amiss, and supplying the particular things which they think deficient
in it, so far as is practicable without endangering the whole.
Bishop Butler[3]

In his great address to both Houses of Parliament in Westminster
Hall in April 1960, General de Gaulle said: 'But in this achievement
of yours, for how much also has counted the value of your institutions. At the worst moments, who ever contested the legitimacy or
the authority of the state? . . . Sure of yourselves . . . you put in
practice in freedom a well founded and stable political system . . .
Thus, without closely correlated constitutional texts but by virtue of
undeniable general consent, you find the means of assuring always
the best results from democracy . . .'

At the time those words seemed a generous but not unjustified
tribute to the British constitution. Now they sound more like a
funeral oration upon it. We are no longer 'sure' of ourselves. 'The
legitimacy and the authority' of the state have been 'contested'; our
political system does not now seem 'well founded and stable'; the
means of achieving the 'best results from democracy' elude us; and
no longer does our constitution rest on 'undeniable general consent'.*

*In *The Body Politic* which was finished in 1968, I quoted de Gaulle's words
without misgivings. In that book, I maintained, against what was then the conventional wisdom, that British Government was not strong. It was stable, but it

The causes of this are not solely political. Had our economy func-
tioned as successfully as, say, that of Germany, the United States, or
Japan, our political institutions might still be admired. All the same,
the working of our political institutions has in its turn affected the
economy. And with the exception of the monarchy none of these
institutions is in good condition.

The Labour Cabinet was for some time the all too willing pawn of
the T U C. The two-party system is groggy. General elections produce
a declining level of support for the main parties and either a minority
Government in the House of Commons or a Government with a
majority of seats derived from a low percentage of the popular vote.
Governments are elected on promises which they are unable to keep.
For instance, the Wilson Government secured re-election in October
1974 by maintaining that inflation was under control and was falling
(8.4 per cent), that unemployment was falling, and under a Labour
Government would not rise – 'I am certain', said Mr Healey, 'that
we shall keep unemployment below a million all next year'* – and
that there would be no prices and incomes policy. On this basis, Sir
Harold Wilson held out a prospect of 'a bit of peace and quiet'.[4] All
this was of course untrue. But when the untruths were duly exposed,
the programme in which they were embedded was not scrapped. It

---

was not strong in the sense of being able to take unpopular decisions before it was
forced to do so. And I ascribed much of the weakness of British Government to
the all-pervading secrecy of the system which so far from helping Whitehall in
fact prevented Government from gaining the consent of the nation. But in
accordance with the conventional wisdom, I believed that the British system
produced sound and moderate, though not strong or imaginative government. I
did not ascribe its weakness to the power of pressure groups; indeed the trade
unions still seemed a force for moderation in the Labour Party. I appreciated
that social forces were more important than constitutional arrangements, but I
did not think British Government suffered from a withholding of consent. The
two-party system and the electoral system which helped to achieve it seemed to
me to have been shown by experience here and elsewhere to be better than
multi-party and proportional alternatives. I favoured fixed-date elections every
four years added to the present power to dissolve and also an elected House of
Lords. Finally I advocated regionalism in England and parliaments for Scotland
and Wales.

   *Sir Harold Wilson was on even less good terms with the truth. In the words
of the authors of the Nuffield Study, 'he used Sir Keith Joseph's remarks on
unemployment to revive the traditional equation, "Tories equal unemployment" '.[5]

had done only half its work: it had ensnared the moderate floating voter into supporting Labour. The other half, which would have repelled the floating voter had it been prominent, was to be enacted in order to appease the sour and dogmatic activists.

The Labour majority in Parliament was mobilized by three-line Whips to vote for these measures, some of which would probably not have secured the support of more than one-fifth of the House if the vote had been secret. The rule of law was broken, and the rules of Parliament were by-passed when they proved inconvenient. Never had the House of Commons seemed so like the despised tool of the executive, as the divisive and unpopular legislation of a bare majority Government was forced through it.

The nominal second Chamber, the House of Lords, did its best. It tried to uphold the rule of law, and with the aid of two courageous Labour MPs, Mr Mackintosh and Mr Walden, who sensibly sat in the press bar while their more timid colleagues voted for legislation which they deplored, it revoked the Government's danegeld to the dockers. It also held up the Aircraft and Shipbuilding Nationaliza-tion Bill, when the Government refused to compromise by agreeing to leave ship-repairing out of the Act. But the composition of the House of Lords, as well as its lack of powers, prevents it from being an effective brake on a Government.

With all Britain's main political institutions either working in-effectively or being perverted by men able to manipulate them, the country was saved from disaster only by the real House of Lords. The effective second Chamber, which has been able to curb Britain's historic political institutions, has been the international financial community: the Gnomes of Zürich, the oil sheikhs, and the Inter-national Monetary Fund. For the assertion of the public interest the British people have had to rely from February 1974 not on their own Government, but on Britain's foreign creditors. Had it not been for their pressure, the Government would not have reversed itself on inflation or, even perhaps, on Europe, and Britain would have been on the rocks instead of merely sinking steadily.

There are three fundamental things wrong with the British system of government at present. Firstly some social forces in Britain today are stronger than the country's political institutions and are not adequately represented in the constitutional process. The trade unions are over-mighty subjects who are not fully subject to control by the ballot box.

Secondly, and partly caused by the first development, politicians have perverted the constitution. The constitution itself has not radically altered during the last few years. But as Coleridge suggested, the idea of the constitution is more important than the constitution itself. And the constitution has lately been operated contrary to that idea. Mme de Staël once gushingly told the Tsar Alexander: 'Your character, Sire, is a constitution.'[6] The British constitution has had more substantial foundations. Nevertheless its workings have depended more upon the self-restraint and traditions of leading politicians than upon its formal provisions. 'The ultimate foundation of every state', said Seeley, 'is a way of thinking.'[7] The same was certainly true of the British constitution, and that foundation has now been sapped.

Thirdly, the Labour Party is not now a reliable defender of freedom and the constitution. This is both cause and effect of the other two developments, and inevitably it has important implications for the future of the two-party system.

In 1968, W. G. Runciman defined a state as 'a human community which successfully claims within a given territory the monopoly of the legitimate use of physical force'.[8] Shortly afterwards Professor Plumb defined political stability as 'the acceptance by society of its political institutions, and of those classes of men or officials who control them'.[9] On those definitions Britain today can scarcely claim political stability, and it is a successful community only if political strikes are not considered to be physical force. Whether or not they should be so considered, they are in this country certainly as effective as other forms of physical force.

It is of course the breakdown of consent that is the root of our troubles. What in the nineteenth century Stendhal called '*the mania of respect*'[10] has been replaced, as he expected, by a waning of authority everywhere. The state, or the government, is overbearing and intrusive. It churns out ever-increasing quantities of detailed and scarcely comprehensible legislation. Yet while the state extends its powers over every aspect of national life, its authority is visibly diminished. It does those things which ought not to be done. And it does not do those things which ought to be done. And more and more people think there is no health in it. Because the state lacks authority (by which I mean the ability to gain consent), it is not able to control the most powerful corporations in the state – the trade unions. Indeed to some extent they control the state. It is as though the Tudors had been unable to impose a centralized authority in England, and the anarchy of the fifteenth century had continued.

If a government does not have sufficient authority to defend the national interest against sectional interests or organized groups, it can either try to increase its authority or it can try to weaken the power of the groups. But since the difficulty is caused by its lack of authority, the first is obviously the more promising approach. Only when the forces of legitimacy have been stripped of all their weakening aspects, only when the constitution is properly designed to mobilize popular consent, and only when under those circumstances sectional forces have proved stronger than the government can one safely say that the problem is intractable.*

The state will be in a better position to deal with the trade unions, if it is seen by the public to be in general acting in a competent, just, restrained and constitutional manner. At present it is regarded as a bull who is afraid to take on other bulls, the big unions, but feels itself entitled to blunder about uncontrolled in the china shop which is the rest of the country. The task of Conservatives therefore is to build up the authority of government while at the same time curbing its powers. This is only superficially a self-contradictory task. A government which is seen to be acting constitutionally and which is forced by the political process to take the people into its confidence, to seek their consent and to govern with it, will enjoy far greater authority than a government whose powers are apparently untrammelled but which because of its behaviour, at once high-handed and craven, is unable to mobilize sufficient public consent either to take unpopular actions in time or to persuade the trade unions to act in accordance with the national interest. At present our institutions which used to be uniquely successful in gaining consent are no longer capable of doing so because they have been perverted from their proper use.

There are, therefore, apart from terrorism, two threats to free and lawful government in Britain. The first threat comes from the inability of a free government elected by universal suffrage to ensure compliance with the law by trade unions and other organizations. Governments both here and abroad find it difficult to control multi-

---

*Of course the process of improving the constitution may include bringing the most powerful social forces within the constitution in new ways.

national companies, but in Britain the main danger is coercion of the government and the country by trade unions not by multi-national corporations.

The second threat to Britain's free institutions comes from the government elected by universal suffrage. Or rather it comes when the government that is elected is a Labour Government. Conservative Governments have many faults, but they do not pose a threat to freedom or to the constitution. Nor, of course, in the past did Labour Governments. The first Macdonald Government was at fault over the Campbell case, and Macdonald lied to the House of Commons. But there is nothing very unusual about that. Otherwise the first and second Labour Governments observed all the constitutional proprieties. Admittedly, in Opposition in the thirties, much of the Labour Party flirted with unconstitutional action, but Ernest Bevin and the trade unions largely kept it from straying far beyond bounds. Attlee's great post-war Government added seventeen seats to those proposed by the Boundary Commissioners. As these seats were all in boroughs, the Government cannot have expected to lose by the increase.[11] But otherwise it fully observed the rules and conventions of the British constitution. Even during Sir Harold Wilson's first period in office, Labour remained within the British constitutional tradition. True, Wilson and his Home Secretary, Mr Callaghan, tried to gerrymander the forthcoming general election by refusing to implement the proposals of the Boundary Commissioners. Those proposals would have stopped Labour winning more constituencies than it deserved. True, the general atmosphere of that Government was not wholesome; and the Crossman diaries make plain that the air in 10 Downing Street was even more foetid than was apparent to most outsiders. True, Sir Harold having declared that the Trade Union Bill was 'essential to the Government's continuance in office'[12] shortly afterwards capitulated to the trade-union chieftains, Mr Callaghan and much of the Parliamentary Labour Party. Yet Wilson was in general at that time trying to act in accordance with the constitutional conventions. His Government was not markedly sectional; on the whole it stayed within the consensus, and the Labour Manifesto of 1970 was a moderate document. That was the end of an era.

It is only since 1970 that the Labour Party has become a threat to the constitution, both in Opposition and in Government. Extremists have penetrated it at every level, and swung it violently to the Left.

As Lord George-Brown said in April 1972, 'in the fifties and sixties the men at the head of the Unions were genuine Social Democrats . . . Now, I think today that the situation is different. The major Unions are the subjects of a different kind of leadership, with a different outlook.' And he added shortly afterwards, 'We have been taken over. And we have been taken over by a collection of people who call themselves "activists". But they are for the most part people who do not believe in our way of life or in our social democratic outlook . . . And these fellows have now captured control of the Labour movement at every level; constituency parties; Trade Union branches; executives of the Trade Unions; the General Council of the TUC; the Labour Party National Executive; and the Shadow Cabinet.'[13] And of course the situation became much worse soon afterwards.

In 1973 the 'proscribed list' which declared various far-left organizations ineligible for application to the Labour Party and members of those organizations ineligible for membership of the party was abolished. This opened the way for far left MPs to cooperate with the Communist Party and with other outside-left organizations. In 1975 Mr Ron Hayward, the General Secretary of the Labour Party, visited East Germany and described the German Communist leader, Herr Honecker, 'as a man of wisdom and experience, very proud of the German Democratic Republic and with every right to be proud'.[14] In 1976 a report on Trotskyist infiltration into the Labour Party was for months ignored by the National Executive Committee, which then appointed a Trotskyist to be the party's youth officer. From 1974 onwards Mr Prentice and other MPs were under threat in their constituencies from various local Soviets and Commissars.

During his leadership, Sir Harold Wilson presided with benign indifference over the increase in the power of the Left at all levels of the party, occasionally indeed as in his support for Mr Hayward's appointment helping it on. Wilson's complacency, as he might have said, was the father and mother of extremism in the Labour Party. Yet after he had retired, Wilson warned an audience in Halifax that democracy was in danger in some European countries because of alliances between Socialist and Communist Parties. And he quoted the well-known limerick of the young lady of Riga who went for a ride on a tiger. Sir Harold knew what he was talking about. After all he had come to power two years earlier through the good offices of

Messrs McGahey, Scargill, Ramelson & Co. Only after he had dismounted from the tiger and left poor Mr Callaghan perched precariously upon it, did Wilson feel free to talk.

Then a few months later in December 1976 Wilson came nearer home and issued in Batley what he called 'a grave warning' about the infiltration into the party by 'small unrepresentative groups' of extremists. This was as though after his ship had been relentlessly sinking for some hours the Captain of the *Titanic* had issued a grave warning to the passengers about the dangers of icebergs. All that Wilson complained of had been clear to virtually everybody else for years, and all of it had taken place without serious obstruction by him while he was leader of the Labour Party.*

Yet even the steadily growing strength of the Left cannot justify the conduct of the Labour leadership after 1970. Except over Northern Ireland, the Labour Opposition ignored the national interest, the party's reputation for consistency, and its leaders' responsibility for the proper workings of the political system. Not for Sir Harold Wilson the courage of an Attlee over German rearmament or of a Gaitskell over unilateral disarmament. For him, party unity was all, and, apart from the temporary resignations of Mr Jenkins, Mr Thomson and Mr Lever, it was achieved at least on the surface. On the reform of industrial relations, on entry into Europe, on the control of prices and incomes, Labour successively repudiated what it had done or tried to do when in office. For Labour MPs, apostasy became not only a habit but a duty. Not even the Conservative Opposition under Bonar Law before the First World War had sunk so low.

If the Conservatives could have anticipated all this, they might have acted differently. Instead of introducing their own measure of trade-union reform, they might have done better to enact Labour's undoubtedly inferior proposals contained in Mrs Castle's 'In Place

---

*In a revealing letter to the *Daily Telegraph* on 17 December 1976, Wilson denied that he had not given similar warnings during his years as Leader of the Party and Prime Minister. But his denial proved the case against him. For even such a diligent historian of his own speeches as Sir Harold was only able to cite two utterances, and both of them were as late as the winter of 1975: his speech at the Party Conference and a later statement to the National Executive. Moreover, his criticism of the Left at the Party Conference of that year was characteristically offset by a harsher attack on the Right. Equally characteristically, Wilson's intervention in the Prentice affair was both late and ineffective.

of Strife'. Sir Harold Wilson and Mrs Castle might perhaps have had difficulty in waging all-out war against their own Bill. But one cannot be sure even of that.

On Europe, there was no chance of Mr Heath being able to appease Labour. After all, every single Labour leader, with the honourable exception of Mr Foot, had been a member of the Labour Government which had refused to 'take "No" for an answer in 1967' and which had renewed its application to join in 1970. Sir Harold Wilson's contention that the Tory terms were worse than Labour would have accepted was clearly untrue. Mr Jenkins, Mr Stewart, Mr Lever, Mr Thomson, and Lord George-Brown belied him. Even taken individually, each one of those men had a larger stock of credibility than Sir Harold Wilson; taken in combination the issue was beyond doubt. Yet Mr Wedgwood Benn and Mr Peter Shore were as happy to sit in a Cabinet intent on entry in 1970, as they were to stump the country in opposition to entry in 1971 and 1972.

On prices and incomes policy, Labour did at least have the excuse that if it had changed sides, so had the Conservatives. The excuse would, however, have been more plausible if Labour had from 1970 to 1972 urged some degree of wage restraint upon its trade-union allies, whose excesses in those years made the imposition of controls inevitable. But the CBI price initiative of 1971 elicited no response; and Sir Harold's maxim when he was in office that 'one man's wage increase is another man's price increase' mysteriously ceased to be true when he was out of it.

Hence the three most important fields of Conservative policy, where there was in reality a considerable measure of agreement between the leaderships of both parties, became party battlegrounds. Monsignor Knox once produced the epigram: 'The Government has turned its back on the people and now has the effrontery to claim that it has the people at its back.' Sir Harold Wilson turned his back on his (and Mr Heath's) policies and then had the effrontery to claim that Mr Heath was pursuing a policy of confrontation with the Opposition.

Sir Harold sank even lower than that. He supported direct action by the unions. The Labour Party officially supported the TUC's one-day general strike against the Government's wages policy and increases in food prices in May 1973. Then Labour did nothing to discourage the miners. Indeed Mr Foot said a victory for the miners would be a victory for the nation.* For parliamentary leaders to support direct action against laws passed by Parliament and to undermine the rule of law should be as inconceivable as the Chief of the Metropolitan Police inciting the police to deal with suspected criminals by force instead of bringing them to court. Indeed, a former leader of the Labour Party, J. R. Clynes, thought a political strike was not 'a blow at a Government, but a blow at democracy'.[15] Yet so far has the Labour Party sunk since then that its leaders have been prepared to support the giving of such blows.

In the British system the duties of the Opposition are almost as important as those of the governing party. Their prime responsibility is to preserve the allegiance of their followers and of the pressure groups that support them to parliamentary democracy and to the freedoms which should go with it. This is in a sense a governing function, and that is why the leader of the Opposition is paid by the state. Plainly that function is not performed if the Opposition deserts the main policies which the party tried to pursue in office. Still more plainly, it is not performed if the Opposition encourages or supports anti-parliamentary action. The Opposition should be helping to deliver the consent of their party to the parliamentary process. Yet from 1970 to 1974 Sir Harold Wilson and the Labour leaders did the exact opposite: they betrayed the Opposition's governing function. Wilson drew his salary as Leader of the Opposition but failed to perform the duties of his office.

The blame for the constitutional crisis cannot be laid exclusively on one party or on one man. Nevertheless the Labour Party, the trade unions and above all Sir Harold Wilson must shoulder by far the major part of the guilt. Anybody who doubts this must ask himself whether he seriously believes that there would have been a constitutional crisis, if Hugh Gaitskell had been leader of the Labour Party throughout the sixties and the early seventies.

Labour's attachment to the constitutional conventions did not grow with its return to office. It had adopted in 1973 an unpreceden-

---

*The Secretary of the TUC, Mr Murray, went to Belfast to take part in a march against the Ulster Workers' political strike in May 1974 and was pelted with eggs for his pains. He displayed admirable courage, but as he had himself only three months before been aiding and abetting a political strike against a lawfully elected Government, the derision he excited in Ulster should not have come as a surprise. But he was not the only Labour leader to exhibit political schizophrenia on this issue.

tly extremist programme, which threatened the mixed economy
and the rule of law. And though the Labour Government had only
a small majority or none at all in the House of Commons and was
supported by a smaller minority in the country than any previous
Government, it proceeded under the orders of the TUC to turn this
extremist programme into legislation.

Of course Governments have long been accustomed to get the
great bulk of the legislation that they want through Parliament. But
previous Governments had gained a much higher proportion of the
public vote, the policies they were pursuing were in general moderate,
and they were not ostentatiously governing in the interest, and at the
behest, of a section of the country. Mr Attlee, when his majority was
reduced by the 1950 election from nearly 200 to 15, realized that his
Government must take account of its reduced circumstances. 'Great
innovations', said Jefferson, 'should not be forced on slender
majorities.'[16] Though technically and legally there was nothing to
stop a Government with a very small majority behaving in the same
way as a Government with a very large one, Attlee knew that to do
so would break the conventions of the British constitution. Unfortunately Sir Harold Wilson had much less regard for the constitutional conventions than Attlee. The constitution for him was, like
everything else, of minor importance compared with the unity of the
Labour Party and the maintenance of a Labour Government in
office.

Yet a Government's outlook and conduct should be conditioned
by its majority in the House of Commons and the degree of support
it gained in the country. This is not merely a constitutional convention; it is a dictate of common sense. Of course a Government
possessing a small majority or none at all and elected with a small
percentage of the popular vote is not condemned to total inactivity.
The Queen's government must go on, and even a minority Government must govern. But the same considerations do not apply to
legislation. Big legislative changes and attempts to make 'an irrevers-
ible shift in the balance of power and wealth' should in those circumstances be removed from the parliamentary and Cabinet agenda.
The reason is simple. It is after all peculiar that a party which
narrowly defeats the other should then enjoy a monopoly of both
executive and legislative power. Such a situation is only tolerable if
the winning party conducts itself in the constant remembrance that
its monopoly is artificial. In other words it should keep its eye on

the majority who did not vote for it, as well as on the minority who did. Moderation is a constitutional convention as well as common prudence.

And that is of course even more true when a Government gained only 39 per cent of the votes cast, and only 28 per cent of those entitled to vote, together with the barest majority in the House of Commons. It is Labour's rejection of this fundamental restraint on Government and Parliament which has produced much of the present constitutional crisis.

Labour has sought to justify its flouting of the constitutional conventions by invoking the doctrine of the mandate. According to this doctrine, a Government has a right or rather a duty to carry into law the policies outlined in its election manifesto. Certainly parties when fighting an election should give the voters a general outline of their policy and as much information about their specific intentions as they feel able to give. Indeed they have no option but to do so, since except in the most exceptional circumstances voters would be reluctant to sign a blank cheque.

A Government should, then, try to keep confidence with the electorate by keeping to the general lines of the programme that it put before the country at the previous election. And if, which is rare, a general election is dominated by a single issue, the winner may be said to have secured a mandate for its policy on that issue. But that is a very different thing from a Government claiming the right or the duty to turn into law any proposal that it happened to mention in its manifesto. Manifestoes, and particularly Labour manifestoes, if we are to believe Richard Crossman, are often drawn up in a haphazard fashion after much haggling.[17] As a result proposals may appear in them which have not been thought out and do not have substantial backing.* In any case all the evidence shows that people decide their vote on general issues and impressions. Most voters are not concerned with the detailed policies, and many are not even aware of them. Besides, the vote is not subject to nuances. The citizen cannot vote 'Conservative, but . . .', or 'Labour, provided that . . .' He has to choose one party or abstain. He may indeed be voting more against the Government than for the Opposition.

*The comedian, W. C. Fields, had a good understanding of this process. Campaign resolutions like New Year resolutions, he wrote, 'are thrown together hastily at the last minute, with never a thought as to how they may be gracefully broken'.[18]

Moreover Labour leaders do not parade their Socialist zeal during elections. They parade their patriotism then; only after the votes have been cast do they sink gratefully back into factional Socialism.*

In these circumstances, the contention that every Labour voter endorsed every Socialist proposal in the Labour manifesto is obviously bogus. By voting Labour, an elector did not, as it were, turn his chosen party's manifesto into an affidavit which he has signed. He cannot reasonably be held to have assented to something that appeared on, say, page 19 in small print – and Sir Harold Wilson was a great artist of the small print – of a document which he has not read, and with much of which he would have disagreed had he in fact read it. Indisputably, for instance, Labour's nationalization proposals are disliked by most Labour voters. Indeed Labour voters often prefer Conservative policies. And in February 1974 Conservative policies were more in line with the preference of the electorate on almost all issues than were Labour policies.[19] But that did not prevent Sir Harold claiming a mandate.

The doctrine of the mandate is therefore fictional even at the best of times. But when a mandate is claimed by a Government that won only 39 per cent of the votes cast, the fiction becomes farce. Not even a notional mandate can be said to have been given, if a policy was not supported by a majority of the electors. Indeed a party which failed to get the support of as many as 61 per cent of the electorate may fairly be said to have obtained a counter-mandate: its controversial proposals have been rejected by the voters and should accordingly be dropped.

But if, despite the absurdity of the mandate doctrine, governments are going to claim a popular *imprimatur* for the small change in their election manifestoes, there surely should be a degree of reciprocity. The Labour claim that the minor parts of its manifesto are binding on Parliament and on the country should be balanced by the admission that the major parts of its manifesto should be binding on the Government. In other words a Government that breaks its major promises to the electorate, as have the Wilson and Callaghan Governments on inflation, unemployment and wage restraint, should feel compelled to go the people and seek a new 'mandate'. In fact the Government claims quasi divine sanction for its minor and divisive proposals which are then forced through Parliament, while giving

*During the February 1974 election Wilson mentioned Socialism precisely twice, and he rarely referred to nationalization except of North Sea oil and land.[20]

itself regular absolution for the breaking of all its major promises. This is proof that the so-called mandate theory is merely a tool of party management. It has no constitutional validity.

Nevertheless, it has damaging constitutional and political consequences. The more disreputable the measure, the more the doctrine is likely to be invoked, since *ex hypothesi* there is little else to be said for it. Parliament is sterilized and political life is impoverished. Parliament can do little to gain consent for a measure if everybody knows that its appearance in an election manifesto is the only argument for it and that parliamentary discussion will be a mere time-wasting ritual with a pre-ordained end. 'If you close the avenues of appeal between the citizen and the state in between elections,' Aneurin Bevan said in another context, 'then you must realise that human beings are not going to have the patience to sit down in resignation for five years until they have another chance.'[21] The mandate theory hinders Parliament from giving legitimacy to legislation, and it lends credence to Rousseau's gibe that the British people are free only at election times.

Either Governments should pay some attention to Parliament, in which case we should once again have a form of parliamentary democracy; or we should have a series of referenda, in which case we should have genuine plebiscitary democracy. Either of these alternatives would be preferable to what we have at present: a sort of plebiscitary democracy without the advantage of plebiscites.*

The mandate theory, then, provides no defence for the Labour Government's disastrous behaviour during its first three years. An extremist programme, which is itself an abuse of the constitution, has been rammed through Parliament, though the Government lacked a proper majority for it either in the House of Commons or in the country. That is another abuse. For a Government to force

---

*There is yet another heavy objection to the mandate theory. It (and also the pressures of two-party politics) encourages a party to enter into cut-and-dried commitments, so that it can then in office claim a mandate for them. But though it has gained a 'mandate', it may not be able to carry its policy out because it has not had the opportunity to discuss it and to negotiate with the interests involved, or it may be stuck with a policy which it then finds in office is not the best way of achieving its object. 'In politics and diplomacy', wrote Lloyd George, 'long intricate persuasion is an essential prelude to action.'[22] By substituting, in its search of a mandate, a blunt commitment for cautious and patient diplomacy, a party is likely to make the best policy both harder to find and more difficult to carry out.

through Parliament extremist legislation, which many of its supporters deplored, which the great majority of the public opposed,
and which it played down at the previous election, is a new and
sinister development. Moreover the Government has cheated in
Parliament itself. When the Aircraft and Shipbuilding Nationalization Bill ran foul of the parliamentary rules of procedure, the Government decided to change the rules. When that piece of cheating looked
like failing, the Government secured a majority for it by cheating
again and breaking a pair.

Again it tried to maintain its majority on Standing Committees
even when it had lost its majority on the floor of the House. And
finally in order to get its programme through, Mr Foot who in 1972
had said that the use of the guillotine showed 'full-hearted contempt
for the normal legislative processes of this country',[23] had to resort
in 1976 to guillotining no fewer than five Bills in three days.

The Labour Governments have thus been breaking the conventions of the constitution and the conventions of the two-party system.
If the British people want a fully Socialist state, presumably they are
entitled to get it. But quite plainly they want no such thing. They are
and for many years have been firmly against nationalization. The
moves towards a Socialist state are therefore taking place against the
wishes of the people. The electoral and parliamentary procedures are
being abused and manipulated by a minority of a minority to secure
an objective disliked by virtually everybody. But still the Left are not
satisfied. They continue to dredge up proposals to take Britain
further down the way to becoming an Eastern-European state.
Labour's Programme for Britain 1976 was overwhelmingly endorsed
by the Labour Party Conference. Yet it could not easily be supported
by anybody who wished Britain to have a solvent mixed economy
and to remain part of the Western Alliance; and one of its more
absurd proposals, the nationalization of the banks and the insurance
companies, was not dismissed out of hand by Mr Callaghan. It was
merely deprecated as being likely to do Labour electoral harm.

The danger is therefore obvious. The Wilson and Callaghan
Governments have done grave damage to the constitution, to the
economy and to personal freedom. The next Labour Government,
led perhaps by Mr Wedgwood Benn, would very likely complete the
process. British freedoms would be obliterated; they could not survive in a fully Socialist economy. The constitution would become an
irrelevance, to be disregarded at will before being finally buried, and

the British people would enjoy an Eastern-European standard of life.

The most important inference to be drawn from this is that the two-party system in this country is crumbling and will continue to crumble unless or until Labour reverts to being a moderate democratic party operating within the British political tradition. The two-party system has anyway been becoming under increasing strain, as the declining share of the electoral vote won by the two major parties clearly shows. In 1951 they gained the support of more than 80 per cent of the electorate; in October 1974 less than 55 per cent supported them. Probably some of this decline was inevitable as regional feeling grew in the Celtic fringe and elsewhere. Yet much of the nationalist feeling is caused by exasperation at British failure. Whether widespread discontent would by itself be enough to crack the two-party system, the continued defection of the Labour Party from it would be conclusive. For a two-party system to have any chance of working, the parties must be fairly close together; they must incline to the Centre rather than to their outside wings; and they must have a deep respect for the constitution. Since Labour's left about turn after the 1970 election, Labour has fulfilled none of these conditions. 'Within reasonable limits', said Salisbury, 'each party should accept the work of its predecessor and try, as far as it can do consistently with the public interest, to work it out to a satisfactory conclusion. And I do not think that in doing so we can be exposed to the imputation of inconsistency or of having changed our opinions.'[24] The Conservative Party has accepted Salisbury's advice. Indeed many of its supporters complain that it has accepted far too much of its opponents' work. Apart from denationalizing road transport and steel – but only once, not twice – and, probably unwisely, abolishing the Consumer Council, the Prices and Incomes Board and the Industrial Reorganization Corporation, incoming Conservative Governments have not sought to overturn the work of their predecessors. Attlee even regarded the denationalization of road transport and steel as 'a regrettable departure from precedent'. He pointed out that it had been the general practice of British politics 'not to seek to reverse the major actions of the preceding Government'. In contrast, Labour under Wilson has accepted no obligations to the continuity of the nation or the continuity of policy. It has even repudiated the policies it pursued when previously in office. That provides a graphic illustration of how far the Labour Party deteriorated under Wilson from the standards it observed under Attlee.

As Attlee put it, 'there is danger here for the stability of the country, especially when the reversal is not based on the national needs but merely on the ideological prejudices of a party'.[25]

In safeguarding and restoring the constitution, then, so that it once again becomes a guarantee of our freedom and a curb both on over-mighty subjects and over-mighty Governments, the Conservatives can expect no help from Labour, unless Labour moves sharply to the Right. The Labour Party as at present constituted is not interested in such things. Only if there is to be a counter-revolution in the Labour Party, and Labour returns to being a genuinely democratic party acting in the free and empirical tradition of British politics, can Labour once again play the honourable role it formerly played.

A Conservative Government with a big working majority and a realization that during the last few years Labour has betrayed itself may produce a revulsion in the Labour Party against extreme-left-wing policies. But since the present balance of forces in the party favours the Left, which may even succeed after an election defeat in transferring the election of the party leader from the Parliamentary Party to the Party Conference, only a determined optimist could be confident of the party's return to sanity.

Since the objective is to preserve parliamentary government, one otherwise theoretically conceivable remedy can be ruled out straight away: to put an end to democracy. Conservatives do not worship democracy. For them, majority rule is a device. Each individual no doubt *should* be the best judge of his own interests, and if he were, majority rule would be more than a device to Tories. But individuals do not always act in their own interest, as Halifax and many others have pointed out; still less do groups. Rational, economic, utilitarian man exists only in the imagination of some economists and philosophers. Similarly, majorities do not always see where their best interests lie and then act upon their understanding. For Conservatives, therefore, democracy is a means to an end not an end in itself. In Dr Hayek's words, democracy 'is not an ultimate or absolute value and must be judged by what it will achieve'.[26]And if it is leading to an end that is undesirable or is inconsistent with itself, then there is a theoretical case for ending it.

Yet as Sir Karl Popper has remarked, 'there are only two kinds of governmental institutions, those which provide for a change of the government without bloodshed, and those which do not. But if the government cannot be changed without bloodshed, it cannot, in most cases, be removed at all . . . I personally prefer to call the type of government which can be removed without violence "democracy", and the other "tyranny".[27] Conservatives wholly accept Popper's distinction, which cuts through much cant and hypocrisy about democracy. 'Numbers in a state', said Burke, 'are always of consideration, but they are not the whole consideration.'[28] In practice, no alternative to majority rule exists, though it has to be used in conjunction with other devices.* And in the Conservative Party, unlike the Labour Party, there is no extreme wing which hankers after the death of parliamentary democracy and the imposition of dictatorship. If our free institutions are overthrown or totally perverted, the Left not the Right will be responsible. There is no danger of a right-wing coup. Only if the constitution had already been destroyed by the Left, might the Right react and the Left find itself overthrown in its turn by a counter-coup from the Right.

Universal suffrage has therefore to be strengthened and supplemented not replaced. The object of constitutional reform is to avoid tyranny not to produce it. One of the justifications of 'prescription' is that constitutions and institutions rarely work as expected. More important than formal constitutions and laws are the customs, manners, traditions and ideas of those who work them. And since the results of conscious reform cannot be accurately predicted, natural evolution is preferred to conscious rational constitution-building. Most of the British constitution is not the product of conscious design. The control of the purse, for example, was Parliament's most effective weapon, but the House of Commons voted both Charles II and James II revenue for life; and the Act of Settlement forbade placemen to sit in the House of Commons, which would have prevented Cabinet government.

Yet plainly 'prescription' does not rule out positive reform. Burke himself led the movement for 'economical reform' which led as he said to constitutional reform;[29] and the Reform Acts, the introduction of the ballot, the elimination of corrupt practices at elections, and the Parliament Act are conspicuous examples of conscious constitutional reform.

*Free states tend to be more efficient than dictatorships. In the end Nazi Germany had two rival general staffs for the army with Hitler arbitrating between them. Hitler even used to instruct two representatives to bid for the same picture. 'The result was', Speer writes, 'that Hitler's two emissaries kept fearlessly outbidding each other long after all other bidders had dropped out.'[30]

Hence, the right Conservative approach to reform is to change enough to preserve freedom, ensure the rule of law, and improve the effectiveness of government, while building so far as is possible on what is already in existence and not carrying out any more alteration or destruction than is absolutely necessary. Within that broad objective the aim must be to increase the prestige and effectiveness of Parliament. The chief function of Parliament is and always has been to gain consent. Even if Parliament itself is working well, that function will not properly be performed if the rest of the system is working badly. Equally, so central is the House of Commons still to our constitution, that the system cannot work well if the House of Commons is despised and disregarded and hence unable to deliver the consent of the nation to acts of government. In 1930 when the crisis was economic not political, Lloyd George said that if Parliament failed, the working population would not 'believe any longer in the old inadequate windmill set up by Simon de Montfort to mill the corn for the people, and they may be incited to do their own milling in their own way'.[31] Today the crisis is political and economic, and unless the whole country begins to find the windmill less inadequate than they do now, parliamentary government may become a thing of the past. As much as in 1832, some alterations in the constitution are necessary, if Parliament is to procure the consent of the nation.

A more powerful second chamber would be a help. The present House of Lords works well enough when the Government and the House of Commons behave themselves. It is then a useful adjunct. But its hereditary and appointed composition emasculate it. 'The House of Lords', Rosebery once said, 'will pass in a storm.'[32] It has lasted longer than expected, but as at present composed it cannot preserve the constitution, and if it did not pass in a storm it could not prevent one. The same would be true of any nominated assembly. The House of Lords can only be strengthened by becoming a predominantly elected body. One or two countries dispense with a second chamber, and in Canada the Senate is nominated. Elsewhere the second chamber is elected, and at least where there is Cabinet government the second chamber does not attempt to rival the other House. The common belief that an elected second chamber would usurp the place of the Commons is therefore ill-founded. Even if Australia in 1975–6 is considered a partial exception, the rule holds.

For the sake of continuity, some of the present hereditary and life peers should probably be included in the reformed Upper House. And the members of the European Parliament probably should also be *ex officio* members of the second chamber. The rest of the House of Lords should be elected preferably on a regional basis for, say, six years with, like the American Senate, a third up for election every two years; and the House's powers of delay except for money bills should be restored to the two years laid down by the Parliament Act of 1911. Such an assembly would enjoy sufficient prestige to be able to hold up hasty and ill-advised legislation, and it would provide some protection for the constitution.*

'How anyone can fear', Sidney Webb told the Labour Party Conference in 1923, 'that the British electorate, whatever mistakes it can make or may condone, can ever go too far or too fast is incomprehensible to me. That, indeed', he added, 'is the supremely valuable safeguard of any effective democracy.'[33] The British House of Commons at present can go too far too fast and in the wrong direction. Effective democracy needs an additional safeguard, and a strengthened House of Lords would keep the Government and the Commons more in tune with the electorate.

Nevertheless there is a limit to what an elected House of Lords could achieve. Incessant quarrels between the two Houses would be likely to bring democratic government into further disrepute, and would not in any case lead to good government. If a Labour Government had much of its legislation held up, there would be a political crisis. And since the Labour Party as at present constituted probably would not accept the increased powers of the second chamber, even if they had been sanctified by a referendum, there might be a constitutional crisis as well. A second chamber is not much of a bulwark against a revolution. The only sure way to prevent a revolution is to prevent a revolutionary situation arising. And a rejuvenated House of Lords would be little help in that. So an elected House of Lords should be an aim, but it would only take us part of the way. It would restore some balance to the constitution. But a second chamber cannot atone for the sins of the first.

Asked on television at the beginning of the 1970 election campaign if he would allow a referendum on the Common Market, Sir Harold Wilson said: 'The answer to that is no . . . I'm not going to trim to win votes on a question like that . . . I shall not change my attitude

*It would also give a useful knock to the mandate theory, since no party could know that it would be able to pass its controversial legislation into law.

on that.'[34] And though Sir Harold Wilson reaffirmed his attitude a year later when he said: 'I oppose a referendum . . . I have always done so,'[35] those who did not take his 'No' for an answer turned out to be fully justified. Sir Harold duly changed his mind for political convenience, and the Labour Party became committed to a referendum.

Fortunately the referendum in England has some more respectable antecedents than that sleazy episode. Balfour, Asquith, Baldwin and Churchill at one time or another all favoured a referendum. Admittedly the expedient was to some extent discredited by its association with dictators seeking to give a democratic façade to their rule. As Attlee put it in his reply to Churchill's suggestion in 1945, 'I could not consent to the introduction into our national life of a device so alien to all our traditions as the referendum, which has only too often been the instrument of Nazism and Fascism.'[36] Yet as Philip Goodhart, the leading advocate of this country of the use of the referendum as a constitutional improvement as opposed to an aid to party unity, has cogently argued,[37] the device has proved a useful adjunct to representative assemblies in a number of successful democracies.

That is just as well, for whatever its merits the referendum is here to stay. Sir Harold Wilson's claim that the referendum on Europe was a unique event never to be repeated was always palpably absurd. As the French say, '*C'est le premier pas qui coûte.*' Almost certainly no great constitutional change could now be introduced by a Government, which was concerned to preserve our constitutional freedoms, without a referendum. The voters would demand their 'rights', and the opponents of the change would have an almost unanswerable case in demanding that the proposal should be submitted to the people. And quite apart from anything else, the referendum is too useful an instrument for Governments in trouble to be now solemnly renounced for ever and ever. The argument therefore is not about whether the referendum should ever be used again but about the circumstances in which an issue should be put directly to the country. It is only in answering this latter question that the merits of the referendum are now relevant.

In 1970, when he was still opposed to referenda, Mr Powell pointed out that if a Government proposed one course and a referendum chose the other, then unless the Government resigned, the result 'would be, quite literally, irresponsible government'.[38]

Again, a Government should have a general strategy, and its range of policies should be consistent with each other. Obviously such consistency becomes very difficult if some of the decisions are made by Parliament and some by referendum. The complexity of modern government is unquestionably very great, and almost every sphere of activity affects every other one. Voters casting a vote on a single issue cannot be expected to be fully aware of all its ramifications. Yet too much can easily be made of this argument; a Government's policies are often quite inconsistent with each other even without the intervention of referenda. A more serious objection is that referenda are easily abused. President de Gaulle was not a dictator, but his referendum on direct election of the President in 1962, which improved his position, broke the constitutional rules.[39] Both the wording of the question and the timing of the poll may be rigged by the Government in its own favour. The holding of a referendum may enable a Government to hang together, when its fall would be in the national interest. Referenda may provide a field day for public-relations firms and the manipulation of opinion as the experience of California has demonstrated.[40] A direct popular vote may be careless of the rights of minorities, but then so may the votes of a temporary majority of the House of Commons. Certainly a referendum cannot take account of the intensity of a vote; the nearly indifferent voter counts as much as the one who has a passionate conviction. Representative assemblies are better able to weigh opinions. These make a formidable array of objections to referenda.

Yet the referendum on Europe was undoubtedly a success. Turnout was high; the great majority of the voters came to the right decision and they refused to be swayed by demagogic scares about unemployment. All the same, it was not wholly reassuring. Though the issue had been on and off the political agenda for nearly fifteen years, public ignorance remained high. More than half of those interviewed were unable to answer correctly a single one of six questions about the EEC.[41] Their knowledge of British politicians was almost as sketchy. In view of Sir Harold Wilson's series of conversions and deconversions, the 13 per cent of the electorate who did not know whether he wanted Britain to stay in Europe or come out can scarcely be blamed. But Mr Powell became anti-European in the late sixties, so the 37 per cent who did not know his position and the 5 per cent who thought he wanted to stay in had less excuse. And Mr Roy Jenkins had been consistent throughout, yet 34 per cent did not know his position and 9 per cent thought he was in favour of leaving Europe.[42] These figures tend to bear out the widely held view that the result of the referendum was determined less by voters' opinion of the European issue than by the fact that the politicians they respected and liked were in favour of Europe, while those they did not like or trust were against it.*

Nevertheless, the referendum effectively settled the European issue. In addition it must have had some beneficent educational results, though it also delayed the taking of urgently needed economic measures. Mr Goodhart is surely right in thinking that the referendum, if judiciously used, is a useful aid to Parliament and not an enemy of it. It is also, the evidence suggests and Lord Hugh Cecil believed, usually conservative in its effects. In any case, as has been said, the referendum is not going to disappear. But the balance of advantage seems to lie in confining it to constitutional issues; otherwise we should run the risk of going over entirely to plebiscitary democracy, and of parliamentary democracy being effectively abandoned.

'The Referendum', wrote Dicey, 'is the people's veto; the nation is sovereign and may well decree that the constitution shall not be changed without the direct sanction of the nation.'[43] Dicey's view was embodied in a new clause which Balfour unsuccessfully moved to the Parliament Bill in 1911. This said: 'A Bill which (a) affects the existence of the Crown or the Protestant Succession thereto; or (b) establishes a National Parliament, or Assembly, or a National Council in Ireland, Scotland, England, or Wales, with legislative powers therein; or (c) affects the qualification for the exercise of the Parliamentary franchise or affects the right to vote at any Parliamentary election, or affects the distribution of Parliamentary seats; or (d) affects the constitution or powers of either House of Parliament or the relations of the two Houses one to the other; shall not be presented to His Majesty nor receive the Royal Assent under the provisions of this Act unless and until it has been submitted to a poll of the electors and approved at such a poll in accordance with the Schedule to this Act.'[44] Those words seem still applicable today.

Although it has obvious dangers, the referendum will thus probably improve our constitution. But it will not be enough to enable

*Mr Powell was a partial exception. Many voters liked and respected him: he was the sixth most popular politician. But many other voters did not like or trust him: only Mr Paisley and Mr Wedgwood Benn were more unpopular.[45]

the two-party system to function, if one of the two parties is determined to break the rules.

A third possibility is to incorporate a strengthened second chamber, the use of the referendum, and other reforms into a grand constitutional settlement. In effect this would mean a new fixed constitution for the country, and there would be a new Bill of Rights. A written constitution has many supporters, the most notable of whom are Lord Hailsham and Sir Leslie Scarman.

The object of the new constitution would be to entrench and safeguard rights which are today threatened by the votes of an unrestrained temporary parliamentary majority. In Scarman's view 'the helplessness of the law in the face of the legislative sovereignty of Parliament . . . makes it difficult for the legal system to accommodate the concept of fundamental and inviolable human rights'. Unless, Sir Leslie believes, there is 'a Bill of Rights protected from repeal, amendment, or suspension by the ordinary processes of a bare Parliamentary majority controlled by the Government of the day, human rights will be at risk'.[46] As well as protecting human rights the new constitution would be able, possibly by introducing federalism, to create a coherent and consistent structure out of the devolution muddle. Conflicts between the various parliaments and assemblies could be settled by the courts. And the judges would also reconcile any conflicts between English law and our international obligations.

Lord Hailsham believes that our constitution shows 'unmistakable marks of disruption and dissolution', and that a new one must be created if our freedoms are to be preserved. Otherwise the 'elective dictatorship' of the House of Commons will filch them one by one. He envisages 'nothing less than a written constitution for the United Kingdom, and by that I mean one which limits the powers of Parliament and provides a means of enforcing these limitations both by political and by legal means'.[47]

The proposal of a new constitution and a Bill of Rights has many attractions, though it is far from being a conservative idea. But there are almost as many difficulties. Fixed constitutions with their guarantees of every known right provide more of an illusion of safety than safety itself. The Soviet constitution guarantees freedom of speech and freedom of assembly. Most fixed constitutions last longer than did the Jacobin constitution of 1793, which was suspended immediately it had been approved and then stuffed into a glass case in the

Hall of the Convention.[48] But with the notable exceptions of the American and the Swiss, fixed constitutions have not had long lives.

They may be better than nothing while they are alive. Yet political questions do not become constitutional or legal merely because they are fought out before judges. Judges and courts are not a constitutional elixir. The record of the American Supreme Court up to 1936 was no better than that of the House of Lords up to 1911.[49] And during the last war the Supreme Court permitted far worse treatment of the Japanese Americans by its Government than anything that was meted out in Britain by a Government less subject to judicial control.[50] 'Judges like other men', as Justice Frankfurter said, 'are too apt to be moved by the deep under currents of public feeling.'[51] Of course, a British written constitution could be less judge-ridden than the American. As in Switzerland, the laws of the subordinate legislatures could be subject to judicial review and the laws of Parliament immune from it. But then that would remove much of the point of introducing a fixed constitution guarded by judges.

A federal solution would be tidy, and it would ensure that every citizen of the United Kingdom had the same rights and obligations. But a federal constitution does not provide immunity from nationalist attack and separatist agitation as the history of Quebec demonstrates. Besides, federalism is usually thought to necessitate a second chamber in which the constituent elements in the federation enjoy virtually equal representation, and for England to have the same representation as Wales or Northern Ireland would seem eccentric. Admittedly there is a greater disproportion between New York and Nevada, but such a discrepancy is less glaring in an assembly of fifty states than one of four. Also a federal Britain would either require a separate English Parliament or produce complications about Celtic representation in the Lower House, much greater than those created by devolution. Some of these difficulties would be removed if England were split into eight regions, but few people want another upheaval in local government, and regional sentiment in England is very unevenly spread.

Yet the British constitution never has been tidy, and to many Conservatives, most notably Burke and Disraeli, that has been one of its principal virtues. And never at any stage of our history has every citizen or every part of the United Kingdom had exactly the same rights and obligations. For example, by the time universal suffrage had been attained Northern Ireland had a devolved assembly. There would therefore be nothing inconsistent with British constitutional history and nothing inimical to Tory constitutional attitudes in making constitutional arrangements for Scotland or for Wales which did not extend to the rest of the country. Such arrangements would merely reflect the fact that the situation was different in the various parts of the kingdom.

To give to Scotland by devolution what was in effect, say, a federal system without imposing federalism elsewhere seems to me quite feasible. Nearly 150 years ago John Galt commented that every new Parliament saw a 'continual increase of Scotchmen'.[52] After devolution, that increase would have to be cut back. The ratio of Scottish MPs to their electors should at the most be no more than the ratio in England. But the objection that Scottish MPs would have a vote on, say, housing and education in England while English MPs (and also Scottish MPs) would have no control over those subjects in Scotland seems legalistic. Whatever happens in England will have great influence on what is done in Scotland, since great disparities between England and the rest would not be tolerated in the devolved areas. It is not therefore unreasonable that the Scots should be allowed some influence on decisions made for England. That surely would not be too high a price to pay for the maintenance of the Union.

Many believe that once devolution for Scotland is embarked upon, there is no logical stopping place before independence. Even if that were true, British statesmen and constitution builders have not previously allowed logic unduly to influence or deter them. The logic of the great Reform Bill pointed to universal suffrage, but there was an interval of ninety-eight years between them. And an independent Scotland seems to me to be far more probable if England blocks devolution than if it promotes it.

'There has been in England', Sir Walter Scott wrote many years ago, 'a gradual and progressive system of assuming the management of affairs entirely and exclusively proper to Scotland, as if we were totally unworthy of having the management of our own concerns.'[53] Over the years there has been much administrative devolution to Scotland. Yet Scotland has not in general been well governed, and the feelings described by Scott are still strong.

Moreover, Britain is one of the most over-centralized countries in the world. Conservatives believe in the dispersal of power not in its concentration, in diversity not uniformity, in constitutions being workable and acceptable not symmetrical, and in solving the problem of the day not those of the distant future. Hence, the strong antipathy to devolution of many Conservatives is not easy to understand. 'For God's sake, sir,' wrote Scott, 'let us remain as Nature made us, Englishmen, Irishmen and Scotsmen! We would not become better subjects, or more valuable members of the common empire, if we all resembled each other like so many smooth shillings.'[54] That surely expresses the proper Tory attitude to devolution and to much else besides.

Devolution aside, a deeper objection to a new grand constitutional settlement is that no Parliament can bind its successors, and that 'constitutional' laws which are entrenched by one Parliament could be dug up again by a future Parliament. They might be treated as open to repeal by a simple majority in the same way as any other laws. Lord Hailsham, a high authority, believes on the contrary that the new constitution could be securely entrenched by a constituent assembly laying down certain categories of laws which could not be changed by a simple majority and then submitting the whole package to the electorate in a referendum.

But even if this solved the legal difficulty, it would not solve the political difficulty. New constitutions do not immediately engender deep and widespread loyalty. They need time to take root in the minds and hearts of both the governors and the governed. And with the Labour Party as it is at present, there is little prospect of Labour fully accepting the sort of fixed constitution which its promoters wish to see established. A constitution which was not accepted by one of the main parties in a two-party system could not possibly achieve its object of preserving constitutional liberties and making the country easier to govern. Even if Labour observed the letter of the new constitution, which in view of its behaviour in Parliament since 1974 is not something that could be taken for granted, it would be likely to break the spirit.

There would be constitutional quarrels. Democracy, as de Tocqueville observed in the last century, is disdainful of forms. Labour would be all the time telling the electorate that measures which were vital for their welfare were being held up by legal and constitutional flummery. The American Fisher Ames described constitutional checks as 'cobweb ties for lions'.[55] Demagoguery would probably overthrow the newly established constitutional checks and balances. In a two-party system a new constitution must have the strong backing of both main parties, if it is to survive. Otherwise the first article of the new constitution and the Bill of Rights would have in effect to read: 'There must always be a Conservative Government.' Until therefore Labour changes its spots, a new constitution is unlikely to be successful. And if Labour does change its spots, a new constitution will lose its urgency.

So far we have been considering ways of restraining potentially tyrannical Governments from further eroding British freedom and imposing their ideological prejudices on the British people, the great majority of whom are strongly opposed to them. A more fruitful approach may be to try to stop such Governments being formed.

An electoral system can only be judged by its results. Arguments about theoretical or practical fairness are irrelevant, unless the alleged unfairness of the system reduces its acceptance in the country. The test of an electoral system is that it should produce good government and that it should enjoy the allegiance of the voters.

Traditionally there have been two chief arguments for the single majority vote used in Britain. The first is that it is the system which is in possession (since 1885) and has by and large been accepted for many years. The second is that it tended to produce a two-party system. Up to 1945 democracies with a two-party system evidently had a better chance of survival than those with multi-party systems. Single-party Governments seemed to be stronger and more stable than multi-party coalitions.

The party system is usually the dominant feature of a constitution. In Britain the two-party system (which may be defined as one in which there are nearly always at least three parties only two of which have any chance of forming a Government) was not intended. It was the outcome of national continuity. And of course it has not always prevailed. But until recently, with one or two obvious exceptions such as the period before the First World War, the party system has tended to unite the country. The parties have been able to deliver the allegiance of their supporters to the constitution. Because they have had to win a majority or a near majority of the country, the main parties have had to be as broad and comprehensive as they could, and to keep their own zealots in control. This entailed at least a blurring of ideology. The parties' search for voters drew them together. Their consequent centrism not only mirrored the centrism of the voters, many of whom often vote for one party while more in agreement with the other, but also prevented violent shifts in policy when there was a change of party in government.*

Recently however these advantages of a two-party system have not been apparent. Indeed the two-party system itself has barely been apparent. In October 1974 more than 45 per cent of the electorate were either unwilling or unable to vote for either of the main parties. In addition, in the election of February 1974 the party winning the most seats did not win the most votes,† and the Liberals won six million votes and only fourteen seats, a result which many people thought massively unfair. Yet the Liberal figures were more the result of a breakdown in the political system than in the electoral system. Many voters support the Liberal Party because they are in agreement with its principles and policies. But most people vote Liberal because they are opposed to the two main parties.‡ When therefore the Liberal Party is able to pick up six million votes, the two main parties have been failing in their job. Still, whatever the cause, a repeated Liberal vote of five or six millions would probably make electoral reform irresistible.

A more likely cause of electoral reform, however, is the failure of the present machinery to deliver either stable, effective and moderate government or the essential consent of the voters. Only two of the last five general elections have produced a Government with a clear working majority, and nobody could accuse the 1974 Labour Governments of moderation. The Labour Party fought the last two elections on more-left-wing platforms than ever before, and Labour's Programme 1976, which was massively endorsed by the Labour Party Conference, is a good deal more Marxist than the programme of Signor Berlinguer's Italian Communist Party.

With the two-party system in its present condition, which is largely caused by the defection from it of the Labour Party but also by the alienation from it of large numbers of voters, and with the failure of British Governments either to pursue consistent policies or to gain

*The two-party system is discussed in *The Body Politic*, pp. 23–62.

†This also happened in 1929 when the Conservatives were again the sufferers and in 1951 when Labour gained 231 000 more votes than the Tories and twenty-six fewer seats. However, in Northern Ireland four Conservative candidates in seats with a total electorate of 292 000 were unopposed.[56]

‡My favourite Liberal voter was the lady at the February 1974 election who complained to me that Sir Alec Douglas-Home had not tried sufficiently hard to reach a settlement 'with nice Mr Ian Smith'. She was therefore going to vote for 'Bomber' Thorpe and the Liberals.

the consent of organized groups, it is only sensible to look at other methods of voting. Since the war, after all, many European countries with proportional systems have fared much better than Britain.

The single transferable vote (STV) in constituencies of five or six members is thought by many reformers to be the best electoral system.* Superficially it is the 'fairest' in the sense that under it fewest votes are 'wasted'. But all electoral systems are to some extent unfair, and as Professor Duncan Black has pointed out 'there is a certain arbitrariness' about STV in that it gives the 'same weight to votes of different kinds'.[57] STV is used by numerous institutions in various countries and by the World Federation for Mental Health. It has also been used with some success in Northern Ireland, but it is the main machinery for political elections in only two countries: Malta and the Republic of Ireland. The list system of proportional representation is much more widely used, and virtually the whole of Western Europe save for France and Germany uses one or other of its forms.

France uses the second ballot, which is a superior form of the alternative vote, but it is the German system which, apart from the STV, has attracted most attention in England. This happily combines first-past-the-post elections in single-member constituencies with an element of proportionality, so that parties end up with seats in the Bundestag in proportion to the votes they received in the country. And if we are to change our electoral system, the German procedure, with the modifications suggested by the Hansard Society's Commission on Electoral Reform which was chaired by Lord Blake, for the House of Commons, and the STV for any assemblies that are set up in Scotland and Wales seem to me the best solution.

No electoral system is ideal, and none is certain in its effects. No change, therefore, can be guaranteed in advance to be beneficial. Yet the dangers and defects of our present system, as it is at present working, are manifest. 'I do not think', Churchill wrote to Beaverbrook in 1930, 'there will ever be a Government in England capable of restoring the position, which has not got behind it a real majority of the Nation.'[58] Since 1918, only in 1931 and 1935 has an elected Government had a real majority of the nation behind it, and our present system is unlikely to produce such a majority. When it could be more or less assumed that decisions taken by Parliament and

*See, for example, Enid Lakeman, *How Democracies Vote*, and Joe Rogaly, *A Handbook of Electoral Reform*.

the Government would be obeyed, the absence of a majority in the country was not a crippling objection. But now the legitimacy and authority of the state are threatened by terrorists and anarchists, by the nationalist movements, and by organized groups, in particular the big trade unions. And a Government which rested on the support not only of a majority of the House of Commons but also of a real majority in the country would surely be in a better position to assert the national over a sectional interest than a Government which had won the support of only 40 or 45 per cent of the electorate. 'Entire nations', Lloyd George wrote, 'are not yet, not even in war, on the parade ground where Ministers can bellow at them orders which must be implicitly and promptly obeyed on peril of the guard-room.'[59] But, too often now, it is not Ministers but trade-union leaders who are bellowing the orders or threatening the disobedient with the guard-room; and the strengthening of the power of the ballot box and of Parliament against extra-constitutional forces would be even more welcome to almost the entire nation than to the Ministers of the day.

No less important, the need for Government to be based on a real majority would demand either a broadening of one of the main parties or a coalition Government so that extremism would be ruled out. In other words electoral reform would help to deal not only with the first threat to the constitution of social forces refusing to obey Parliament but also with the second threat of an extremist Labour Party imposing Marxist chains upon an unwilling country. After electoral reform, no Labour Party led by Mr Wedgwood Benn, say, would ever win a majority in the country. If the Labour Party wished to participate in government it would have to shed its Marxist–Trotskyist wing or make it impotent. Thus the main argument for electoral reform is that it would prevent control of Governments by extremist minorities.[60]

Namier thought that by the eighteenth century the House of Commons had come 'to represent, not so much the sense of the community, as the distribution of power within it . . .'[61] Now it does not represent either. The economic power of the community is not properly represented in it, and because of the growing power of the left wing of the Labour Party the sense of the community is not properly represented in it. A glance at the legislation passed by the Labour Government in 1974–6 is sufficient to establish that. De Gaulle's belief that parties are more a barrier between the people and

H

Inside Right

their destiny than a channel between people and government has certainly been true of the Labour Party of the last three years.[62] If the House of Commons cannot be reformed so as to represent both the power and the sense of the community, it can be reformed so as to represent at least one of them. And electoral reform on the German model should ensure that the sense of the community was properly represented. Any such change in the electoral system, together with a reformed second chamber and the rules for future referenda, would presumably have to be approved by the country in a referendum.

Naturally electoral reform would not be unalloyed gain. The Liberals would probably gain many more seats in the House of Commons, and the Conservatives when in office would normally be in coalition with the Liberals or with the resuscitated Social Democrats. Coalitions bring their own problems. But the idea that coalition leads to weak government is quite as mythological as the idea that a single-party Cabinet leads to strong government. In any case coalition, or even opposition, would be a small price to pay for saving British freedom.

Besides, as was pointed out in Part Three, Chapter 3, there is nothing new in Conservatives being partners in a coalition. They would merely be once more putting the interest of the country and of Conservatism above the narrower interests of the Conservative Party. In the years ahead Conservative Governments are going to have to do so many difficult and unpopular things that they will need a real majority of the nation behind them. And of course electoral reform would only be a recognition of what is at present an accomplished fact: Labour's effective desertion of the two-party system.

In my view, a two-party system and an unfixed constitution is the highest form of political development yet seen. Unfortunately owing to the current political infantilism of the Labour Party it seems at present too high for Britain. It depends upon informal checks and balances and the self-restraint of politicians. As Coleridge might have said, the 'idea' of the two-party system is vital to its success. And the Labour Left certainly have no 'idea' of a two-party system. Their idea is a one-party system. Should Labour regain its maturity and return to what it once was, then electoral reform would be unnecessary though some constitutional reform would still be vital. Maybe the next Conservative Government will be faced by a moderate responsible Labour Opposition determined to observe the conventions of parliamentary democracy. In that case the two-party system can resume its sway, and the constitutional crisis will have been resolved with merely piecemeal constitutional reform. But if Labour moves Left instead of Right, then a change in the electoral system seems to me the most conservative as well as the most effective way of preserving and strengthening the British constitution.

6. The Economy

Why remember we not, what, and, how many contradictions we
finde and feele even in our owne judgement? How many things
served us but yesterday as articles of faith, which today we deeme
but fables?

Montaigne[1]

I have no great faith in political arithmetic.

Adam Smith[2]

This coal strike is the beginning of a revolution. Power has passed
from the King to the nobles, from the nobles to the middle classes
and through them to the House of Commons and now it is passing
from the House of Commons to the Trade Unions . . . There are
unpleasant years before us.

Sir Edward Grey in 1912[3]

And happed to hear the land's practitioners
Steeped in conceit sublimed by ignorance,
Prattle fantastically on disease,
Its cause and cure . . .

Browning[4]

'We are not cotton-spinners all,'[5] Tennyson rejoiced in 1852. Had he
been living now, his scorn would have been directed at other
targets. He would probably have written 'We are not civil servants
all – at least not yet.' Tennyson could afford to despise commercial-
ism and the bawling of the 'niggard throats of Manchester'; Britain
was then the leading industrial nation. Today we cannot afford to
disdain those who manufacture wealth; Britain has been declining
industrially for over a century. And now not nearly enough of us are
'cotton-spinners' or engaged in profitable industry and commerce.

As Messrs Bacon and Eltis have convincingly shown there are too
few producers[6] in this country and far too many people trying to live
off them. The number of people employed in industry fell by nearly

two million from 1966 to 1974. Between 1961 and 1974 employment by local authorities rose by 54 per cent and by central government by 9 per cent. The ratio of non-market expenditure to marketed output increased from 41 per cent to 60½ per cent (before tax) in the same period. Bacon and Eltis's explanation of Britain's poor economic performance is that 'successive governments have allowed large numbers of workers to move out of industry and into various service occupations where they still consume and invest industrial products and produce none themselves; their needs have, therefore, been met at the expense of the balance of payments, the export surplus of manufacturers, and investment in industry itself . . .' The taking away by taxation of 'an increasing proportion of what workers produce' explains the great acceleration of wage inflation. 'The militant and obstructive trade union activity from which Britain has suffered' has been the consequence not the cause of Britain's economic failures.[7]

Bacon and Eltis have done as much as anybody else to illuminate Britain's economic problems. We suffer from high inflation, high unemployment, low production, low growth and an unstable exchange rate. Some of the disciples of Bacon and Eltis seem to think that the structural fault in Britain's economy of too few people in the productive sector is the sole explanation of our poor economic performance. This seems unlikely. Nothing explains everything. Moreover Bacon and Eltis themselves show that in Sweden, Norway and Denmark there was an even faster shift into public services than in Britain without those countries experiencing the difficulties suffered here.[8] And there are a number of other likely causes of Britain's economic decline: a ramshackle trade-union structure, too much inefficient management, too many changes in government policy, too much nationalization and state control, inadequate incentives, a fairly widespread reluctance to work hard, bad industrial relations, excessively high taxation, hostility to change, obsessive Treasury secrecy, restrictive practices, etc.

For a Tory, politics are more important than economics: political and social consequences are more important than purely economic considerations. Coleridge taught the importance of each individual, and stressed that no human being can be treated merely as a means to an end. Thus labour is not, and *a fortiori* should not be treated as, a normal commodity; and it is perhaps insensitive to talk of the labour market, and thus implicitly to ignore the wider human considerations. The good of the community must rank far higher than any so-called principle of economic orthodoxy – especially since there is no Tory economic orthodoxy. As Baldwin said in answer to those who claimed that the Ottawa Agreement of 1932 had imposed a permanent system of protection on the country, 'Nothing is permanent except the folly of mankind . . . if it fails, the system will be changed, and that is the common sense of the matter.'[9]

Certainly there is nothing permanent about the wisdom of economists. In the mid-sixties Professor Devons remarked that 'the speed at which fashion changes in current [economics] theory . . . is quite staggering',[10] and in his Keynesian days Mr Brittan was 'struck by the enormous power of fashion in economic policy'.[11] That is still true.

The Times is now a citadel of monetarism, from which have been launched thunderbolts against the economic policy of the last Conservative Government. It was not always so. Shortly before Lord Barber introduced the second of his expansionist budgets in 1972, *The Times* was clear that 'political and economic judgement alike require the Chancellor to go all out for full employment'. And after Lord Barber cut taxes by £1200 million in his budget with the intention of raising the rate of growth to 5 per cent, *The Times*'s verdict was not that he had been too ambitious: '. . . it is by no means certain', *The Times* considered, 'whether he has done all that was required of him on either economic or social grounds'.[12]

Mr Patrick Hutber of the *Sunday Telegraph* is now an uncompromising if entertaining Friedmanite. Yet he greeted Lord Barber's 1971 Budget with the words 'it's a long time since there has been a Budget with so much to applaud in it'. Of the 1972 Budget, after saying he had 'always been a Barber fan', Mr Hutber wrote that 'every rational man would risk stop–go again rather than endure a million unemployed'. It was, he concluded, 'unquestionably a great Budget'.[13] The thinking of the doyen of economic journalists, Mr Samuel Brittan, has undergone a similar evolution during recent years, but Mr Brittan's conversion was completed by the early seventies.

Mr Heath and Lord Barber were criticized by Mr Bacon and Mr Eltis for damaging British industry by their imposition of price controls in order to secure wage restraint.[14] But in 1962 Mr Eltis made the opposite criticism of the then Conservative Government. 'In the two years 1958–60 . . . dividends on ordinary and preference shares increased by 34 per cent, while weekly wage rates increased by $5\frac{1}{2}$ per cent and weekly earnings by $11\frac{1}{2}$ per cent. 'This kind of "free for all",' he commented, 'is naturally very discouraging to wage restraint.'[15] Again, Mr Eltis savaged the Keynesian conventional wisdom in the *Lloyds Bank Review* of December 1976. But in 1962 he was telling his readers that the solution to the problem of unemployment was well known, and that any British Government which allowed substantial unemployment was 'guilty of negligence'. The solution was 'to give people all over the country more money to spend'.[16] Was ever the Keynesian conventional wisdom more pungently expressed?

Of course distinguished economists, newspapers and financial commentators have at least as much right to change their minds as politicians. And indeed in allowing their views to be altered by changed 'circumstances', they can be said to have behaved in a proper conservative manner. But changes of doctrine of an absolutist kind by experts, often in a short space of time, as well as the great differences of opinion between experts, provide a warning to Conservatives not to be too influenced by the prevailing economic fashion. Many Conservatives became hooked on Keynesianism; they should now beware of addiction to the harder drug of monetarism. Much as well dressed women do not slavishly follow every outlandish whim of the fashion designers, but adapt the changes in fashion to suit themselves, so Conservatives, whether or not they agree with Professor Nisbet that economists 'know very little',[17] are wary of wholeheartedly embracing every new economic doctrine and prefer to make only cautious adjustments to their economic views. No doubt there is a tendency for Conservatives, like Keynes's practical men, to be addicted to the last economic orthodoxy but one, and to be the slaves of some defunct economist. But even that may be better than to be the slaves of the current economic orthodoxy. At least old-fashioned orthodoxies have been mellowed by time, and their adherents are less likely to cling to them with the proselytizing zeal of converts.

The natural Tory scepticism about the claim of any economic theory or orthodoxy to a monopoly of the truth has a stronger foundation than merely the frequent changes of mind by the experts and the mutations of orthodoxy into heresy and back again to orthodoxy. It is not unusual in any kind of science for there to be two competing and incompatible theories; indeed for long periods they may coexist and be used side by side when relevant despite their incompatibility. Sir Karl Popper discusses a classic instance in his autobiography, when between the wars 'modern physics was in turmoil'. One theory was based on the idea of particles, and the other on waves.[18] Eventually the incompatibility was resolved by a higher hypothesis. Popper's basic philosophic position, that our understanding of the world proceeds by a series of decreasingly unreliable hypotheses which are gradually reconciled and strengthened by testing, offers impressive philosophic support to a pragmatic attitude to economics. 'Strictly logical conclusions based on insufficient data', Namier pointed out, 'are a deadly danger',[19] and in politics and economics our data are invariably insufficient. Strict application of a theory whose truth is far from being certain is no less dangerous. Explanation, in Popper's words, 'is always incomplete'. And theories, he thinks, 'can only be understood as tentative solutions of problems . . .'[20] This well fits the Tory position that no single economic doctrine or policy is capable of wholly explaining, guiding, or predicting economic activity, in the same way that all political doctrines and policies are themselves defective.

Accordingly, in a period of competing theories, the wise Tory will be eclectic. He will agree with Harold Macmillan's remark about Enoch Powell that in the study of financial and economic problems 'fanaticism' is 'inappropriate'.[21] He will not look for single causes or total solutions. He will instead use whatever aid is at hand, and with many theoretical doubts he will proceed with cautious empiricism. In economics as in politics, abstraction is the Tory enemy.

The eclectic Conservative feels no call to become either a card-carrying Keynesian or a card-carrying Friedmanite. He carries no cards. He is not adverse to governmental intervention in the economy. He sees it as a fact of life throughout the Western world. But he does not believe that a Government can now necessarily spend itself out of a recession without causing unacceptable inflation. In the last three years he has seen high public expenditure in conjunction with both inflation and unemployment. He accepts that monetary policy is important, and he considers it to be an essential weapon against inflation. He has noted that even some anti-monetarist economists concede its usefulness.* But he does not believe that monetarism has turned economics into one of the natural sciences, so that an increase in the money supply can be infallibly predicted to produce a given rise in prices two years later. He agrees with Keith Joseph that 'Monetarism is not enough'.[22]

*For example, Sir John Hicks in *Lloyds Bank Review*, July 1976, p. 18, and Francis Cripps and Martin Fetherston in *Economic Policy Review*, March 1977, pp. 48–54.

The eclectic Conservative, then, eschews what may be called vulgar Keynesianism and vulgar monetarism. He may even like to think that his position is close to that of Keynes himself. Just as Marx was not a Marxist, and St Simon not a St Simonian, Keynes was not a Keynesian. He was for much of his life a monetary economist. Had he lived, he would surely not have allowed his pre-war insights during a depression to ossify into post-war dogma during an inflation. He believed in interfering with capitalism to make it work and to make it acceptable, and there the cautious Conservative accompanies him. But in his earlier writings he emphasized the importance of the quantity of money; and there, too, he is accompanied by the cautious Conservative.

Eclectism is appropriate for the Conservative not merely because economic theories conflict but because the British economy fits into no clearly defined category. The Conservative is not faced with a consistent or logical construction. He is faced with a mixed economy – Professor Ball has called it 'the mixed-up economy'[23] – in which market forces, producer groups, nationalized industries, the welfare state, multi-national companies, powerful trade unions, the Government and the consumer are all thrown together without pattern, without agreement as to means or ends, in an astonishing, if not particularly productive, diversity. Any theory that was able adequately to comprehend so variegated a scene without distortion could not be simple.

Rejecting reliance on any single theory and rejecting all simple solutions, the Conservative is naturally predisposed in favour of a market economy, that is to say an economy in which the consumer rather than the politician or bureaucrat decides what shall be produced. He prefers the market (or workable competition) for both political and economic reasons. It is decentralized and pluralistic. It operates by consent not coercion. It is libertarian not bureaucratic. It is much more efficient.

The City of London is a good example of the market in action. It is highly competitive, and there is no monopoly. As Humbert Wolfe who worked in the Board of Trade put it:

> 'In the City
> they sell and buy
> and nobody ever
> asks them why.

> But since it contents them
> to buy and sell,
> God forgive them!
> They might as well.'

We may not only forgive them but thank them. We need not be effusive about it; people in the City are generally quite well rewarded for their efforts. But we should be quietly grateful. The City of London is one of the parts of our economic system that works undeniably well. It makes an indispensable contribution to the balance of payments; and if the rest of the economy was anywhere near as successful, Britain would not have an economic problem. The City with its full range of financial and commercial services embraces probably the least imperfect markets in Britain, and it should suffer the minimum of state interference.

Yet the Conservative is fully aware that in some other parts of the economy there is either a very imperfect market or none at all. Plainly there is no market when there is a state monopoly, which is one of the reasons for Conservatives being in general opposed to nationalization. Even many so-called Socialists are doubtful of the benefits brought by state monopolies, and a Conservative can hardly be expected to be more Socialist than they are. He remembers the reasons Socialists used to give for nationalization. Not even Herbert Morrison's worst enemy would have accused him of being a starry-eyed idealist. Yet he said when moving the nationalization of coal in the House of Commons in 1946: '. . . and particularly to the miners I would say, emancipate yourselves from the understandable inhibitions created by the past. Emancipate yourselves from the mentality thrust upon you by a crude capitalism. This is vital, this is essential, if this socialized industry is to take with it miners and management, to become co-operators and partners in a great and worthy adventure for the common good.'[24]

Fantasy apart, the record of the nationalized industries has been poor. Virtually everybody knows this except the British Labour Party. After forty years of Social Democratic government in Sweden, only 7 per cent of Swedish industry was nationalized. The Conservative does not rule out nationalization if, as with Rolls-Royce, for defence or other reasons a company has to be kept in existence. But he will only nationalize if there is no alternative, and for both economic and political reasons he will be looking for ways of reducing the over-grown nationalized sector.

Nor, clearly, is there a market in the welfare services provided by the state. Even if, as is almost certainly necessary as well as desirable, some of those services are financed by charges as well as by taxes, there will still not be a market.

In the private sector of industry there is obviously more of a market. But the Conservative appreciates that there must be a framework of rules or laws to ensure the fulfilment of those conditions which make a market desirable. A market without a legally enforced framework would be as absurd as a society without government or laws; it would be a jungle in which the politically and economically powerful prevailed to the growing disadvantage of the rest of the community. Untrammelled market forces are likely to lead to the destruction of the market. That is why a Conservative Government is always prepared to intervene to improve the functioning of the market, and why for example the Conservative Governments in the 1950s passed legislation on monopolies and mergers in the private sector. Besides, such things as the planning of cities, the building of roads, the prevention of pollution cannot be left to the market. And elsewhere very large companies, monopoly unions (which are not subject to the laws against monopoly) or the presence of the Government as a monopolistic buyer, as it is in defence, often prevent a market in the classic sense from operating. So, often, does the complexity of modern life. Companies are frequently unaware of opportunities to export. They may not know enough about what is happening in the rest of industry. They often cannot find out what the Government's policy is going to be on, say, energy; and impending changes in taxation are normally concealed from them. For the market to work properly, the competitors in it need much greater knowledge than they can on their own usually possess.

For all these reasons the Conservative does not regard the market as something sacrosanct on which a profane government should not intrude. Certainly a business man has better things to do than to fill in government forms or bury himself in volume after volume of statutes to find out if his company is breaking one of the myriad laws which bind it. Yet while bureaucratic interference can be diminished, it cannot be abolished. In a highly interdependent society and economy, government and industry have to live together, not apart. 'Government', Harold Macmillan said when he was Prime Minister, 'has to appear as the partner of industry, which shares its profits and losses, as its patron, as the user of its products, as the champion of the consumer, as the director of scientific research, as providing educational facilities for technical and industrial staff, as the initiator of new policies, as the creator of a spirit of confidence and enterprise.'[25] Government is inextricably involved in every free economy even in those which are the most market orientated, such as the German, the Japanese and the American. Indeed today the state with its specialized services is a vital and central part of the market mechanism.

There is no ideal extent of governmental intervention. 'The position of government in industry', as Mr Macmillan once put it, is 'not a principle, it is an expedient.'[26] What that position should be varies from time to time and from country to country. In Britain the pendulum has swung too far. There has been too much government meddling, and too much of it has been incompetent.

It is, above all, the trade unions which make the application of any simple theory to the British economy virtually impossible. The unions are of course as great a stumbling block to Socialist or egalitarian theories as they are to free market or other economic doctrines. While professing to be Socialist, their Socialism is strictly for others. They favour the progressive extension of law and controls throughout all the rest of society, while providing virtually unlimited licence for themselves. They preach Socialism, while themselves remaining the last bastions of nineteenth-century *laissez-faire*. If anything in this country would be improved by a little Socialism, it is the structure and attitude of the trade-union movement. But nothing is further from the minds of trade unions, which creates a difficulty for Socialists as well as for the unions. As Oliver Lyttelton said in 1948, 'the Socialist General in the Socialist-run battle commands everything except the troops'.[27] Left-wing union leaders can combine extreme Socialist beliefs and extreme *laissez-faire* behaviour only in a free society. In the Socialist society of their dreams they would have to behave very differently. In a fully Socialist country, the unions would be fully socialized, that is to say wholly controlled by the state, or they would not exist at all. For the time being the difficulty is resolved by pretending it does not exist.

Trade-union egalitarianism is also only for others. Privileges are not objectionable provided they are trade-union privileges. And differentials are for all except the most unskilled unions an essential element of Socialism in action.

In any case the British trade unions are probably the most powerful politically of any in the world. They are formally united: the Communists work within the T U C instead of as in many other countries having their own confederation; and there is no Catholic or Liberal trade-union body. Moreover the Labour Party is now probably more dependent on the unions than is any other Socialist party. This is partly due to the constitution of the Labour Party, which gives a preponderant place to the unions, in contrast with Germany, for example, where there is no organic connection between the S D P and the unions, and where indeed any such connection is forbidden by the constitution. But in recent years it has been due more to the decline of the constituency Labour Parties. The unions are virtually the only things that are left. And they provide the money.

Whereas American trade-unionism has in numbers scarcely advanced in the last quarter of a century,[28] British trade-unionism has gone on expanding and there are now eleven million people in trade unions affiliated to the T U C. The British unions combine large membership and great power with widespread unpopularity. Hostility to them is not confined to people who have been inconvenienced by their anti-social behaviour. It extends to the union membership itself. In 1976 two out of three trade-unionists thought that trade unions had too much power, and well over half thought that the unions were 'controlled by a few extremists and militants'.[29]

The trade-union bosses have often been compared to the robber barons of the late Middle Ages. And certainly in the damage they have inflicted on the economy, and in their ruthless disregard for everybody's interests but their own, the comparison is reasonably close. But by itself it underestimates the trade unions. A closer comparison is with the late medieval Church shortly before the Reformation. Like the medieval Church, the British trade-union movement has been a strong brake upon the country's economic progress, and like the Church it has steadily amassed political and economic power. Just as the Church claimed and achieved great privileges from the state, so have the trade unions. In industrial disputes, trade unions are allowed to do many things which would be illegal if done by anybody else. And recently they attempted to extend this very broad 'benefit of clergy' to individual breakers of the criminal law. Hence the agitation on behalf of the so-called 'Shrewsbury Two'.

The trade-union leaders are as unrepresentative of their rank and file as was the medieval Church of the laity, or as were the bishops of the inferior clergy. And as the medieval Church was heavily involved in politics, so is the trade-union movement. Similarly much as bishops looked to Rome as well as to Whitehall, so do some trade-union leaders look to Moscow rather than to Westminster. The existence of the medieval Church created for its more fervent adherents a conflict of loyalties. Their loyalty to the Church competed with their loyalty to the Crown. Similarly the existence of the trade unions has created a dual loyalty among trade-unionists, for many of whom their trade union seems more legitimate than the state. Indeed for the more extreme there is no dual loyalty. Their only loyalty is to the trade-union movement. The British state is merely the class enemy.

This trade-union legitimacy has been enhanced by customs, ritual and incantations which have attained a quasi religious status. Thus to handle goods that have been 'blacked' is as unthinkable as was sacrilege for the devout. And for some trade-unionists the picket line has become as sacred as any image or holy place. To join a picket line is as meritorious as going on a pilgrimage, while in British life today the only mortal sin is to cross one. The ultimate sanction of trade unions like that of the Church is excommunication.

Finally, much as Luther believed that the Church of his day was a barrier between the Christian and his God, so trade unions are now an obstacle to the prosperity of their members. By their insistence on restrictive practices, overmanning, government *pourboires*, and inflationary wage claims and strikes, trade unions have slowed economic growth, fuelled inflation, increased unemployment, and undermined the authority of the state. Whatever the other reasons for Britain's economic failure, strong trade unions are certainly one of them. Although they did so in the past, these costly antiques do not now further the interests of their members.

Nevertheless Britain is heavily unionized and is likely to remain so. The average trade-unionist regards union membership as insurance against unemployment and hardship. The average householder probably would not insure his house, if to do so meant that he was more likely to be burgled or that his house was more likely to be burned down. And that is the situation of trade-unionists as a whole. But it is not true of individual trade-unionists. So long as other people are in trade unions, the trade-unionist usually does not suffer more by being in a union than outside one. And often, of course, he has little choice.

Trade-unionism is not going to fade away. Indeed trade-union failure has a self-reinforcing element: the worse the economy performs because of trade-union action or other reasons, the more do people feel the need of protection by trade unions. The political task therefore is to make trade-union activity less self-destructive and to bring home to the average trade-unionist that union power is only legitimate within limits, that it should be subject to the rule of law and parliamentary government, and that he has obligations to his country, to the community, and to his family as well as to his union. Most trade-unionists are patriotic, moderate and law-abiding citizens who are well aware of all these things. But they are unable for various reasons to put their beliefs into action. Yet in the course of time there is no reason why nearly all trade-unionists should not come to realize how damaging trade-unionism, as at present practised in this country, is to them and everybody else. British trade unions, instead of being a rein on economic progress, will then become like unions in some other countries. Duelling, which was every bit as irrational a custom as some trade-union 'blacking' and instant strikes, died out when public opinion no longer tolerated it and the duelling class came to realize its folly. With luck the same processes are even now at work on trade-unionism as practised in Britain since the war. But whereas the Reformation in the sixteenth century caused a proliferation of Churches, any trade-union reformation will need to involve a shrinking in the number of unions. The shipbuilding industry in Britain, for example, has fourteen unions; in other countries there is one or at the most two.

Restrictions on combinations were removed in this country long before they were removed elsewhere,[30] and trade unions in the past performed a useful political and social function. They were voluntary associations, which Conservatives welcome as giving their members a sense of belonging and as blurring the harsh line between the state and the individual. They also provided some protection for their members. Up till the mid-sixties, moreover, the trade unions were more often than not a brake on Labour's extremists. 'Our job now', Vic Feather told me in 1962, 'is to keep the Labour Party sensible, to support Gaitskell and squash Mikardo and Silverman.' But now that they are compulsory coercive institutions trade unions do not perform a useful social role, and their political power has in the last decade all too seldom been exercised in favour of moderation.

Trade-union influence on government may perhaps be dated from the Treasury Agreement between Lloyd George and the trade-union leaders in 1915. According to Lloyd George, Balfour who was present seemed bewildered by seeing 'those stalwart artisans . . . on equal terms negotiating conditions with the Government of the day' and 'by this sudden revelation of a new power'. Lloyd George himself was clear that government could not be carried on during war or peace 'without . . . the cooperation of Labour'.[31] Between the wars the General Secretary of the TUC once told Sidney and Beatrice Webb that Conservative Governments had consulted the TUC more than Labour had,[32] but it was only with the arrival of Ernest Bevin as Minister of Labour in the wartime coalition that consultation with the TUC became normal. It has remained normal, and union power and influence have been considerable ever since.

This growing power is not trammelled by the legal curbs that trade unions are subject to in every other country. Carson said that, as a result of the 1906 Trades Disputes Act, the situation was 'the King can do no wrong: neither can a Trade Union . . .'[33] Since then trade unions have had privileges heaped upon them, notably by the second Wilson Government, but have given little in return. The law does not control the TUC; the TUC does not control individual unions; and many unions do not control their members. The resultant anarchy is not amiable, and British industrial relations are more chaotic than those of any of our competitors. Sir Harold Wilson tried to bring some law and order into union affairs, but was foiled by Mr Callaghan and others. Then he himself joined with his erstwhile opponents to sabotage Mr Heath's attempt to do the same thing. Hence the unions are largely above the law, and in addition to their political power have unusually great industrial strength.

There are several possible ways of dealing with trade-union power. The first method is the so-called social contract, which Sir Harold Wilson modestly called 'the boldest experiment in civilized government' that the world had ever seen.[34] So much for Athens, Rome, the American constitution and the growth of parliamentary democracy! To many of those whom allegedly it was intended to help as well as to those who were always beyond its pale, the social contract has seemed more like a suicide pact than anything else. Many people's savings have been wiped out, taxes and inflation have rocketed, and hundreds of thousands of jobs have been lost. The social contract resolved the conflict between the unions and the state by effectively giving the control of the Government to the TUC. No wonder more than half the public recently thought Mr Jack Jones was the most powerful man in the country, and only 25 per cent thought that accolade should be awarded to the Prime Minister, poor Mr Callaghan. The country has been a heavy loser from the social contract. Its results have always been disastrous except for the TUC and the leaders of the Labour Party. The talents possessed by trade-union chieftains do not include those necessary to govern the country.

Another method has been proposed by Mr Peter Jay, who believes that the combination of a commitment to full employment, powerful trade unions, the inherent impossibility of a sensible and effective incomes policy, and 'trade union monopoly bargaining' produces a level of inflation that in the not-so-long run is bound to lead to the collapse of parliamentary democracy. For Mr Jay, whose despair has presumably been heightened by the failure of the Social Democrats, the only way to salvation is to 'disalienate' the workers by turning them into 'the entrepreneurs of the firm' in which they work. 'Ownership and ultimate control of enterprises' would be given 'to the people employed by them', trade unions would wither away, and everybody would live happily ever afterwards in a world of workers' cooperatives and strict monetary policy.[35] Mr Jay's economic qualifications are considerable, the democratic illness he diagnoses is undoubtedly real, much must be done to 'disalienate' the workers, and there is certainly a place for more workers' cooperatives. But his proposed remedy for the British disease is a prime example of what Reinhold Niebuhr once called 'the strategy of fleeing from difficult problems by taking refuge in impossible solutions'. There is not the remotest chance of Mr Jay's plan being carried out in the foreseeable future, and not the remotest chance of its working as he envisages if it were. The idea that a change of ownership leads to a change of attitude among the work force, which as we have seen used to be naively entertained by Socialist politicians, has been disproved by the experience of nationalization. The miners, say, would be unlikely, merely because they were now the owners, to split themselves up into competing 'entrepreneurial' entities and to forgo the power that a monopoly gives them. And if they were split, they would be unlikely to remain split if their interest lay in recombining. Hence the only difference made by a change of ownership would be, by eliminating the National Coal Board, say, slightly to increase the power the unions already possess to hold the community to ransom. (This is also the objection to Peter Walker's suggestion that we should consider denationalizing some of the nationalized industries – though not the mines – by making their employees the owners.)[36] Mr Jay thinks his 'formula' might 'not be applicable to certain reserved sectors of the economy, such for example as the public utilities'.[37] But in some of these sectors the workers have the power to do enormous damage to the economy and even to bring it to a stop. If these workers saw themselves compulsorily excluded from the joys of Mr Jay's Arcadia, they could scarcely be expected to be more amenable than they are today. So if Mr Jay's formula is more applicable to them, it becomes less not more feasible. In any case, as Michael Oakeshott has reminded us, syndicalism is an even greater threat to freedom than collectivism.* And Mr Jay's proposals would be much more likely to lead to a syndicalist state with the trade unions even more belligerent and powerful than they are today than to the cooperative bliss of a world without union coercion.

A third possibility, favoured by some, is to smash union power by very high unemployment. The trouble is that the free society would probably be smashed at the same time. At the very least, high unemployment is unlikely to help the promulgation of free-market doctrines or to cement loyalty to the country's free and democratic institutions. Those who talk, Lord Butler said after the war, 'about creating pools of unemployment should be thrown into them and made to swim'.[38] In any case, quite apart from the waste and misery involved, the ambition is unattainable. 'A monetary policy that would break the coercive powers of the Unions by producing extensive and protracted unemployment must be excluded', Dr Hayek has laid down, 'for it would be politically and socially fatal.'[39]

A fourth method is to deny that the problem exists. For those who hold this view trade unions are not powerful. A sensible financial policy and sufficient competition in the economy are all that are required to ensure peace and prosperity. To such people any co-operation or even discussion between Government and the unions and industry is the beginning of the corporate state. Any such corporate hanky-panky is a derogation of parliamentary sovereignty, and if the corporative forces will not go away they will be kept in their proper place by the pressures of the market.

*See Part II, ch. 8.

These thinkers maintain that trade unions have no direct role in generating inflation, since excessive wage claims will not produce a general increase in the price level unless the Government expands demand to accommodate the wage increases. Inflation is thus entirely the fault of Governments which in their cowardice have increased the money supply instead of permitting large-scale unemployment and industrial difficulties. This attitude is an example of the urge for dogma, for certainty and for single-cause explanations in economics and politics. After all nobody would ever be run over if pedestrians always kept away from roads. But that does not lead people to blame every road accident upon the pedestrian instead of upon the motorist. To put all the blame for inflation on Governments is no more sensible. The absolution of trade unions from direct responsibility for the inflation resulting from their wage claims seems, as Lord Robbins delicately puts it, 'a slightly fanciful . . . approach to the explanation of what happens'.[40] Besides even if the Government does not expand demand after an excessive wage round, it will not necessarily prevent a rise in the price level. There will be a rise in bankruptcies, a rise in unemployment and probably higher prices as well.

Curiously, many who denounce an incomes policy as a dread step down the path to corporatism often take a very corporatist attitude to unemployment. They say that under a system of cash limits in the public sector and with the increase in the money supply unalterably fixed, unions will have to decide whether they want higher wages or higher unemployment. Now this may well be sheer realism and common sense; if unions insist upon pricing their members out of jobs, perhaps nobody can stop them. But to welcome private bodies or organizations rather than the Government fixing the level of employment is surely corporatist. And the difficulty cannot be avoided by pointing to the allegedly democratic features of trade unions. Trade-union leaders are not representative of their rank and file, as a wide range of Labour politicians has from time to time testified and as public-opinion polls have confirmed. There is a fundamental difference between handing over the making of decisions to private individuals and giving the power of decision to large conglomerates of power. So an anti-corporatist policy leads to corporatism.

The fifth possibility is to recognize the power of the trade unions and other producer groups and to try to work with them through consultative procedures, called in Germany and France 'concerted action', as suggested in the Conservative Party document 'The Right Approach'. This idea is in no way at variance with the Tory tradition, though it is contrary to other traditions.

For authoritarians of the Left and the Right, interest groups are anathema. They themselves embody the public interest, and therefore interest groups can only distort that interest and thwart the wishes of the ruler. Thus Hobbes complained of corporations in the state being 'worms in the body politic'.[41]* And Rousseau believed that if 'the general will' was to be truly expressed, it was 'essential that there be no subsidiary groups within the state . . .'[42] (French society under the *ancien régime* had been pluralist.[43]) The Abbé Sieyès followed Rousseau in repudiating pluralism and maintained that 'corporate interest' led to 'conspiracy and collusion'; therefore social order inflexibly required 'that no citizens must be allowed to organize themselves in guilds'.[44]

Conservatives are on the other side. They are aware of the corporatist tradition in England. 'The representatives who appeared in Parliament', wrote Maitland, 'were not representatives of inorganic collections of individuals, they represented shires and boroughs.' Maitland thought it was only a 'little too definite to say that they represented corporations aggregate'.[45] Leo Amery also thought that representation in the House of Commons originally had 'a real functional basis'. But, he said in 1947, 'our geographico-arithmetical constituencies' had largely 'lost their justification as the basis of a representative system', and he advocated a new Reform Act, which would create 'a "separate House of Industry" or "Sub-Parliament" ' so that 'the new principle of functional representation can in this way be tried, without destroying the existing geographical principle'.[46]

Earlier, in 1930, Winston Churchill after wondering 'whether institutions based on adult suffrage could possibly arrive at the right decision upon the intricate propositions of modern business and finance', suggested an 'Economic Sub-Parliament, debating day after day with fearless detachment from public opinion . . . without caring a halfpenny who won the general election'.[47] Lord Eustace Percy favoured a similar body.[48] The Economic Council recommended by

---

*Mussolini pretended that his fascist state was a 'corporate state'. But in Italy as in Spain the trade unions and other corporations were entirely under the control of the state,[49] and Mussolini's Italy and Franco's Spain were no more corporate than they were democratic.

Harold Macmillan in 1938 would have been composed of 'representatives of every department of Government concerned with economic
policy; representatives of the Central Bank, the Investment Board,
the Foreign Trade Organization, and the Industrial Advisory
Council; representatives of the appropriate National Organization
of Employers; representatives of the Trade Union Congress General
Council; and selected individuals of eminence in the fields of
economic science and any other branches of learning from which
expert assistance could usefully be recruited'. For Macmillan, the
Economic Council would have been 'the keystone of the structure
of a planned economy'.[50]

This line of thought was continued after the war by Walter Elliot
as well as by L. S. Amery. 'A new entity has emerged in the body
politic', Elliot said in 1955, 'the power of the Trade Unions to intervene in an organised fashion in our lives, either to promote or to
bring to a dead stop the intricate processes upon which a modern
state depends . . . Are we not', he asked, 'witnessing the emergence of
a new Estate of the Realm – a new strand in our national make up
lacking which the nation cannot work. It is the hall mark of an
Estate of the Realm that it can vote supplies. We can vote the supply
of money; . . . the Trade Unions can vote the supply of labour
without which, equally, the affairs of the state can not be conducted.'[51]
Elliot's conclusion was that an industrial parliament was needed.

Very recently Mr Vernon Bogdanor, after quoting Disraeli's
remark in the *Vindication* that 'the great art in creating an efficient
representative government is to secure its representation of those
interests of the country which are at the same time not only considerable, but in their nature permanent', has advocated the integration
of the two types of representation 'territorial representation through
the House of Commons and functional representation through
interest groups'. Interest groups would be 'organized in a proper
representative system', and a House of Industry which would be able
to propose legislation but which would be an advisory not a legislative assembly would be created.[52]

The degree of corporatism in a country is determined not by the
presence or absence of corporate institutions but by the nature and
extent of corporate power. An ill man does not become healthy by
refusing to recognize his illness, nor does he become more ill if his
illness is diagnosed and treated. He may even be cured. Despite the
great strength of producer groups in Britain, especially the trade

unions, Britain is less well endowed with organizations of cooperation than other countries and with the traditions of communication needed to make them work. Moreover the British party system and the centralization of the country have placed the making of nearly all political decisions in Whitehall. The deference the executive used to pay to Parliament has disappeared in the last few years. Parliament can still not be separated from the executive; nevertheless any sharing of power – indeed even of thought – with producer groups would, if anything, be more a loss of power by Whitehall than by Westminster. In reality, of course, it would not be a loss of power by either. It would merely be the recognition of loss of power – a very different thing.

During his premiership Mr Macmillan set up the National Economic Development Council, which is a recognizable sketch of his grand design of the 1930s. The Council has done much valuable work, and it should now be strengthened, as the last Conservative election manifesto 'Putting Britain First' suggested, in order to make it 'a better industrial forum'. Its membership should be widened, and some of its proceedings should be in public and preferably televised. Both sides of industry would be subject to public scrutiny. No longer would they be able to get away with the easy assumptions or obvious contradictions which can pass unchallenged in the trade-union conference hall or in the directors' board room. Trade unions would be forced to argue how higher wages could be paid without adding to inflation or increasing unemployment. Industry would be forced to explain the defects of management, obsolete techniques and inadequate training.

'In a period of freedom for all', the leader of the transport workers, Frank Cousins, said with apparent logic in 1956, 'we are part of the all'.[53] Unfortunately there is no reason why the collective pursuit of self-interest should be in the public interest. Adam Smith's 'invisible hand' is not laid upon collectivities. 'When a gang of real-estate agents, bond salesmen and automobile dealers gets together to sob for service', H. L. Mencken pronounced, 'it takes no Freud to surmise someone is about to be swindled.' Adam Smith made the same point with more restrained irony.[54] Trade unions would not necessarily be led to act in the public interest at all times and in all respects, even if they were purely economic institutions. In fact they are more political than economic. They are affiliated to the Labour Party, and their leaders have strong political, if often conflicting and contradictory, ideas and ambitions. Many of them seek to further those ideas and ambitions even to the detriment of the interests of their own members. Their belief in competition is confined to their right to compete with other unions to secure the largest possible wage claim. And even if they try to hold back, they are pushed on by militants on the shop floor. The enforcement of cash limits and a strict monetary policy will do much to promote realism. But unions may call strikes against cash limits or even against a refusal to increase the money supply. In addition even the enlightened self-interest of a union may be contrary to the public interest: an excessive wage claim by a union may lead not to its members but to the members of other unions or to non-unionists losing their jobs. And Britain's primitive trade-union structure with its multiplicity of unions makes rational behaviour far from easy.

The great advantage of a public industrial forum would be that union leaders would have to argue their claim against other union leaders. At present wage claims still tend to be regarded, erroneously, as struggles between the unions and the employers or between the unions and the Government, instead of as a struggle between unions as to the relative amounts each group should get. This truth is obscured by the present system and would become clearer after argument in an industrial forum.

People get very excited over incomes policies. It is hard to understand why. There is much dogma on both sides, none of it helpful. Certainly in this country incomes policies have not always worked well. But then not having an incomes policy has not worked well either. So long as there is a large public sector, no Government can avoid having an incomes policy for the public sector. After all, on any economic view, public-sector wages are an important part of public expenditure. And the Government's incomes policy is more likely to work in the public sector, if wages there do not fall too far out of line with wages in private industry. Unquestionably a statutory policy should be avoided if at all possible. Unquestionably an incomes policy should not disturb differentials. Unquestionably, too, a Government should not pay a high price to the unions for an incomes policy, which is as much in the unions' interest as in that of everybody else. And such a policy must be backed up by a strict financial policy not wrecked by profligate public expenditure. An incomes policy, formal or informal, cannot tackle inflation by itself.

But, when all is said, the object of an incomes policy is to further the public good by persuading people to behave more responsibly in their own interest. Yet they can scarcely be persuaded to behave in such a way, indeed it may not be in their interests to do so, unless other people do the same. And they cannot know that other people will so behave unless there is an incomes policy. Besides, as was argued earlier, to leave decisions on the level of employment in the hands of union leaders is far more corporatist than for the Government to take them together with the unions and industry. The level of unemployment has in any case implications for the survival of a free society, and a number of union leaders do not believe in a free society. They are therefore peculiarly unsuitable people to be put in sole charge of decisions about employment.

Again the discussion, and if possible the achievement, of an incomes policy should take place in public in an enlarged NEDC. This body, incidentally, would be useful even to those who do not believe in incomes policies. 'Under a monetarist theory', James Douglas has written, 'the subject matter of the dialogue with the Trade Unions would be different (demarcation rules, apprentice arrangements, etc. rather than wage rates) but the Unions' voice and their consent would be as crucial as before'.[55] There would therefore be plenty to discuss.

In his original, suggestive and occasionally not wholly clear book *Centripetal Politics*, Professor Ionescu writes that 'faced with the prospect of increasingly ungovernable societies . . . the representative governments relinquish their positions as unique national policy-makers and seek "partnerships" or "contracts" with' the most important 'corporate forces'. For Ionescu, the ' "politics of concertation" is the technique of policy-making in which the horizontal process of consultation–commitment replaces the vertical process of command–obedience'. He points out that 'the thoroughly liberal, and thoroughly parliamentary German system of politics' borrowed the French 'concept of "concertation" and embodied it in three Acts of Parliament: the Stability and Growth Act (1965), Principles of Sectoral Policy (1966), and the Principles of the Federal Government's Sectoral and Regional Economic Policy (1968). ' "The politics of concertation" ', Ionescu writes, 'combines the political dualism, corporate and representative, characteristic of the industrial–technological society with the economic need of that society for the regulatory functioning of the market and its natural competitiveness', and he observes that Britain has lagged behind France and

Germany and also Sweden in adopting the technique of concertation.[56]

We are perhaps on more familiar ground in regarding corporate forces as having much in common with Calhoun's idea of rule by the concurrent majority. According to Calhoun, an American conservative, 'there are two different modes in which the sense of the community may be taken . . . one regards numbers only . . . The other, on the contrary, regards interests as well as numbers; – considering the community as made up of different and conflicting interests, as far as the action of the government is concerned; and takes the sense of each, through its majority or appropriate organ, and the united sense of all, as the sense of the entire community'. The first was the numerical, and the second, 'the concurrent, or constitutional majority'.[57]

All free countries are governed by a combination of both majorities. In Sweden and Norway, both of which have successful economies, the concurrent majority is probably more important than the numerical majority. That would be undesirable in this country. The proposed 'House of Industry' would be only advisory, and it should be joined to the House of Commons by a parliamentary Select Committee. The creation of a functionally representative body would not be an attack on geographical representation and the House of Commons. It would merely be a recognition of the strong pressures that exist in our society and an attempt to bring them away from the backstairs and out of the recesses of Congress House and the CBI into full visibility by the public. Such a body would demonstrate that while competition is necessary both for an efficient economy and a free society, cooperation and consensus are also necessary for the preservation of that society.

'Concerted action' is not a panacea – there are no panaceas for the British economy. Some extremist union leaders might initially refuse to take part; others would remain as unreasonable as they are now. Dr Haseler has pointed out that the Marxist-controlled unions 'don't want to be reconciled to the bourgeois state – they want to destroy it'.[58] Certainly trade-union leaders and Labour MPs who feel at home in East Germany, will not go out of their way to make a free economy work. Nevertheless the refusal of extremists to join in 'concerted action', and extremist behaviour in a House of Industry, would have the useful side-effect of revealing to the rank and file how badly represented they were by some of their leaders.

Trade unions have shown a greater interest in the sort of industrial democracy that would increase their own power in industry than in the sort that would bring more democracy into trade-unionism. Trade-union leaders tend to be elected for life, and often only a minute percentage of the union bothers to vote. Conservatives therefore favour the election of union leaders by postal ballots, and want to see firms provide time for union meetings on their premises.

Conservatives want greater participation in companies as well as in unions. The crudities of the Bullock Committee have not been helpful. The German system has worked well, but it is much less radical than the scheme recommended by the majority of Bullock. Moreover, Germany has an effective trade-union structure and a law of industrial relations which prevents the absurdities of the British industrial scene. No one model would be suitable for all large companies in this country, and each should choose the most appropriate form of participation. Peter Walker has cogently argued that legislation should require every large firm to adopt one out of a listed range of schemes within three years.[59] In any event, company law should be altered so that firms are required to take into account the interests of their employees as well as those of their shareholders. This is already the practice in all good companies.

It is Conservative policy to encourage share-ownership by employees. Here once again we are well behind the United States, Germany, France and other countries. By giving tax incentives to firms wishing to develop deferred profit-sharing and employee share-ownership, the Conservatives aim to spread ownership of capital and to make employee share-ownership in this country as widely spread as it is elsewhere. By all these measures the Conservative hopes to further 'disalienation' and to accommodate and domesticate trade-union power in Britain. The dual loyalty of trade-unionists will in future, it is hoped, not always be resolved in favour of the union but more often in favour of the community, the firm and the family.

The British economy is out of balance, as Messrs Bacon and Eltis have shown. Public expenditure is greater than we can afford, and resources must be diverted to manufacturing industry. It is only in the manufacturing sector of industry that high rates of growth are possible – much higher than in the service sector – and unless manufacturing industry is restored to health, British growth will continue to be much slower than that of our competitors, and the gap between the British standard of living and that of the rest of Western Europe will continue to grow.

Conservatives are better able than Labour to encourage an industrial renaissance, since they genuinely believe in private enterprise, and in the social value and economic importance of small business. They regard industrialists as national assets, whereas in Socialist demonology business-men are selfish and unscrupulous exploiters of the poor. Conservatives would not go so far as President Coolidge in proclaiming that 'the man who builds a factory builds a temple'.[60] Nor do they agree with Bishop Lawrence of Massachusetts that 'godliness is in league with riches'.[61] But they salute those who broaden our industrial base and increase the national wealth. Even Coolidge's classic confusion of God and Mammon is healthier than the contemporary snobbery, which decrees that almost any career is more useful and admirable than a career in industry or commerce.

The Conservatives are also well placed to foster industrial expansion by their attitude to taxation. The present Socialist Government has pushed taxes to a ridiculous level, as did its Socialist predecessors. 'I am convinced', R. A. Butler said in his Budget speech in 1952, 'that the present weight of direct taxation, particularly on the lower- and middle-income groups, acts as a very positive discouragement to extra effort . . . Austerity and restriction are not enough – we must give positive encouragement if we are to pull through together.' And he described the purpose of his second Budget as being 'designed to encourage industry both as a corporate whole and as a living structure of human beings'.[62] Today the situation is far worse. The taxation system is not merely restrictive and discouraging; it is penal and unintelligible. The only incentive it provides is to emigrate.

Many people pay income tax even though they are earning less than some of those who receive supplementary benefit. Income tax in Britain is paid at a very low level of income, and its starting rate is the highest in the world. Only four countries impose a higher rate of tax on large earned incomes than the British rate of 83 per cent: Algeria, Egypt, Tanzania, Portugal. These countries are either dictatorships or are less punctilious in their tax paying than the British. So Britain effectively leads the world in paying income tax, if in almost no other field of economic activity. Unquestionably taxation is too high – even Mr Healey has noticed this. Taxation must be moderated, and the balance between taxes on earning and on spending must be tilted towards the latter.

Manufacturing industry needs a more stable environment than it has recently enjoyed. Admittedly the UK economy does not appear to be more unstable than other countries.[63] And admittedly a comparative study of British and West German industry found little evidence that the growth of industries was 'greatly affected by instability'.[64] Nevertheless the chopping and changing of Government policies in all spheres of the economy can scarcely fail to unsettle industry and harm our industrial performance. So long as they are confronted by opponents who are intent on ever-increasing state control, an incoming Conservative Government cannot just leave things as they are. That would be to choose the stability of quicksand. Everybody would go on sinking. But it will be mindful of the benefits of steadiness and continuity.

Finally the Conservatives will help industry by mastering inflation. In the past successive British Governments have been swayed too much by the prevailing economic fashion. Too much reliance has been placed on one or other instrument of economic policy at the expense of others. Yet Conservative eclecticism requires that in tackling inflation no tool of economic management should be discarded. To conquer inflation the British Government will need to maintain strict control of public expenditure and the public-sector borrowing requirement; it will need a strict monetary policy; it will need some form of incomes policy; and it will need to develop its policies in consultation with all sides of industry.

Conservatives will provide a favourable climate for the British to work in. They will strive for simple and undogmatic goals: a more balanced economy, more economic freedom, the creation of wealth not its confiscation, lower taxation and greater incentives. They will seek to reconcile competition and corporatism. They will make the state an aid to industry and commerce, not a burden. All this will benefit the economy.

Yet at the end of the day none of it may make very much difference. Governments have limited power and influence, and well established attitudes may be immune to governmental persuasion or action. Common observation and experience as well as the figures of low productivity here compared with other countries suggest that taken together the British at all levels and in all walks of life work less hard and less efficiently than their competitors. 'There is in England', Sydney Smith wrote about a century and a half ago, 'almost a love of difficulty and needless labour . . . If the English were in a paradise of spontaneous productions, they would continue to dig and plough, though they were never a peach nor a pineapple the better for it.'[65] Nobody would say that today. But even in the 1930s, two American observers compared British industrial relations favourably with American. 'Every man', they said, 'was diligently at work, never loafing, never killing time. All were as busy as beavers, trying to turn out a full day's work.'[66]

If the British prefer to go on sinking towards an Eastern European standard of life, if they persist in maintaining what used to be considered a Mediterranean attitude to work, if they insist on demanding more than they are prepared to produce, there is not much any Government can do. Not even North Sea oil will save us. Yet the British mood has changed before. It may now change again. In the past, people have been badly wrong in their assessment of this country's economic future. Conservatives will do their utmost to prove the gloomsters wrong again.

7. The Immediate Future

We are to consider . . . whether, according to reason and judgement,
the spirits and temper of the people of this nation are prepared to
receive and to go along with it.
Oliver Cromwell[1]

Nothing can be more impertinent than good reasons, when they
are misplaced or ill-timed.
Halifax[2]

The young stand by principle, the old by law, the wise by expediency,
and the foolish by their own opinion.
John Galt[3]

In Britain the date of the general election is seldom known in
advance. Now to the ordinary uncertainty created by the Prime
Minister's right to seek a dissolution of Parliament is added the
uncertainty created by the Government not possessing a majority in
the House of Commons and therefore liable to be driven to dissolve
against its own wishes. While this makes the political scene more
exciting, especially for the Opposition, it is undeniably inconvenient
for a writer of a book on politics, who has no means of knowing if it
will appear before, during or after an election. The Lib–Lab pact
seems unlikely to endure; two drowning men do not keep each other
afloat for long. But nobody can be sure at exactly what point they
will sink beneath the waves.

When the election does come, the Conservatives will be facing a
Prime Minister who, like his predecessor, is much better at gaining
power than at using it. In the forties Mr Callaghan gave Lord Wigg
his 'recipe for political success: wait till the trade unions decide their
line and follow them'.[4] To all appearances Mr Callaghan has consistently cooked according to that recipe, and he has produced for
himself some succulent dishes. Nobody else has headed the three

great Departments of State and then become Prime Minister. Unfortunately Mr Callaghan's formula, while excellently designed to secure good jobs, provides no guidance as to how the jobs should be performed to the public advantage. And indeed probably no leading politician this century had a worse record as a Departmental Minister than Mr Callaghan. Sir John Simon is perhaps his only serious rival. Charity demands that little should be said about Mr Callaghan's years at the Treasury – Richard Crossman has anyway left little unsaid – yet his behaviour in 1966 cannot be entirely glossed over. Although his Treasury advisers had told him that the post-election budget would have to be deflationary, Mr Callaghan announced on 1 March, just before the campaign began, that he did not 'foresee the need for severe increases in taxation'.[5] With the election duly won, the Selective Employment Tax was imposed; an economic crisis followed in July.

As Home Secretary Mr Callaghan went down well with the crowds in Northern Ireland. But he panicked over the Kenyan Asians, he lost the confidence of the police, and he was responsible for (unsuccessfully) gerrymandering the 1970 election. (In that grimy episode Mr Foot was his chief cheerleader.) Even worse, Mr Callaghan was at that time the Mr Benn of the Cabinet. In accordance with his formula, he sided with the trade unions and the National Executive Committee against the Government's proposals to reform industrial relations.

His record as Foreign Secretary was no less dismal. Even if, charitably once more, we exclude Cyprus and Angola from the accounts, we are left with his embarrassing handling of the EEC 'renegotiations', the fiasco over Britain's seat at the Energy Conference, and the blundering over the Cod War with Iceland. His unswerving obedience to Dr Kissinger proved small compensation for a vacuum in diplomatic skills and knowledge. After a visit by Wilson and him to Moscow, he claimed that it had 'heralded a period of particularly close Anglo-Soviet co-operation'.[6] As this was the time of Portugal and Angola, as well as Russia's arms build up, the fruits of this close co-operation were not apparent to anybody else.

In view of Mr Callaghan's formula for self-advancement none of this is surprising. All the time he was watching his popularity with the party and the trade unions, and 'a lifetime in watching the cat jump', Kipling pointed out, 'does not breed liontamers'.[7] All the same, Mr Callaghan unquestionably has cross-party appeal. He did more than any other Labour politician to win the election of February 1974. His air of a rather puzzled policeman is vaguely reassuring, and he has been slightly better at 10 Downing Street than he ever was in any of his other offices.

He will presumably present himself at the election as somebody untainted by the shortcomings of his predecessor and as somebody only loosely connected with all those left-wing extremists in the Parliamentary Party and on the National Executive Committee. This will be difficult. He was after all the second most important man in the Wilson Government, and he is the Leader of the Labour Party. During the campaign he can hardly keep both Mr Benn and Mr Healey concealed from the public view. Mr Benn is the most vivid reminder of Labour's lurking extremism, and Mr Healey is the living embodiment of the dishonest economic prospectus on which Labour got itself elected. Admittedly Mr Healey has evolved for himself a personal doctrine of movable infallibility. Whatever he says or does is at any given moment infallibly right. No matter that it is quite different from what he was saying and doing a few months before, and is quite different from what he will be saying and doing in a few months' time. The policy changes, but the Chancellor remains infallible. Even Britain's final bankruptcy, one imagines, would be just another demonstration that Mr Healey had been right all the time. Yet three years of economic failure and incompetence, comprising rocketing inflation, doubled unemployment and a depreciated pound, will prevent the voters taking Mr Healey at his own valuation.

Mr Callaghan and Mr Healey will certainly be able to say that the economy is in better shape than it was before the bailiffs from the IMF were called in. They will claim credit for the improvement in the balance of payments due to North Sea oil and for a reduction in the inflation rate from the astronomical levels to which they raised it; and they will demand another period of power in order to 'finish the job'. In this they will be like incendiarists, who having set fire to a building and seen it partly destroyed, belatedly make a few tentative efforts to put the fire out and helped by others are partially successful. Then instead of being prosecuted for arson, they demand a reward for having summoned the fire brigade. Yet to secure re-election after its inventory of folly, dishonesty and rancour during the last few years, the Labour Government would have to induce amnesia on a massive scale among the voters, and the by-election results suggest that the task will be beyond it.

Nor, probably, will the Liberals fare any better. The Liberal vote has increased after every Conservative Parliament since the war and decreased after every Labour Parliament. This time that trend is likely to be accentuated. The Liberals will be blamed for Labour's failures and will receive little credit for Labour's successes, if any. Their claim to be a moderating influence upon Labour is fraudulent. Before the Lib–Lab pact Mr Callaghan was in a minority and had already had to drop contentious Socialist legislation. It was mathematics not Liberals that took Socialism off the Labour Government's agenda. Mr Steel postponed his appointment with the electorate as though with a dentist. But in doing so he sold himself cheaply to Labour. Almost certainly the voters will not want to buy him back.

Nothing is certain about a general election. But a Conservative victory looks by far the most likely result. Probably the only thing that could prevent it would be for the Tories to go on an ideological 'trip' and scare the voters. But at present, as the intelligent moderation of the party document 'The Right Approach' bears witness, there is little danger of a relapse into ideology.

Labour can win elections despite an extremist programme, as was demonstrated all too clearly in 1974. Many Labour voters support the party for reasons of class and not because of its policies. It is a myth that so-called 'deference' has led voters to eschew left-wing policies close to their hearts and vote Conservative. The opposite has happened. Voters sympathetic to the Tory outlook and policies have voted Labour out of class solidarity.[8]

The Conservatives could not imitate Labour even if they wished. They are not a class party. Even in the October 1974 election, when they secured only 35 per cent of the vote, the Conservatives had a wider base of support and were a far more national party than Labour.[9] The Conservatives have lost every election since the war when they did not get 50 per cent of their vote from the working class; and they have won every election since the war when they got 50 per cent of their vote or more from the working class. For the Tory Party, depending as it does equally upon the working and the middle classes for support, ideology and extremism are therefore out of the question. The party can only remain national by remaining moderate. 'The Conservative Party', said Baldwin, 'must recruit from the left.'[10] Moreover as Dr Butler and Dr Stokes have shown, the renewal of the electorate has been helping Labour; there are more new electors reaching voting age from Labour than from Con-

I

servative homes, and as there are more elderly Conservative than Labour voters more of them are dying. The swing to Labour in 1964 would not have been enough to produce a Labour Government if the 1959 electorate had still been in existence.[11]

By and large, the Conservatives have been successful in recruiting from the Left; since the war, they have shared power equally with the Labour Party. The Tory Party has been able to wean Labour voters away from supporting Socialism because it has usually been considered more competent than its opponents, and because Tory policies have been more in line with the ideas and wishes of the British people than those of the Labour Party. The great majority dislike nationalization and state control; they do not want to be pushed around by the bureaucracy; they are happy to pay taxes to help those in real need, but they do not like to see their money wasted and they think taxation is excessive; they want to own their homes and to be liberated from what Peter Walker has called the 'permanent tenantry' of the Council estates.[12] Since the war Tory policies have been more popular than the Tory Party, and as we saw earlier there is no basis for the belief that those policies have not been Conservative. It is the Tory Party not Tory policies which have failed to please the voters. Hence the importance of the party being embedded in the life of the community at all levels throughout the country. Hence the importance of the tone of the party. Hence the importance of its message being fully comprehensible to ordinary people. 'For purposes of conversation, especially on matters of business', Tolstoy once observed, 'it is not at all necessary to understand what is said to you – the only thing necessary is to remember what you want to say yourself.'[13] Too often the Tory Party (like other parties) has seemed not sufficiently ready to listen to the public and too intent on just saying its piece. Yet because the Tory Party is untainted by ideology, it should find it easy to forgo soliloquies and to conduct a dialogue with the voters.

Be that as it may, Margaret Thatcher and the Tory Party will fight the next election on a moderate non-dogmatic programme consisting of common-sense policies and not many promises. The ensuing Conservative Government will have a more difficult task than faced the Heath Government in 1970. The international outlook is much bleaker. There has been what the Supreme Allied Commander in Europe, General Haig, has called 'an explosion' in Russia's military capabilities. The Soviets have not been spending 13 per cent of their gross national product building up a vast offensive potential as part of a grandiose Keynesian job-creation programme. They have been turning Russia into a vast arsenal because they wish to increase Russian influence and eventually dominate the world. Labour's succession of unilateral cuts in defence have been a sacrifice of the national interest to the anti-West and anti-democratic wing of the party. The Conservatives will restore the faith of our allies in Britain's will to resist by seeing that our armed forces are once more properly equipped to fight. Only a strengthened and united West will be able to ensure that Russia pursues a non-aggressive course. Genuine détente and the reduction of forces on both sides will only be achieved from a position of strength.

At home, the new Government will be taking over with both inflation and unemployment far higher than they were in 1970. Britain has slipped even further behind her neighbours, and economic failure does not predispose people to make the compromises necessary for their own and the country's well being.

The Tory Party (and the country) have not been lucky in recent years. The Conservatives lost narrowly both in 1964 and in 1974. Writing with the benefit of hindsight and the knowledge that the election of February 1974 was lost, one can see that the Government might have been wise to accept the TUC's offer to treat the miners as a special case, and only hold the election when the unions did not keep their word.* 'Everything', Dostoyevsky said, 'seems stupid when it fails.'[14] Yet had it not have been for a misleading unattributable briefing given by one of the members of the Pay Board,[15] the Conservative Government would probably have been re-elected. In any case the Tory Party does not set 'the people in the papal chair'.[16] It does not believe the voters are always right. It believes they were disastrously wrong in 1974, though it takes its share of responsibility for the result. But the fact that the voters gave the wrong answer does not necessarily mean that it was wrong to ask the question. 'In international affairs', Mr George Kennan has laid down, 'the proof of the pudding is always in the eating.'[17] But in internal affairs and in party politics failure may be unavoidable, or it may be a prelude to future success.

The nation has now seen extremism at work in the Labour Government and in the Labour Party, and it does not like what it has

*At the time, I was in favour of an election, though I would have preferred an earlier date.

seen. There are signs also of greater economic realism in the country. Moreover with the decline of the Social Democrats and the increased strength of the Far Left, it should be plain after the election that there is no sensible alternative to sound moderate Tory Government and a freer more energetic economic system. Probably the only alternative on offer will be Mr Wedgwood Benn.

Nobody can pretend that Britain is now an easy place to govern. But under the next Conservative Government the country will have the opportunity to end its long decline and start on the road to recovery. One does not have to be a wholly irrational optimist to believe that she will take it.

Bibliography

There is a fairly full bibliography in my previous book *The Body Politic* (1969). I have included here only books I have quoted from, books I have found especially useful, and books published since 1968.

The books listed below, are except where stated, published in Great Britain.

ABBOTT, W. C., *The Writings and Speeches of Oliver Cromwell* (4 vols.), Cambridge, Mass., 1937–47.

ACHESON, DEAN, *An American Vista*, 1956.

ADDISON, PAUL, *The Road to 1945*, 1975.

AGAR, HERBERT, *The United States*, 1950.

ALLEN, V. L., *Trade Unions and the Government*, 1960.

AMERY, L. S., *My Political Life* (3 vols.), 1953–5.

—, *Thoughts on the Constitution* (2nd ed.), 1953.

ANGELL, NORMAN, *The Press and the Organisation of Society* (rev. ed.), 1953.

ARISTOTLE, *Politics* (trans. and ed. by Ernest Barker), 1948.

ASPINALL, A., *Lord Brougham and the Whig Party*, 1927.

ATTLEE, C. R., *As It Happened*, 1954.

BACON, ROBERT, and ELTIS, WALTER, *Britain's Economic Problem: Too Few Producers*, 1976.

BAECHLER, JEAN, *The Origins of Capitalism*, 1975.

BALFOUR, A. J., *Chapters of Autobiography*, 1930.

BASSETT, R., *The Essentials of Parliamentary Democracy* (2nd ed.), 1964.

BEER, S. H., *Modern British Politics*, 1965.

BEER, S. H., and ULAM, A. B., (eds.), *Patterns of Government* (2nd ed.), New York, 1962.

BELL, DANIEL, *The Coming of Post-Industrial Society*, 1973.

—, *The Cultural Contradictions of Capitalism*, 1976.

BELOFF, NORA, *Freedom Under Foot*, 1976.

BENINDER, ROBERT, *White House Fever*, 1960.

BENNEY, MARK, *et al., How People Vote*, 1956.

BERLIN, ISAIAH, *Montesquieu*, 1955.

—, *Two Concepts of Liberty*, 1958.

BIRCH, A. H., *Representative and Responsible Government*, 1964.

BIRKENHEAD, Lord, *Walter Monckton*, 1969.

BLACK, DUNCAN, *The Theory of Committees and Elections*, 1958.

BLAKE, ROBERT, *The Unknown Prime Minister*, 1955.

—, *Disraeli*, 1966.

—, *The Conservative Party from Peel to Churchill*, 1970.

—, *The Office of Prime Minister*, 1975

—, *Conservatism in an Age of Revolution*, 1976.

BLAKE, Lord, and PATTEN, JOHN (eds.), *The Conservative Opportunity*, 1976.

BLOCK, GEOFFREY, *A Source Book of Conservatism*, 1964.

BLONDEL, J., *Voters, Parties and Leaders*, 1963

BOOTHBY, ROBERT, *I Fight to Live*, 1947.

BOSWELL, JAMES, *Life of Johnson*, 1952.

BOYSON, RHODES (ed.), *1985*, 1975.

BRAHAM, C., and BURTON, J., *The Referendum Reconsidered*, 1975.

BRENAN, GERALD, *The Spanish Labyrinth* (2nd ed.), 1950.

—, *A Holiday by the Sea*, 1961.

BRINTON, CRANE, *Political Ideas of the English Romanticists*, 1926.

—, *English Political Thought in the Nineteenth Century*, 1933.

BRITTAN, SAMUEL, *The Treasury under the Tories, 1951–1964*, 1964.

—, *Steering the Economy*, 1971.

—, *Capitalism and the Permissive Society*, 1973.

BRITTAN, SAMUEL, and LILLEY, PETER, *The Delusion of Incomes Policy*, 1977.

BROADWAY, FRANK, *State Intervention in British Industry, 1964–68*, 1969.

BROGAN, D. W., *The Free State*, 1945.

—, *The Price of Revolution*, 1951.

—, *An Introduction to American Politics*, 1954.

BRUCE-GARDYNE, JOCK, and LAWSON, NIGEL, *The Power Game*, 1976.

BRUUN, G., *Europe and the French Imperium*, New York, 1938.

BUCK, PHILIP W. (ed.), *How Conservatives Think*, 1975.

BULGAKOV, V., *The Last Year of Leo Tolstoy*, 1971.

BULLOCK, ALAN, *The Life and Times of Ernest Bevin* (2 vols.), vol, I: *1881–1940*, 1960; vol. II: *1940–1945*, 1967.

BULLOCK, ALAN, and SHOCK, M., (eds), *The Liberal Tradition*, 1956.

BUNDY, MCGEORGE, *The Strength of Government*, Cambridge, Mass., 1968.

BURKE, EDMUND, *Works* (16 vols.), 1826–7.

BURN, W. L., *The Age of Equipoise*, 1964.

BUTLER, R. A., *The Art of the Possible*, 1971.

—, *Our Way Ahead*, 1956.

BUTLER, D. E., *The British General Election of 1951*, 1952.

—, *The Electoral System in Britain since 1918* (2nd ed.), 1963.

BUTLER, D. E., and ROSE, RICHARD, *The British General Election of 1959*, 1960.

BUTLER, DAVID, and KAVANAGH, DENNIS, *The British General Election of February 1974*, 1974.

—, *The British General Election of October 1974*, 1975.

BUTLER, DAVID, and KITZINGER, UWE, *The 1975 Referendum*, 1976.

BUTLER, DAVID, and STOKES, DONALD, *Political Change in Britain*, 1969.

BUTLER, DAVID, and PINTO-DUSCHINSKY, MICHAEL, *The British General Election of 1970*, 1971.

BUTTERFIELD, HERBERT, *The Whig Interpretation of History*, 1931.

—, *The Statecraft of Machiavelli*, 1940.

CALLAGHAN, JAMES, *Challenges and Opportunities for British Foreign Policy*, 1975.

CAMPBELL, PETER, *French Electoral Systems*, 1958.

CARLYLE, THOMAS, *The French Revolution* (3 vols.), 1837.

—, *Letters and Speeches of Oliver Cromwell* (3 vols.: 2nd ed.), 1846.

—, *Latter Day Pamphlets*, 1870.

CARR, E. H., *The Bolshevik Revolution, 1917–1923* (3 vols.), 1950–3.

CARTER, B. E., *The Office of Prime Minister*, 1956.

CECIL, Lord, HUGH, *Conservatism*, 1912.

CHADWICK, OWEN, *From Bossuet to Newman*, 1957.

CHURCHILL, WINSTON S., *Lord Randolph Churchill*, 1907.

—, *The Dawn of Liberation*, 1945.

—, *The Gathering Storm*, 1948.

—, *Europe Unite*, 1950.

—, *The Hinge of Fate*, 1951.

—, *Triumph and Tragedy*, 1954.

—, *The World Crisis 1911–1918* (1-vol. ed.), 1964.

CITRINE, LORD, *Men and Work*, 1964.

CLARKE, DAVID, *The Conservative Party*, n.d.

CLAYTON, JOSEPH, *The Rise and Decline of Socialism in Great Britain 1884–1924*, 1926.

CLUTTERBUCK, RICHARD, *Protest and the Urban Guerilla*, 1973.

COBBAN, ALFRED, *Edmund Burke*, 1929.

—, *Rousseau and the Modern State*, 1934.

COIT, M., *John C. Calhoun*, 1950.

COLE, MARGARET, *The Story of Fabian Socialism*, 1961.

COLERAINE, Lord, *For Conservatives Only*, 1970.

COLERIDGE, S. T., *On the Constitution of the Church and State* (Everyman ed.), 1972.

—, *Biographia Literaria* (Everyman ed.), 1965.

COMMAGER, H. S., *Freedom, Loyalty, Dissent*, 1954.

CONGAR, M. J., *Divided Christendom*, 1939.

CONQUEST, ROBERT, *Lenin*, 1972.

COOPER, DUFF, *Old Men Forget*, 1953.

CORNFORD, F. M., *Microcosmographica Academica* (5th ed), 1953.

COXON, A. P. M. and JONES, C. L. (eds.), *Social Mobility*, 1975.

CRANSTON, MAURICE, *Freedom: A New Analysis*, 1953.

CROSLAND, C. A. R., *The Future of Socialism*, 1956.

—, *Socialism Now*, 1975 (i).

—, *Social Democracy in Europe* (2 vols.), 1975 (ii).

CROSS, COLIN, *Philip Snowden*, 1966.

CROSSMAN, RICHARD, *Inside View*, 1972.

—, *The Diaries of a Cabinet Minister* (2 vols.), vol. I: *1964–1966*, 1975; vol. II: *1966–1968*, 1976.

CRUIKSHANK, R. J., *Charles Dickens and Early Victorian England*, 1949.

CROZIER, BRIAN, *A Theory of Conflict*, 1974.

DAHRENDORF, RALF, *The New Liberty*, 1975.

DAHL, ROBERT A. (ed.), *Political Oppositions in Western Democracies*, New Haven, 1966.

DALTON, HUGH, *Call Back Yesterday*, 1953.

—, *The Fateful Years*, 1957.

—, *High Tide and After*, 1962.

DAVENPORT, NICHOLAS, *The Split Society*, 1964.

DICEY, A. V., *Law and Public Opinion in England* (2nd ed.), 1962.

DICKENS, CHARLES, *Bleak House*.

DICKINSON, H. T., *Bolingbroke*, 1970.

DISRAELI, BENJAMIN, *Vivian Grey*, 1826.

—, *Popanilla*, 1827.

—, *Vindication of the English Constitution*, 1835.

—, *Coningsby*, 1844.

—, *Sybil*, 1845.

—, *Tancred*, 1847.

—, *Lord George Bentinck*, 1852.

—, *Endymion*, 1880.

—, *Tory Democrat* (Disraeli's Manchester and Crystal Palace Speeches), 1950.

DOSTOYEVSKY, *Notes from Underground*.

—, *The Idiot*.

—, *Crime and Punishment*.

—, *Pushkin Speech*.

DOUGLAS, NORMAN, *Old Calabria* (4th ed.), 1935.

EDEN, Sir ANTHONY, *The Eden Memoirs: Facing the Dictators*, 1962; *Full Circle*, 1960; *The Reckoning*, 1965.

EHRMANN, HENRY W. (ed.) *Interest Groups on Four Continents*, Pittsburgh, 1958.

ELIOT, T. S., *Notes towards the Definition of Culture*, 1948.

EISENHOWER, DWIGHT D., *Mandate for Change*, 1965.

EMDEN, C. S., *The People and the Constitution* (2nd ed.), 1956.

EYCK, ERICH, *Pitt versus Fox*, 1950.

FABER, RICHARD, *Beaconsfield and Bolingbroke*, 1961.

FAIRLIE, HENRY, *The Life of Politics*, 1968.

FEILING, KEITH, *History of the Tory Party 1640–1714*, 1924.

—, *The Second Tory Party 1714–1832*, 1938.

—, *The Life of Neville Chamberlain*, 1946.

FIELDS, W. C., *Fields for President*, 1972.

FIGGIS, J. N., *From Gerson to Grotius* (2nd ed.), 1931.

FINER, HERMAN, *The Major Governments of Modern Europe*, 1960.

FINER, S. E. (ed.), *Adversary Politics and Electoral Reform*, 1975.

FISHER, NIGEL, *Iain Macleod*, 1973.

FLEMMING, JOHN, *Inflation*, 1976.

FOOT, MICHAEL, *Aneurin Bevan*, vol. I: *1897–1945*, 1962.

FOOT, PAUL, *The Rise of Enoch Powell*, 1969.

FRIEDMAN, MILTON, *The Counter-Revolution in Monetary Theory*, 1970.

—, *Unemployment* versus *Inflation?* 1975.

—, *From Galbraith to Economic Freedom*, 1977.

FULFORD, ROGER, *The Prince Consort*, 1949.

GALBRAITH, J. K., *Economics, Peace and Laughter*, 1971.

—, *Economics and the Public Purpose*, 1974.

GALT, JOHN, *The Member*, 1831.

GASH, NORMAN, *Politics in the Age of Peel*, 1953.

—, *Mr Secretary Peel*, 1961.

—, *Reaction and Reconstruction in British Politics 1832–1852*, 1965.

—, *Sir Robert Peel*, 1972.

GIBBON, EDWARD, *The Decline and Fall of the Roman Empire*, 1776–88.

GILBERT, MARTIN, *Winston S. Churchill*, vol. V: *1922–1939*, 1976.

GLASS, S. T., *The Responsible Society*, 1966.

GOLLIN, A. M., *Proconsul in Politics*, 1964.

GOOCH, G. P., *Political Thought from Bacon to Halifax* (new ed.), 1946.

GOODHART, PHILIP, *Referendum*, 1971.

—, *Full-Hearted Consent*, 1976.

GRAY, ALEXANDER, *The Socialist Tradition*, 1946.

GREVILLE, CHARLES, *The Greville Memoirs* (8 vols.), 1874–87.

GRIERSON, H. J. C., *Cross Currents in English Literature of the Seventeenth Century*, 1929.

—, *Criticism and Creation*, 1949.

K

GRIFFITHS, BRIAN, *Inflation*, 1976.
GUEDALLA, PHILIP, *Palmerston*, 1926.

HAILSHAM, Lord, *The Purpose of Parliament*, 1947.
—, *The Conservative Case* (rev. ed.), 1959.
—, *Science and Politics*, 1963.
—, *New Charter*, 1969.
—, *The Acceptable Face of Western Civilisation*, 1973.
—, *The Door Wherein I Went*, 1975.
—, *Elective Dictatorship* (the Dimbleby Lecture in the *Listener* 21 October 1976), 1976.
HAINES, JOE, *The Politics of Power*, 1977.
HALÉVY, ELIE, *The Growth of Philosophic Radicalism*, 1928.
—, *A History of the English People in the Nineteenth Century* (6 vols.), 1934–47.
HALIFAX, Marquess of, *Complete Works* (ed. by W. Raleigh), 1912.
HAMILTON, ALEXANDER et al., *The Federalist* (ed. by Max Beloff), 1948.
HAMMOND, J. L., and FOOT, M. R. D., *Gladstone and Liberalism*, 1952.
HANHAM, H. J., *Scottish Nationalism*, 1969.
HANSARD SOCIETY, *Report of the Commission on Electoral Reform*, 1976.
HARRIS, NIGEL, *Competition and the Corporate Society*, 1972.
HARRIS, RALPH, and SEWELL, BRENDON, *British Economic Policy 1970–74: Two Views*, 1975.
HARRISON, MARTIN, *Trade Unions and the Labour Party since 1945*, 1960.
HARROD, R. F., *The Life of John Maynard Keynes*, 1951.
HART, JEFFREY, *Viscount Bolingbroke*, 1965.
HASELER, STEPHEN, *The Death of British Democracy*, 1976.
HAYEK, F. A., *The Constitution of Liberty*, 1960.
—, *The Road to Serfdom*, 1944.
HAYWARD, J. E. S., *Private Interests and Public Policy*, 1966.
HEILBRONNER, ROBERT L., *The Quest for Wealth*, 1958.
HEUSTON, R. F. V., *Lives of the Lord Chancellors 1885–1940*, 1964.
HICKS BEACH, Lady VICTORIA, *The Life of Sir Michael Hicks Beach* (2 vols.), 1932.
HILL, B. W. (ed.), *Edmund Burke on Government, Politics and Society*, 1975.
HILL, CHRISTOPHER, *Oliver Cromwell 1658–1958*, 1958.
—, *The Century of Revolution, 1603–1714*, 1961.
—, *God's Englishman*, 1970.
HIRSCH, FRED, *Social Limits to Growth*, 1977.
HIRSCHMAN, ALBERT O., *Exit, Voice and Loyalty*, Cambridge, Mass, 1970.
HOBHOUSE, CHRISTOPHER, *Fox* (2nd ed.) 1947.
HOGG, QUINTIN, see HAILSHAM, Lord.
HOLMES-LASKI, *Letters* (2 vols)., 1953.

HOME of the Hirsel, Lord, *The Way the Wind Blows*, 1976.

HOOK, SIDNEY, *Revolution, Reform, and Social Justice*, 1976.

HOWARD, MICHAEL, *The Continental Commitment*, 1972.

HUME, DAVID, *A Treatise of Human Nature, 1739–40*, Oxford ed., 1888.

—, *Essays, Moral Political and Literary, 1741–2*, Oxford ed., 1963.

—, *Enquiries Concerning Human Understanding and Concerning the Principles of Morals* (posthumous edition), 1777, Oxford ed., 1975.

HURD, DOUGLAS, *The Arrow War*, 1967.

HUTBER, PATRICK, *The Decline and Fall of the Middle Class*, 1976.

HUTCHINSON, GEORGE, *Edward Heath*, 1970.

HYDE, MONTGOMERY, *Carson*, 1953.

IONESCU, GHITA (ed.), *The New Politics of European Integration*, 1972.

—, *Between Sovereignty and Integration*, 1974.

—, *Centripetal Politics*, 1975.

JACKSON, ROBERT LOUIS, *Dostoyevsky's Quest for Form*, New Haven, 1966.

JAMES, ROBERT RHODES, *Memoirs of a Conservative*, 1969.

—, *Ambitions and Realities: British Politics 1964–1970*, 1972.

JAY, DOUGLAS, *Socialism in the New Society*, 1962.

JAY, PETER, *Employment, Inflation and Politics*, 1976.

JENKINS, PETER, *The Battle of Downing Street*, 1970.

JENNINGS, Sir I., *The Growth of Parties*, 1961.

JONES, AUBREY, *The New Inflation*, 1973.

JONES, THOMAS, *Lloyd George*, 1951.

—, *A Diary with Letters 1931–1950*, 1954.

—, *Whitehall Diary* (3 vols.), 1969–71.

KELF-COHEN, R., *Nationalisation in Britain* (2nd ed.), 1961.

KELLEY, STANLEY, *Professional Public Relations and Political Power*, Baltimore, 1956.

KELLNER, PETER and HITCHENS, CHRISTOPHER, *Callaghan: The Road to No. 10*, 1976.

KENNAN, GEORGE, *Memoirs 1925–1950*, 1968.

KENNEDY, A. L., *Salisbury 1830–1903*, 1953.

KEY, V. O., *Politics, Parties and Pressure Groups* (5th ed.), New York, 1964.

—, *Public Opinion and American Democracy*, New York, 1961.

KEYNES, J. M., *The General Theory of Employment, Interest and Money*, 1936.

KEYNES, MILO (ed.), *Essays on John Maynard Keynes*, 1975.

KING, ANTHONY (ed.), *Why is Britain Becoming Harder to Govern?*, 1976.

KIRK, RUSSELL, *The Conservative Mind*, 1954.

LAKEMAN, ENID, *How Democracies Vote*, 1974.

LASKI, HAROLD J., *The Rise of European Liberalism*, 1936.

—, *Parliamentary Government in England*, 1938.

LEON, DERRICK, *Tolstoy*, 1944.

LETWIN, S. R., *The Pursuit of Certainty*, 1965.

LICHTHEIM, GEORGE, *A Short History of Socialism*, 1975.

LINCOLN, ABRAHAM, *Speeches and Letters* (Everyman ed.), 1957.

LINDSAY, A. D., *The Essentials of Democracy* (2nd ed.), 1948.

LLOYD GEORGE, DAVID, *War Memoirs* (2 vols.), 1938.

LONGFORD, ELIZABETH, *Wellington, Pillar of State*, 1972.

LOW, SIDNEY, *The Governance of England*, 1904.

LYMAN, R. W., *The First Labour Government 1924*, 1957.

MACAULAY, Lord, *The History of England* (6-vol. ed.), 1913.

MACCOBY, S., (ed)., *The Radical Tradition*, 1952.

MACCUNN, JOHN, *The Political Philosophy of Burke*, 1913.

MACDONALD, J. F., *The State and the Trade Unions*, 1960.

MCDOWELL, R. B., *British Conservatism 1832–1914*, 1952.

MACK, MARY P., *Jeremy Bentham*, 1962.

MCKENZIE, ROBERT, *British Political Parties* (2nd ed.), 1963.

MCKENZIE, ROBERT, and SILVER, ALLAN, *Angels in Marble*, 1968.

MACKINTOSH, J. P., *The Devolution of Power*, 1968.

MACLEOD, IAIN, *Neville Chamberlain*, 1961.

MACMILLAN, HAROLD, *The Middle Way* (1966 ed.).

—, *Winds of Change 1914–1939*, 1966.

—, *Tides of Fortune 1945–55*, 1969.

—, *Riding the Storm 1956–1959*, 1971.

—, *Pointing the Way 1959–61*, 1972.

—, *At the End of the Day 1961–63*, 1973.

—, *The Past Masters*, 1975.

MAITLAND, F. W., *The Constitutional History of England*, 1908.

MANCHESTER, WILLIAM, *The Sage of Baltimore*, 1952.

MARX, KARL, and ENGELS, F., *Selected Works* (2 vols.), Moscow, 1950.

MAUDE, ANGUS, *The Common Problem*, 1969.

MAYHEW, CHRISTOPHER, *Party Games*, 1969.

MENCKEN, H. L., *A Carnival of Buncombe,* Baltimore, 1956.

MEREDITH, GEORGE, *Beauchamp's Career* (3 vols.), 1876.

MICHELS, R. W. E., *Political Parties* (Dover ed.), 1950.

MIDDLEMAS, KEITH, and BARNES, JOHN, *Baldwin*, 1969.

MILIBAND, RALPH, *Parliamentary Socialism*, 1961.

MILL, JOHN STUART, *On Liberty*, 1859.

MILNE, R. S., and MACKENZIE, H. C., *Straight Fight*, 1951.

—, *Marginal Seat 1955*, 1958.

MITCHELL, BROADUS, *Alexander Hamilton*, 1976.
MONTAIGNE, MICHAEL, Lord of, *Essays* (Temple Classics ed.), 1898.
MONTHERLANT, HENRI DE, *The Bachelors*, 1960.
MONYPENNY, W. F., and BUCKLE, G. F., *The Life of Benjamin Disraeli* (6 vols.), 1914–20.
MORLEY, JOHN, *The Life of Gladstone* (2 vols.), 1905.
MOSS, ROBERT, *The Collapse of Democracy*, 1975.
MOSSE, GEORGE L., *The Culture of Western Europe*, 1963.
MOSSNER, E. C., *Life of David Hume*, 1954.
MOWAT, C. L., *Britain Between the Wars 1918–1940*, 1955.

NAMIER, L. B., *England in the Age of the American Revolution*, 1930.
—, *The Revolution of the Intellectuals*, 1946.
—, *Personalities and Powers*, 1955.
NEVINS, ALLEN, and COMMAGER, H. S., *A Short History of the United States*, New York, 1945.
NEWMAN, Cardinal, *Apologia Pro Vita Sua* (1946 ed.).
NISBET, ROBERT, *Twilight of Authority*, 1976.
NORDLINGER, ERIC A., *The Working Class Tories*, 1967.
NORTON, D., and POPLIN, R., *David Hume: Philosophical Historian*, New York, 1965.

OAKESHOTT, MICHAEL, *Rationalism in Politics*, 1962.
—, *On Human Conduct*, 1975.
ORWELL, GEORGE, *Shooting an Elephant*, 1950.
OSTROGORSKI, M. Y., *Democracy and the Organisation of Political Parties* (2 vols.), 1902.

PANIC, M. (ed.), *The U.K. and West German Manufacturing Industry 1954–1972*, 1976.
PATON, H. J., *The Claim of Scotland, 1968*.
PEACOCK, ALAN, *The Credibility of Liberal Economics*, 1977.
PEARSON, HESKETH, *The Smith of Smiths*, 1934.
PELLING, H., *A Short History of the Labour Party*, 1961.
—, *A History of British Trade Unionism* (1963 ed.).
—, *The Challenge of Socialism*, 1954.
PETRIE, Sir CHARLES, *Bolingbroke*, 1937.
PLUMB, J. H., *The Growth of Political Stability in England 1675–1725*, 1967.
POPPER, K. R., *The Open Society and its Enemies* (2 vols.), 1945.
—, *Conjectures and Refutations*, 1963.
—, *Unended Quest*, 1976.

RAISON, TIMOTHY (ed.), *The Corporate State – Reality or Myth?* 1977.

REES-MOGG, WILLIAM, *The Reigning Error*, 1974.
RIDLEY, F., and BLONDEL, J., *Public Administration in France*, 1964.
ROBBINS, Lord, *Aspects of Post-War Economic Policy*, 1974.
—, *Political Economy Past and Present*, 1976.
ROBERTS, B. C., *Trade Unions in a Free Society* (2nd ed.), 1962.
ROCKEFELLER, NELSON A., *The Future of Federalism*, Cambridge, Mass., 1962.
ROGALY, JOE, *Parliament for the People*, 1976.
ROLO, P. J. V., *George Canning*, 1965.
ROOTS, IVAN, *The Great Rebellion 1642–1660*, 1966.
ROSE, KENNETH, *Superior Person*, 1969.
—, *The Later Cecils*, 1975.
ROSKILL, STEPHEN, *Hankey*, vol. I, 1970.
ROSTOW, EUGENE V. *The Sovereign Prerogative*, New Haven, 1962.
ROUSSEAU, J. J., *Social Contract* (World's Classics ed.).
RUNCIMAN, W. G., *Social Science and Political Theory*, 1963.
—, *Relative Deprivation and Social Justice*, 1966.
RUSSELL, BERTRAND, *A History of Western Philosophy*, 1946.

SAMPSON, ANTHONY, *Macmillan*, 1967.
SCARMAN, Sir LESLIE, *English Law – The New Dimension*, 1974.
SCHLESINGER, ARTHUR M., *The Coming of the New Deal*, 1960 (i).
—, *Kennedy or Nixon?*, New York, 1960 (ii).
SCHONFIELD, ANDREW, *British Economic Policy since the War*, 1958.
—, *Modern Capitalism*, 1965.
SCHUMPETER, JOSEPH A., *Capitalism, Socialism and Democracy* (3rd ed.), 1950.
SHAW, G. B., *The Intelligent Woman's Guide to Socialism and Capitalism*, 1928.
—, *Plays*, 1930–34.
—, *Everybody's Political What's What*, 1944.
SIEYÈS, ABBÉ, *What is the Third Estate?*, 1963.
SIMON, Viscount, *Retrospect*, 1952.
SKIDELSKY, R., *Politicians and the Slump*, 1967.
SMELLIE, K. B., *A Hundred Years of British Government* (2nd ed.), 1950.
SMITH, ADAM, *The Wealth of Nations* (Everyman ed.), 1954.
SMITH, PAUL (ed.), *Lord Salisbury on Politics*, 1972.
SOLZHENITSYN, ALEXANDER, *Lenin in Zürich*, 1976 (i).
—, *Warning to the Western World*, 1976 (ii).
SOMERVELL, D. C., *Stanley Baldwin*, 1953.
SORENSON, THEODORE C., *Decision-Making in the White House*, 1963.
SOUTHGATE, DONALD (ed.), *The Conservative Leadership 1832–1932*, 1974.
SPEER, ALBERT, *Inside the Third Reich*, 1970.

STEEL, RONALD, *Pax Americana*, 1968.
STEINER, GEORGE, *Tolstoy or Dostoevsky*, 1960.
STENDHAL, *The Charterhouse of Parma*.
STEWART, DESMOND, *The Middle East: Temple of Janus*, 1972.
STEWART, JOHN B., *The Moral and Political Philosophy of David Hume*, New York, 1963.
STUART, JAMES, *Within the Fringe*, 1967.

TALMON, J. L., *The Origins of Totalitarian Democracy*, 1952.
TAYLOR, A. J. P., *English History 1914–1945*, 1965
—, *The Origins of the Second World War*, 1961.
THOMPSON, J. M., *Leaders of the French Revolution*, 1932.
THORNTON, A. P., *The Habit of Authority*, 1966.
TOCQUEVILLE, ALEXIS DE, *Democracy in America* (World's Classics ed.).
TOLSTOY, *Polikushka*.
TREVELYAN, G. M., *The Peace and the Protestant Succession*, 1934.
TREVOR-ROPER, HUGH, *Historical Essays*, 1957.
TROLLOPE, ANTHONY, *Phineas Finn*.
TROYAT, HENRI, *Tolstoy*, New York, 1967.
TRUMAN, DAVID B., *The Governmental Process*, New York, 1951.

ULAM, ADAM B., *Lenin and the Bolsheviks* (Fontana ed.), 1969.
UTLEY, T. E., *Enoch Powell*, 1968.

VICTORIA, Queen, *Letters* (Second Series, 3 vols.), 1926–8.
VIERECK, PETER, *Conservatism Revisited*, 1950.
VILE, M. J. C., *Constitutionalism and the Separation of Powers*, 1967.
VINCENT, JOHN, *The Formation of the Liberal Party 1857–1868*, 1966.

WALKER, PETER, *The Ascent of Britain*, 1977.
WATSON, GEORGE (ed.), *Radical Alternative*, 1962.
WATSON, J. STEVEN, *The Reign of George III 1760–1815*, 1960.
WEBB, BEATRICE, *Our Partnership*, 1948.
WHEARE, K. C., *Modern Constitutions*, 1951.
—, *Legislatures*, 1963.
WHEELER-BENNETT, Sir JOHN, *John Anderson, Viscount Waverley*, 1962.
WHITE, R. J. (ed.), *The Conservative Tradition*, 1950.
WIGG, Lord, *George Wigg*, 1972.
WIGHAM, ERIC, *Strikes and the Government, 1893–1974*, 1976.
WILLEY, BASIL, *The Eighteenth Century Background*, 1949.
—, *Nineteenth Century Studies*, 1949.
WILLIAMS, BASIL, *The Whig Supremacy 1714–1760* (2nd ed.), 1962.
WILLIAMS, DUNCAN, *Trousered Apes*, 1971.
WILLIAMS, MARCIA, *Inside Number 10*, 1972.

WILSON, HAROLD, *The Labour Government 1964–1970* (Pelican ed.), 1974.

WOODHOUSE, A. S. P., *Puritanism and Liberty*, 1938.

WOODWARD, Sir LLEWELLYN, *The Age of Reform 1815–1870* (2nd ed.), 1962.

WOOLTON, Earl of, *Memoirs*, 1959.

YOUNG, G. M., *Stanley Baldwin*, 1952.

YOUNG, KENNETH, *Arthur James Balfour*, 1963.

ZAGORIN, PEREZ, *The Court and the Country*, 1969.

References

HALF TITLE PAGE

Hume, 'Of the Liberty of the Press'; Galt, p. 97.

PART ONE *(page 9)*

1. Gash (1965), p. 132.

Part One, Chapter I: Post-War Conservatism (pages 11–21)

1. Emden, p. 70.
2. Byron, *Childe Harold's Pilgrimage*, IV, XII.
3. Smellie, p. 129.
4. Hicks Beach, vol. I, pp. 301–2.
5. Shaw (1928), p. 344.
6. Howard, pp. 95, 103, 138.
7. ibid., p. 11.
8. James (1972), p. 293.
9. Blake (1970), pp. 188, 255.
10. Bruce-Gardyne and Lawson, pp. 92–112.
11. Longford, p. 110.
12. Feiling (1938), p. 333.
13. Gash (1972), p. 360.
14. McDowell, p. 36.
15. Guedalla, p. 128.
16. Disraeli (1844), Book II, ch. V; Book V, ch. II.
17. Blake (1966), p. 408.
18. Paul Smith, pp. 62–3.
19. ibid., p. 84.
20. Kennedy, p. 59.
21. ibid., p. 147.
22. Webb, pp. 140–1.
23. Blake (1955), p. 14.
24. ibid., p. 130.
25. ibid., p. 299.
26. Hyde, pp. 465, 466.
27. Middlemas and Barnes, p. 435.
28. Southgate, p. 24.
29. Macleod, pp. 161–2.
30. Cooper, p. 254.
31. Eden (1965), pp. 33, 57–8.
32. Stuart, p. 147.
33. Boswell, p. 424.
34. Woolton, p. 379.
35. R. A. Butler (1971), p. 132.
36. Addison, p. 14.
37. Churchill (1945), pp. 262–3 – 29 November 1944.
38. Addison, p. 14.
39. Miliband, p. 277.
40. Kellner and Hitchen.
41. Churchill (1954), p. 509.
42. Butler and Pinto-Duschinsky, p. 92.
43. Dalton (1957), p. 151.
44. Somervell, p. 42.
45. Taylor, p. 382.

Part One, Chapter 2: Origins (pages 22–6)

1. Hume 'Of the Parties of Great Britain', p. 68.
2. Boswell, pp. 1154–5.
3. Disraeli (1847), Book I, ch. IV.
4. Halévy (1928), p. 378.
5. Bosewll, p. 973.

K*

6. Figgis, p. 7.
7. Zagorin, p. 225.
8. Feiling (1924), p. 62.
9. Roots, p. 36.
10. Kirk, p. 202.
11. Heuston, p. 326.
12. Brenan (1950), p. 57.
13. Hill (1970), p. 22.
14. Woodhouse, p. 97.
15. Carlyle (1846), vol. III, p. 53.
16. Abbott, vol. I, p. 472.
17. Lindsay, p. 69.
18. Hill (1970), pp. 197–8.
19. Halifax, p. 136 (a letter to a Dissenter).
20. Plumb, p. 151.
21. ibid., p. 172.
22. Namier (1930), p. 219.
23. Feiling (1938), p. 166.
24. J. Steven Watson, p. 441.
25. Feiling (1938), p. 162.
26. Agar, p. 118.
27. Blake (1970), p. 8.
28. ibid., pp. 8, 60.

Part One, Chapter 3: A Glance Backwards (pages 27–39)

1. Burke, 'Thoughts on the Cause of the Present Discontents'.
2. Bolingbroke, *Letters on the Study and Use of History*.
3. Swinburne, 'Hymn of Man'.
4. Gash (1961), p. 107.
5. Feiling (1938), p. 277.
6. Oakeshott (1962), p. 114.
7. Rolo, pp. 213–14.
8. Gash (1961), p. 335.
9. Woodward, p. 74.
10. Aspinall, p. 129.
11. Gash (1961), p. 457.
12. Feiling (1938), p. 363.
13. Longford, p. 227.
14. Gash (1972), p. 96.
15. Gash (1961), pp. 230–31, 621–2.
16. Gash (1972), pp. 154–5.
17. Gash (1961), p. 622.
18. Gash (1972), pp. 318–19.
19. Byron, *Don Juan*, XI, LXXXII.
20. Longford, p. 156.
21. Greville, Diary – 13 July 1847.
22. Halévy, vol. IV, p. 138.
23. Vincent, p. 38.
24. Gash (1972), pp. 494–5.
25. Hurd, p. 54.
26. White, p. 171.
27. Boothby, p. 382.
28. Kenneth Young, p. 196.
29. Burn, 'English Conservatism: the Nineteenth Century and After', p. 67.
30. Blake (1955), p. 433.
31. Kenneth Young, p. 59.
32. Schumpeter, p. 366.
33. James (1969), p. 136.
34. Taylor, p. 237.
35. Feiling (1946), p. 136.
36. Macleod, p. 116; Taylor, p. 354.
37. Addison, p. 33.
38. Pelling (1961), p. 96.
39. Gilbert, pp. 92–100.
40. Amery (1953–5), vol. II, pp. 299–300.
41. Macmillan (1975), p. 96.
42. Macleod, p. 146.
43. Feiling (1946), p. 203.
44. Mowat, p. 453.
45. Cross, p. 66.
46. Pelling (1954), vol. II, pp. 321–2.
47. Feiling (1946), p. 229.
48. Hayek (1944), p. 9.
49. Wheeler-Bennett, p. 186.
50. Feiling (1946), p. 115.
51. Dicey, p. 259.
52. R. A. Butler (1956), p. 10.
53. Disraeli (1880), ch. XL.
54. Burn (1964), pp. 287–8.
55. Agar, p. 215.
56. Bullock and Shock, p. 23.

PART TWO *(page 41)*

1. Hume, 'Of Commerce'.
2. Burke, 'First Letter on a Regicide Peace'.

3. Halifax, 'The Character of a Trimmer', p. 62.

Part Two, Chapter 1: George Savile, Marquis of Halifax (pages 43–7)

1. Macaulay, vol I, p. 232.
2. ibid., vol. V, p. 2484.
3. Preface to 'The Character of a Trimmer', p. 47.
4. ibid., p. 48.
5. Trevor-Roper, p. 256.
6. '. . . Trimmer', pp. 80, 95.
7. 'A Rough Draft of a New Model at Sea', p. 168.
8. '. . . Trimmer', pp. 61–3, 50.
9. 'Political Thoughts and Reflections', p. 224.
10. 'Cautions for the Choice of Members in Parliament', p. 156.
11. '. . . Trimmer', pp. 55–6.
12. ibid., pp. 64–5.
13. 'Political Thoughts and Reflections', p. 221.

14. Trevor-Roper, pp. 256–9.
15. '. . . Trimmer', p. 67.
16. 'Cautions . . .', pp. 159–60.
17. 'Political Thoughts . . .', pp. 225–7.
18. ibid., pp. 173–4.
19. 'Moral Thoughts and Reflections', p. 240.
20. 'Miscellaneous Thoughts and Reflections', p. 254.
21. 'A Rough Draft . . .', p. 170.
22. 'Political Thoughts . . .', pp. 209–14.
23. '. . . Trimmer', p. 85.
24. Miscellaneous Thoughts . . .', pp. 244–5, 249.
25. '. . . Trimmer', p. 100.
26. ibid., p. 103.

Part Two, Chapter 2: Henry St John, Lord Bolingbroke (pages 48–52)

1. Trevelyan, p. 230.
2. Petrie, p. 311.
3. Dickinson, p. 311.
4. *Journal to Stella*, quoted in Hart, p. vii.
5. Faber, p. 40.
6. Hart, p. 51.
7. Boswell, p. 189.
8. Dickinson, p. 309.
9. *Letters on the Study and Use of History* quoted in Basil Williams (1962), p. 394.
10. 'The Idea of a Patriot King'.

11. 'A Dissertation on Parties.'
12. ibid.
13. 'The Idea of a Patriot King'.
14. 'A Dissertation on Parties'.
15. ibid.
16. Tennyson, 'You ask me why tho' ill at ease . . .'
17. 'The Idea of a Patriot King'.
18. *Letters on the Study and Use of History*.
19. 'The Idea of a Patriot King'.
20. Letter to Sir William Wyndham.
21. 'A Dissertation on Parties'.

Part Two, Chapter 3: David Hume (pages 53–8)

1. 'Of Some Remarkable Customs', *Essays*, p. 372.
2. 'My Own Life', ibid., p. 609.

3. Russell, p. 685.
4. Boswell, pp. 1214–15.
5. *Treatise*, Bk I, pt III, s. 8, p. 103.

6. ibid., Bk II, pt III, S. 3, p. 415.
7. *An Enquiry . . . Morals*, s. 3, pt I, p. 188.
8. *Treatise*, Bk III, pt II, s. 2, pp. 481–95 *passim*; *Enquiry*, s. 3, pt I, p. 188.
9. *Enquiry*, s. 3, pt II, p. 195; *Treatise*, Bk III, pt II, s. 6, p. 520.
10. *Enquiry*, s. 3, pts II and I, pp. 192,183.
11. Mack, p. 120.
12. Norton and Popkin, pp. 109–10.
13. John B. Stewart, p. 233.
14. ibid., p. 234.
15. 'Of the Coalition of Parties', p. 482.
16. Birch, p. 49.
17. 'Idea of a Perfect Commonwealth', p. 499.
18. 'Of the Original Contract', p. 463; 'Idea of a Perfect Commonwealth', pp. 499, 500.

19. *Enquiry*, s. 3, pt II, p. 193.
20. 'Of Commerce', p. 271.
21. *Enquiry*, s. 3, pt II, p. 194.
22. 'Of Commerce'; 'Of the Protestant Succession', pp. 266, 492.
23. 'That Politics may be Reduced to a Science', p. 24.
24. 'Of Parties in General', p. 58.
25. 'Of the Parties of Great Britain', pp. 68–9.
26. 'Of the Coalition of Parties', p. 478.
27. Taylor (1965), p. 195.
28. John B. Stewart, p. 281.
29. *Enquiry*, s. 9, pts I and II, pp. 270,277,280, 279.
30. 'Of Refinement in the Arts', pp. 275, 287–8.
32. *Treatise*, Bk I, pt IV, ss. 2 and 7, pp. 218, 268.
32. ibid., s. 7, p. 273.

Part Two, Chapter 4: Edmund Burke (pages 59–67)

1. Coleridge, *Biog. Lit.*, p. 122.
2. Boswell, p. 696.
3. Goldsmith, 'The Retaliation'.
4. Wordsworth, *The Prelude*, Bk VII, 519–30.
5. 'Eloquence of the British Senate' quoted in B. W. Hill, p. 61.
6. 'Thoughts on the Present State of the Nation'.
7. ibid.
8. 'Thoughts on the Cause of the Present Discontents'.
9. Coleridge, *Biog. Lit.*, pp. 104–5.
10. Speech on Reform of Representation of the Commons, 1782.
11. MacCunn, p. 42.
12. Speech on the Petition of the Unitarians, 11 May 1792.
13. *An Appeal from the New to the Old Whigs*, 1791.
14. *Reflections on the Revolution in France*.

15. Letter to a Member of the National Assembly, 1791.
16. Speech, 11 May 1792.
17. *Reflections*.
18. Rousseau, Bk IV, ch. VIII.
19. *Reflections*.
20. 'Remarks on the Policy of the Allies', quoted in MacCunn, pp. 96–7.
21. Speech, 11 May 1792.
22. Observations on a Late Publication on the Present State of the Nation.
23. *Appeal*.
24. *Reflections*.
25. ibid.
26. Speech on Representation, 1782.
27. ibid.
28. ibid.
29. *Reflections*.
30. *Appeal*.
31. *Reflections*.
32. *Appeal*.

33. **Letter** to Captain Mercer, 26 February 1790.

34. Speech on Representation, 1782.

35. *Reflections*.

36. ibid.

37. Speech on His Arrival at Bristol.

38. Letter to M. Dupont, 1789.

39. *Reflections*.

40. *Appeal*.

41. Speech, 7 May 1782.

42. *Reflections*.

43. *Appeal*.

44. Letter to M. Dupont, October 1789.

45. Cobban (1929), p. 106.

46. Speech on Conciliation with America, 1775.

47. ibid.

48. Speech on the Plan for Economical Reform, 1780.

49. *Reflections*.

50. Speech on Representation, 1782.

51. Letter to O'Hara, 24 May 1766, quoted by L. B. Namier in the *Spectator*, 19 December 1958.

52. Cobban (1929), p. 191.

53. 'Thoughts and Details on Scarcity'.

54. *Capital*, quoted in Thornton, p. 320.

55. Robbins (1976), p. 128.

Part Two, Chapter 5: Samuel Taylor Coleridge (pages 68–73)

1. *Biog. Lit.,* p. 284.

2. Quoted in notes to *On the Constitution of the Church and State – Lay Sermons*, p. vi.

3. 'Sonnets on Eminent Characters'.

4. *Biog. Lit.* p. 124.

5. Cobban (1929), p. 157.

6. 'Sonnets on Eminent Characters'.

7. *Church and State*, p. 53.

8. ibid., p. 51.

9. Cobban (1929), p. 166.

10. ibid., pp. 167–8.

11. *Church and State*, p. 15.

12. ibid., p. 4.

13. ibid., p. 9.

14. ibid., pp. 16–22, 33–4.

15. ibid., pp. 43, 58–9.

16. ibid., pp. 80, 81.

17. ibid., pp. 5–7.

18. ibid., p. 52.

19. Cobban (1929), p. 203.

20. *Church and State*, p. 50.

21. Cobban (1929), p. 214.

22. *Church and State*, pp. 67–8.

23. *Biog. Lit.*, p. 101.

24. Cobban (1929), pp. 172, 177.

25. *Church and State*, p. 134.

26. ibid., p. 9.

27. ibid., pp. iv–v.

28. ibid., p. vi.

29. ibid., p. iv; *Biog. Lit.*, p. 121.

Part Two, Chapter 6: Benjamin Disraeli (pages 74–86)

1. *Vindication of the English Constitution*, p. 193.

2. Victoria, vol. I, p. 550.

3. Beninder, p. 141.

4. *Sybil or The Two Nations*, Bk IV, ch. xii.

5. Preface to the Hughenden edition of the novels.

6. *Coningsby*, Bk IV, ch. xiii.

7. *Vindication*, pp. 15–17.

8. *Vindication*, p. 32.

9. ibid., pp. 63–4.

10. *Popanilla*, ch. iv.

11. *Vindication*, pp. 22–5.

12. *Coningsby*, Bk II, ch. i.

13. *Sybil*, Bk II, ch. v.

14. ibid., ch. x.

15. *Sybil*, Bk I, ch. iii.

16. *Coningsby*, Bk II, ch. i.
17. *Sybil*, Bk I, ch. iii.
18. ibid.; *Vindication*, p. 180.
19. ibid., p. 181.
20. ibid., pp. 183–4.
21. Dickens, *Bleak House*, ch. iv.
22. Cruikshank, p. 12.
23. *Coningsby*, Bk II, ch. i.
24. *Sybil*, Bk I, ch. iii.
25. ibid.
26. *Coningsby*, Bk II, ch. i.
27. ibid.
28. ibid.
29. *Sybil*, Bk I, ch. iii.
30. ibid.
31. ibid.
32. ibid., Bk IV, ch. xiv. f
33. ibid., Bk VI, ch. xiii.
34. Preface to the 5th edition of *Coningsby*, 1849.
35. Speech at Crystal Palace, 24 June 1872 in *Tory Democrat* p. 42.
36. Blake (1966), p. 281.
37. Gash (1956), p. 147.
38. *Lord George Bentinck*, pp. 554–7
39. *Vindication*, pp. 181–2.
40. Namier (1946), p. 24.
41. Blake (1966), p. 504.
42. Preface to the 5th edition of *Coningsby*, 1849.
43. Woodward (1962), p. 116.
44. Speech at Manchester, 3 April 1872 in *Tory Democrat*, p. 26.
45. *Vindication*, pp. 137–8.
46. *Tory Democrat*, p. 24.
47. Monypenny and Buckle, vol. II, pp. 460–1.
48. *Tory Democrat*, p. 25.
49. Preface to the Hughenden edition of his novels.
50. *Vindication*, pp. 192–3.
51. Southgate, p. 90.
52. Faber, p. 18.
53. Mill, p. 130.
54. *Tory Democrat*, pp. 42–3.
55. ibid., p. 46.
56. Southgate, p. 99.
57. Blake (1966) p. 556.
58. ibid., p. 555.
59. ibid., p. 553.
60. *Vindication*, pp. 204–5.
61. Blake (1966), p. 482.
62. ibid., p. 455.
63. Taylor (1961), esp. pp. 108, 131–4, 166, 212, 217, 249–50, 254–5 246.
64. Brinton (1926), p. 136.

Part Two, Chapter 7: Lord Hugh Cecil (pages 87–91)

1. *Conservation*, p. 251.
2. Rose (1975), p. 248.
3. ibid., p. 232.
4. ibid., p. 235.
5. Thomas Jones (1969–71), vol. III, pp. 3–4.
6. *Conservatism*, pp. 116–17.
7. Rose (1975), p. 263.
8. *Conservatism*, p. 144.
9. Rose (1975), pp. 263–4.
10. *Conservatism*, p. 218.
11. Rose (1975), pp. 245–7, 235.
12. ibid., pp. 244–5.
13. *Conservatism*, pp. 237–9.
14. ibid., pp. 244, 9, 36.
15. ibid., pp. 39, 61–2.
16. *Conservatism*, p. 67.
17. Hobhouse, p. 235.
18. *Conservatism*, p. 70.
19. Paul Smith, pp. 279, 268.
20. *Conservatism*, pp. 118–22.
21. ibid., p. 154.
22. ibid., p. 158.
23. ibid., pp. 89–92, 95–6.
24. ibid., pp. 195, 246–8.
25. ibid., pp. 248–9, 185, 169.
26. ibid., p. 246.

Part Two, Chapter 8: Michael Oakeshott (pages 92–100)

1. *Rationalism in Politics*, p. 170.
2. ibid., p. 127.
3. ibid., pp. 112–14, 118–19, 121.
4. ibid., pp. 123–4.
5. ibid., pp. 124–6.
6. ibid., pp. 1, 6–7, 28.
7. ibid., pp. 1–2, 11, 4–6.
8. ibid., p. 21.
9. ibid., pp. 26, 30.
10. ibid., p. 77.
11. ibid., pp. 35–6.
12. ibid., pp. 40, 41, 44.
13. ibid., p. 41.
14. ibid., pp. 44–5, 41.
15. ibid., pp. 42–3.
16. ibid., pp. 46–7.
17. ibid., pp. 48, 50–2.
18. ibid., pp. 53–4.
19. ibid., pp. 55–8.
20. *On Human Conduct*, pp. 115, 157, 315.
21. ibid., pp. 60–81, 108–84.
22. ibid., pp. 185–326.

Part Two, Chapter 9: Lord Hailsham of St Marylebone (pages 101–6)

1. MacCunn, p. 47.
2. *The Door Wherein I Went*, p. 224.
3. *The Conservative Case*, p. 19.
4. ibid., p. 19.
5. ibid., pp. 21–2.
6. *Science and Politics*, pp. 13, 97.
7. Brenan (1961), p. 217.
8. *The Door Wherein I Went*, pp. 69, 71, 79, 107.
9. *The Conservative Case*, pp. 12–13.
10. *The Door Wherein I Went*, p. 113.
11. *The Conservative Case*, pp. 15–16.
12. ibid., pp. 16–17.
13. ibid., pp. 57, 64.
14. ibid., pp. 61–2.
15. *The Acceptable Face of Western Civilisation*, p. 7.
16. *The Door Wherein I Went*, pp. 124, 212, 239, 229–31, 152.
17. ibid., p. 94.
18. *The Conservative Case*, pp. 50–1.
19. ibid., pp. 72–4.
20. ibid., pp. 77, 79.
21. Burke, *Reflections*.
22. *The Conservative Case*, p. 36.
23. *New Charter; Elective Dictatorship*.
24. ibid., pp. 36–9.

PART THREE *(page 107)*

1. Burke, Speech on the Duration of Parliament, 1790.
2. Halifax, p. 130.
3. Cecil, pp. 249–50.

Part Three, Chapter 1: Conservative Philosophy (pages 109–29)

1. Rolo, p. 165.
2. Duncan Williams, p. 63.
3. Leon, p. 11.
4. Buck.
5. Rose (1969), p. 317.
6. Quoted in Introduction to Bulgakov, p. v.
7. Talmon, p. 35.
8. Popper (1945), vol. II, p. 102.
9. Dostoyevsky, *Notes from Underground*, I, VII.
10. Leon, p. 250.
11. Viereck, p. 124.
12. Cole, pp. 196–7, 252–5.
13. Orwell, p. 122.
14. Cobban (1929), p. 164.

15. Byron, *Childe Harold's Pilgrimage*, IV, cxxv.
16. Russell, p. 667.
17. Hayek, (1960), p. 506.
18. Brittan (1973), p. 132.
19. Robbins (1976), p. 115.
20. Oakeshott (1962), p. 21.
21. Hayek (1960), pp. 397–8.
22. Hayek (1960), pp. 398–401, 411. (In the last phrase Hayek is quoting Adam Smith).
23. Bullock and Shock, p. 53.
24. Mitchell, pp. 104, 216–21.

25. Steel, p. 50.
26. Hayek (1960), p. 284.
27. Hayek (1944), p. 13.
28. Hirschman, p. 18.
29. Brogan (1951), p. 79.
30. Bullock and Shock, p. 212.
31. Hume, 'The Sceptic', in *Essays*, p. 161.
32. Cobban (1929) p.165.
33. Dostoyevsky, *Notes from Underground*, I, VIII.
34. Thompson, p. 15.
35. Troyat, p. 144.

Part Three, Chapter 2: What Conservatism is Not (pages 121–43)

1. Eisehnower, p. 36.
2. Oakeshott (1962), p. 48.
3. Hansard, 3 May 1952, col. 33.
4. Hill (1961), p. 106.
5. Fulford, p. 2.
4. Hill (1961), p. 106.
6. Paul Smith, p. 94.
7. Wordsworth, 'On the Projected Kendal and Windemere Railway'.
8. Meredith, ch. XXVII.
9. Trollope, ch. LXX.
10. Paul Smith, p. 39.
11. Ostrogorski, vol. I, p. 97.
12. Eyck, p. 296.
13. Churchill (1948), p. 27.
14. Thomas Jones (1951), p. 47.
15. Roskill, vol I, p. 135.
16. Newman, p. 65.
17. Popper (1963), p. 124.
18. Cornford, p. 15.
19. De Montherlant, ch. VI.
20. Blake (1966), p. 482.
21. Jennings, pp. 60–1.
22. Middlemas and Barnes, p. 99.
23. Churchill (1964), p. 798.
24. McDowell, p. 90.
25. Newman, p. 137.
26. Macmillan (1973), p. 398.
27. G. M. Young, p. 247.

28. *Daily Telegraph*, 16 February 1967.
29. Paul Foot, pp. 66–7.
30. Hailsham (1975), p. 230.
31. Utley, p. 61.
32. Speech in Glasgow, 13 March 1976.
33. Hansard, 22 September 1971, cols. 44–5.
34. *Sunday Express*, 5 January 1971 and speech in East Belfast, 2 June 1971.
35. *Daily Telegraph*, 7 September 1974.
36. Utley, p. 61.
37. Quoted in Berlin (1955), p. 293.
38. Fisher, p. 17.
39. Utley, p. 114.
40. Election address, 1966.
41. Balfour, pp. 198–9.
42. Morley, vol. I, p. 211.
43. Guedalla, p. 182.
44. Coleridge, *Biog. Lit.*, p. 109.
45. Burke, 'Thoughts on the Cause of the Present Discontents'.
46. Simon, p. 70.
47. Nevins and Commager, p. 306.
48. Burke, Letter to the Sheriffs of Bristol.
49. De Tocqueville, p. 274.
50. Churchill (1954), p. 306.

Part Three, Chapter 3: Tory Themes (pages 144–71)

1. Quoted in Grierson (1929), p. 15.
2. McDowell, p. 9.
3. Holmes–Laski, vol. I, p. 331.
4. Michael Foot, vol. I, p. 505.
5. Blake (1970), p. 274.
6. Chadwick, p. 80.
7. Laski (1936), p. 68.
8. Address at Sanitary Fair, Baltimore 1864 – Lincoln, p. 266.
9. Brinton (1933), pp. 68–9.
10. Burke, 'Remarks on the Policy of the Allies'.
11. Halévy (1928), p. 374.
12. White, p. 211.
13. Boswell, p. 723.
14. Burke, *Reflections*.
15. Hume, *An Enquiry concerning the Principle of Morals*, s. 3, pt II, p. 190.
16. Brinton (1933), pp. 68–9.
17. Gooch, p. 18.
18. 'Proposals for Wider Ownership', Conservative Central Office, 1977.
19. Bell (1973), p. 456.
20. Jackson, p. 47.
21. Popper (1945), vol. II, p. 317.
22. Quoted in Feiling (1946), p. 217.
23. Popper (1963), pp. 345, 361.
24. *New Society*, 17 June 1976.
25. Douglas Jay, p. 180.
26. Amery (1953–5), vol. III, p. 29.
27. Beloff (1976), p. 61.
28. Haseler, p. 104.
29. Schlesinger (1960 i), p. 63.
30. Hume, 'Of some Remarkable Customs, pp. 379–80.
31. Quoted in Cranston, p. 88.
32. Popper (1945), vol. I, p. 222.
33. Woodhouse, p. 37.
34. Leon, p. 290.
35. Cole, p. 60.
36. Talmon, p. 211.
37. Dostoyevsky, *Pushkin Speech*, III.
38. Brogan (1954), p. 184.
39. Cruikshank, p. 173.
40. Manchester, p. 60.
41. MacCunn, p. 1.
42. Douglas, p. 158.
43. Commager, p. 72.
44. Burke, 'Letter to a Member of the National Assembly'.
45. Troyat, p. 423.
46. Dostoyevsky, *The Idiot*, pt III, ch. x.
47. Macmillan (1966), p. 3.
48. Hirschman, p. 75.
49. Burke, 'Regicide Peace', quoted in MacCunn, pp. 30–1.
50. Churchill (1950), p. 312.
51. Letter to his constituents in Bristol, South East, 14 November 1970.
52. Churchill (1950), p. 312.
53. Southgate, pp. 40–4.
54. Paul Smith, p. 61.
55. ibid., p. 91.
56. ibid., p. 108.
57. Feiling (1946), p. 81.
58. Eden (1965), pp. 522, 545.
59. Sampson, pp. 83–4.
60. Middlemas and Barnes, p. 533.
61. Macmillan (1969), p. 365.
62. Balfour, p. 113.
63. Hammond and Foot, p. 171
64. Carter, p. 125.
65. Blake (1955), p. 457.
66. Churchill (1954), p. 509.
67. Speech at Party Conference, 8 October 1976.
68. Congar, p. 44.
69. Grierson (1929), p. 207.
70. Hayek (1944), p. 52.
71. Macmillan (1966), p. 110.
72. Cruikshank, p. 8.
73. Burke, Speech on Economical Reform.
74. McDowell, p. 136.
75. Middlemas and Barnes, p. 170.
76. Somervell, pp. 29–30.
77. Grierson (1949), p. 64.

282 References

Part Three, Chapter 4: The British Social Democrats (pages 172–94)

1. Desmond Stewart, p. 59.
2. Brogan (1951), p. 11.
3. Mencken, p. 13.
4. Crosland (1975 ii), pp. 1–2.
5. Clayton, pp. vii, viii.
6. Crosland (1975 ii), p. 2.
7. Crosland, (1975 ii), p. 2.
8. Miliband, p. 333.
9. Crosland (1975 i), pp. 16–17.
10. Maccoby, p. 202.
11. Douglas Jay, pp. 7–9.
12. Maude, p. 129.
13. Marx, *Critique of the Gotha Programme* quoted in Bell (1976), p. 262.
14. Aristotle, 1280A.
15. Russell, p. 753.
16. Crosland (1975 ii), p. 7.
17. ibid., p. 7.
18. ibid., p. 5.
19. Carlyle (1837), Pt. II, Bk. V, ch. iv.
20. Leon, p. 86.
21. Gray, p. 101.
22. Dahl, p. 156.
23. Crosland (1975 i), p. 18.
24. Wilson, pp. 17–18, 74, 180, 256, 768–70.
25. Crossman, vol. II, p. 331.
26. Gibbon, ch. lxiii.
27. ibid., p. 73.
28. Douglas Jay, p. 16.
29. Beer and Ulam, p. 595.
30. Crosland (1956), p. 190; (1975 ii), p. 6.
31. Crosland (1975 ii), p. 6.
32. Crosland (1975 i), p. 84.
33. ibid., p. 58.
34. Hamilton *et al.*, p. 294.
35. Crosland (1956), p. 205.
36. Burke, 'Thoughts and Details on Scarcity'.
37. Miller, 'Comparative Social Mobility' in Coxon and Jones; Blondel p. 42.
38. Michels, p. 212.
39. Dalton (1957), p. 65.
40. Crosland (1975 ii), p. 4.
41. Douglas Jay, p. 6.
42. Berlin (1958), p. 10.
43. Popper (1976), p. 36.
44. Crosland (1975 ii), p. 5.
45. ibid.
46. De Tocqueville, pp. 370, 588. (See also pp. 301, 368, 550, 579, 587).
47. Birch, 'Economic Models in Political Science' *British Journal of Political Science*, January 1975, pp. 77–9.
48. Crosland (1975 ii), p. 10.
49. See for example, Crosland (1975 i), p. 38; (1975 ii), pp. 10–11; Douglas Jay, pp. 319–24.
50. Crosland (1975 i), p. 44.
51. ibid., pp. 99, 105.
52. ibid., p. 53.
53. Carlyle (1837), Pt III, Bk III, ch. iii.
54. Solzhenitsyn (1976 ii), pp. 31, 35–6.
55. Conquest, p. 127.
56. Clutterbuck, pp. 3, 15–18.
57. Douglas Jay, pp. 390, 205, 375, 384, 347.
58. Shaw, *Man and Superman*, Act III.
59. Churchill (1951), p. 824.
60. Speech at Solihull, 9 July 1976.
61. Crosland (1975 i), p. 40.
62. Haines, p. 203.
63. Lyman, p. 274.
64. Solzhenitsyn (1976 ii), p. 43.
65. Hayek (1944), p. 89.
66. Conquest, p. 121.
67. Steiner, p. 259.
68. Carr, vol. I, p. 32.
69. ibid., p. 33.
70. ibid., p. 168.
71. Ulam, pp. 618–20.
72. Talmon, p. 258.
73. Conquest, p. 121.
74. Crosland (1965), pp. 20–1.
75. Crosland (1950), p. 49.

Part Three, Chapter 5: The Consitution (pages 195–227)

1. Hume, 'Idea of a Perfect Commonwealth', p. 515.
2. Quoted in Schlesinger (1960 ii), p. 45.
3. Quoted in Kennedy, p. 19.
4. Bolton, 29 September 1974 – Butler and Kavanagh (1975), p. 291.
5. Butler and Kavanagh (1975), p. 134.
6. Brunn, p. 203.
7. Angell, p. 28.
8. Runciman (1963), p. 35.
9. Plumb, p. xvi.
10. Stendhal, ch. vii.
11. Butler (1963), pp. 142–3.
12. Jenkins, p. 102.
13. Haseler, p. 125.
14. ibid., pp. 123–4.
15. Bullock, vol. I, p. 104.
16. Sorenson, p. 48.
17. *Daily Mirror*, 16 August 1957.
18. Fields, p. 67.
19. Butler and Kavanagh (1974), pp. 141–2.
20. Ibid., p. 125.
21. Michael Foot, vol. I, p. 162.
22. Lloyd George, vol. I, p. 1008.
23. Hansard, 2 May 1974, col. 235.
24. Low, pp. 129–30.
25. Attlee, pp. 214–15.
26. Hayek (1960), p. 106.
27. Popper (1963), pp. 344–5.
28. Burke, *An Appeal from the New to the Old Whigs*.
29. ibid.
30. Speer, pp. 242, 179.
31. Thomas Jones (1951), p. 233.
32. Laski (1938), p. 125.
33. Cole, p. 175.
34. Goodhart (1971), p. 17.
35. Goodhart (1976), p. 45.
36. Attlee, p. 137.
37. Goodhart (1971), pp. 82–98.
38. Goodhart (1976), pp. 55–6.
39. Braham and Burton, p. 11. (The Fabian Tract succinctly states the case against referenda.)
40. Kelley, p. 43.
41. Butler and Kitzinger, p. 213.
42. Goodhart (1976), p. 152.
43. Goodhart (1971), p. 21.
44. Goodhart (1976), pp. 197–8.
45. ibid., p. 152.
46. Scarman, pp. 15, 69.
47. Hailsham (1976).
48. Talmon, p. 105.
49. *The Body Politic*, pp. 298–9.
50. Rostow, pp. 193–266.
51. Acheson, p. 103.
52. Galt, p. 54.
53. Paton, p. 125.
54. ibid., p. 126.
55. Vile, p. 161.
56. Butler (1952), pp. 237, 249.
57. Black, pp. 80–1.
58. Gilbert, pp. 365–6.
59. Lloyd George, vol. x, p. 1587.
60. Finer, p. 287.
61. Namier (1930), p. 3.
62. Goodhart (1971), p. 77.

Part Three, Chapter 6: The Economy (pages 228–53)

1. Montaigne, vol. I, p. 275.
2. Adam Smith, vol II, p. 35.
3. Wigham, p. 28.
4. Browning, 'An Epistle – Karshish'.
5. Tennyson, 'The Third of February 1852'.
6. Bacon and Eltis.
7. ibid., pp. 62, 13, 24, 8, 29.
8. ibid., p. 32.
9. Middlemas and Barnes, p. 669.
10. *Lloyds Bank Review*, July 1965, p. 22.
11. Brittan (1964), p. 173. Also Britton and Lelley, p. 42.
12. *The Times*, 21 and 22 March 1972.

13. *Sunday Telegraph*, 4 April 1971; 26 March 1972.
14. Bacon and Eltis, pp. 60–1.
15. George Watson. p. 78.
16. ibid., pp. 70–2.
17. Nisbet, p. 122.
18. Popper (1976), pp. 90–6.
19. Namier (1955), p. 5.
20. Popper (1976), pp. 130, 135.
21. Macmillan (1971), pp. 372.
22. Joseph, Stockton Lecture, 1976.
23. R. J. Ball, Ernest Sykes Memorial Lecture, 1976.
24. Kelf-Cohen, pp. 28–9.
25. Nigel Harris, p. 335.
26. ibid., pp. 245–6.
27. ibid., pp. 138–9.
28. Bell (1973), p. 139.
29. *Economist*, 10 January 1976 (reporting a poll conducted by Mr R. Worcester of MORI).
30. Macdonald, p. 24.
31. Lloyd George, pp. 177, 627.
32. Citrine, p. 270.
33. Hyde, p. 217.
34. Speech at Cardigan, 28 September 1974.
35. Peter Jay, pp. 27–34.
36. Walker, pp. 94–7.
37. ibid., p. 29.
38. R. A. Butler (1971), p. 61.
39. Hayek (1960), pp. 281–2.

40. Robbins (1976), p. 73.
41. Herman Finer, p. 9.
42. Rousseau, p. 275.
43. Ridley and Blondel, pp. xii–xiii.
44. Sieyès, pp. 158–9.
45. Maitland, p. 85.
46. Amery (1953), pp. 64–7.
47. Romanes Lecture, in Gilbert, pp. 361–2.
48. James Douglas, 'The Overloaded Crown', *British Journal of Political Science*, October 1976, p. 498.
49. Ionescu, pp. 19–20.
50. Macmillan (1966), pp. 291, 293.
51. Wigham, p. 112.
52. 'A House of Industry' in Raison.
53. Wigham, p. 114.
54. Adam Smith, vol. I, p. 117.
55. James Douglas, op. cit., p. 490.
56. Ionescu, pp. 1–2, 8, 135–8.
57. Kirk, p. 157.
58. Haseler, p. 73.
59. Walker, p. 77.
60. Truman, p. 249.
61. Heilbronner, p. 200.
62. Hansard, 11 March 1952, col. 1302; 14 April 1953, col. 61.
63. Panic, p. 10.
64. ibid., p. 14.
65. Pearson, pp. 300–1.
66. Wigham, pp. 81–2.

Part Three, Chapter 7: The Immediate Future (pages 254–60)

1. Woodhouse, p. 8.
2. Halifax, 'A Rough Draft of a New Model at Sea', p. 174.
3. Galt, p. 77.
4. Wigg, p. 254.
5. Butler and Pinto-Duschinsky, p. 7.
6. Callaghan.
7. Gollin, p. 314.
8. Butler and Rose, p. 199; Benney *et al.*, pp. 142–6; Milne and McKenzie (1951), p. 108; (1955), p. 119; Butler and Kavanagh (1974), pp. 141–2.

9. *Financial Times*, 25 October 1974 (Harris poll reproduced and commented upon by David Watt).
10. James (1972), pp. 89–90.
11. Butler and Stokes, pp. 63, 285–8.
12. Walker, pp. 163–81.
13. Tolstoy, *Polikushka*.
14. Dostoyevsky, *Crime and Punishment*, Pt V, ch. VII.
15. Haines, p. 192.
16. Dryden, 'The Medal'.
17. Kennan, p. 363.

Index

The capacity destroying itself but not quite — eversion

brinkmanship
Part 1880 — Schism
1914-1918 — Some Players